The Successful Business Plan:
Secrets & Strategies

By Rhonda M. Abrams

The Oasis Press® / PSI Research
Grants Pass, Oregon

081895

Published by The Oasis Press

The Successful Business Plan: Secrets & Strategies
© 1991, 1993 by Rhonda M. Abrams

This publication is designed to provide accurate and authoritative information
in regard to the subject matter covered. It is sold with the understanding that the
publisher is not engaged in rendering legal, accounting, or other professional
service. If legal advice or other expert assistance is required, the services of a
competent professional person should be sought.
> —*from a declaration of principles jointly adopted by a committee of*
> *the American Bar Association and a committee of publishers*

Second Edition
Editor and Typographer: Melody Joachims

First Edition
Editor and Page Design: Virginia Grosso
Formatting: Darrin Clay, Melody Joachims, Constance Dickinson
Editorial Assistance: Vickie Reierson, Rosanno Alejandro, Mark Hasting
Typographic Assistance: Jan Olsson

Please direct any comments, questions, or suggestions regarding this book to
The Oasis Press, Editorial Department, at the address below.

The Oasis Press offers companion business software for sale.
For information, contact:

PSI Research
300 North Valley Drive
Grants Pass, OR 97526
(503) 479-9464
(800) 228-2275

The Oasis Press® is a Registered Trademark of Publishing Services, Inc.,
an Oregon corporation doing business as PSI Research.

Library of Congress Cataloging-in-Publication Data
Abrams, Rhonda M.
   The successful business plan : secrets & strategies / Rhonda M.
Abrams. -- 2nd ed.
     p. cm. -- (PSI successful business library)
Includes index.
   ISBN 1-55571-194-4 (pbk.) : $21.95. -- ISBN 1-55571-197-9 (binder)
$49.95. -- ISBN 1-55571-199-5 (pbk. with disk) : $39.95
   1. New business enterprises--Planning. 2. New business
enterprises--Management. 3. New business enterprises--Finance.
I. Title. II. Series.
HD62.5.A344 1993
658.4 ' 012--dc20
                                 93-21563
                                 CIP

Printed in the United States of America
Second edition

To my clients, who have shared with me their enthusiasm for the entrepreneurial spirit and have shown me that business can be a career for people of integrity, intelligence, and honor; and to the memory of my parents, who would have been proud.

About the Author

Rhonda M. Abrams

Nationally-syndicated columnist Rhonda M. Abrams heads Abrams Business Strategies, a management consulting firm which works with both new enterprises and established companies facing new challenges. Headquartered in San Francisco, California, her company develops and reviews business plans, solves marketing and administrative problems, and devises long-term strategic goals for businesses. Clients range in size from sole proprietors to corporations with over $500 million in revenues to major city governments and are in diverse industries nationwide.

Rhonda Abrams writes a syndicated column, "Small Business Strategies," which is distributed by the Gannett News Service to over 100 newspapers throughout the country. The column focuses on the concerns of small businesses and suggests approaches to solving common business problems, as well as addressing public policy issues of importance to the the small business community.

Educated at Harvard University and UCLA, where she was named Outstanding Senior, Ms. Abrams also attended the London School of Economics.

A popular lecturer and seminar-leader, Ms. Abrams is regularly invited to address MBA programs at leading universities. She has been featured in The New York Times, Nation's Business, and other major business publications.

Ms. Abrams works with business plans on a daily basis, which gives her extraordinary depth of experience, common sense, and real-life understanding of the problems facing entrepreneurs.

About the Contributors

Eugene Kleiner
Founding Partner, Kleiner Perkins Caufield & Byers

Eugene Kleiner is a legend in venture capital. He is a founding partner of one of the nation's leading venture capital firms, Kleiner Perkins Caufield & Byers, which has invested more than $400,000,000 in entrepreneurial companies. Currently, he also serves on the advisory boards of PaineWebber R&D Partners, Intersouth Partners, and Capital Resource Partners, in addition to being active in venture capital on his own behalf.

Mr. Kleiner was a founder of Fairchild Semiconductor where he played a key role in the growth of the company. The eight founding members of Fairchild are generally considered to be the "fathers" of California's Silicon Valley. Mr. Kleiner has served as founder or director of many of the nation's leading high technology firms; in recent years, these have included Tandem Computers and Genentech. Mr. Kleiner is a trustee of the Polytechnic University of New York.

Ann Winblad
Partner, Hummer Winblad Venture Partners

In high technology circles, Ann Winblad is a well-known software entrepreneur and venture capitalist. In 1976, she co-founded Open Systems with a $500 investment and sold the company in 1983 for $15.1 million. Prior to starting her venture capital firm with partner John Hummer, she served as a consultant to clients such as IBM, Microsoft, Apple, Price Waterhouse, and numerous start-up companies. Her venture capital firm has helped launch leading software companies, including Central Point Software, which publishes *PC Tools,* Powersoft, and Slate Corporation.

Bill Walsh

Head Football Coach, Stanford University
Former Commentator, NBC Television,
and Coach and President, San Francisco 49ers

When Bill Walsh was hired as head coach of the San Francisco 49ers football franchise in 1979, the team was hardly taken seriously. But within three years, under his innovative management, the 49ers had won a Super Bowl. He went on to win two additional world championships and was named "Coach of the Eighties." His management style was marked by intelligent, strategic planning of every detail and contingency. Formerly a commentator on NBC Television, he is a frequent speaker to business audiences.

Andre S. Tatibouet

President, Aston Hotels and Resorts

At the age of 19, Andre S. Tatibouet developed his first hotel and has been a force in the hospitality industry ever since. Aston is the largest condominium resort and hotel operator in Hawaii and the fourth largest in the nation. The rapidly growing chain also includes properties in California and Mexico. Mr. Tatibouet was named one of the top five entrepreneurs in the hotel industry and is active in numerous philanthropic and civic organizations.

Robert E. Price

Chairman of the Board, The Price Club

When Robert Price co-founded The Price Club with his father, Sol Price, in 1976, he revolutionized the retail industry. By introducing the nation to the concept of the warehouse club, he brought the buying power of large corporations to small businesses and individual shoppers. Originally started with one warehouse in San Diego, California, the Price Club concept was an astounding success, and there are now Price Clubs throughout the United States and Canada. Mr. Price previously served as Vice President of FedMart Corporation, a chain of discount department stores.

Charles Orr

President, Productivity Point International

Charles Orr is one of the original founders of Productivity Point International, a franchisor of computer training services and the largest, independent provider of instructor-led training services in North America. As the owner of Training Works, a software training company in San Francisco, California, Mr. Orr recognized the coming trend of franchised business services and helped establish the Productivity Point system in 1990. Previous to purchasing Training Works, Mr. Orr owned and operated three San Francisco ComputerLand franchises. He has more than twenty years in the computer industry.

Deborah Mullis
Owner, D.A.M.E.'S Foods

For twelve years, Deborah Mullis helped shape and launch products for some of the world's largest companies as Vice President/Associate Creative Director at Lintas, an advertising agency. Her love of food and her understanding of marketing led her to create D.A.M.E.'S Foods. After successfully launching D.A.M.E.'S Nutsy Noodle Sauce and Nutsy Noodles in San Francisco, she returned to her home state of Florida. She continues to operate D.A.M.E.'S while also serving with an advertising agency in Orlando.

Christine Maxwell
President, Research on Demand

Christine Maxwell is active in many phases of the information services industry. Not only does she head Research on Demand, a market research firm in Berkeley, California, but Ms. Maxwell also serves as Senior Vice President for Macmillan Publishers, Director of Pergamon Press, and the Chair of the Advisory Board of Maxwell Communications Corporation. Research on Demand is one of the nation's most effective providers of on-line database information and business research services.

Robert M. Mahoney
Executive Director of Corporate Banking, Bank of Boston

In this leadership position, Robert Mahoney is responsible for commercial lending and services throughout the New England states for the Bank of Boston, a bank that has earned the reputation as one of the nation's most receptive of entrepreneurial companies. During his eighteen years with the bank, Mr. Mahoney has served as President of Massachusetts Banking and Vice President for corporate banking in the United Kingdom.

Larry Leigon
President, Ariel Vineyards

Ariel Vineyards was founded in 1985 to produce and market premium dealcoholized wines. In its first four years of operation, Ariel grew to be larger than 95% of all the wineries in the United States. Larry Leigon is one of the four founding principals of Ariel and has served as President since its inception. He has primary responsibility for all marketing and distribution strategy, a unique challenge since Ariel created a new product category. Mr. Leigon is also a founding member of The Wine Trust, a wine marketing and sales company. Previously, he was Vice President of Clos du Bois Vineyards.

Martha Johnson
Co-owner, Suppers Restaurant

In 1977, after a decade as a successful management consultant, Martha Johnson changed careers and followed her love of cooking into the food business. After writing a thorough business plan, she and partner Susan Snider opened their first restaurant with an investment of $10,000. Six years later, she sold the restaurant for $175,000. In 1985, the two partners opened a European coffee bar/cafe, Trio Cafe, in San Francisco, California. In 1991, they launched Suppers, a restaurant serving regional American cuisine. Suppers has received substantial critical acclaim and have been featured in national publications such as *Food and Wine*.

George B. James
Senior Vice President and Chief Financial Officer
Levi Strauss & Company

As Chief Financial Officer, George James is responsible for all planning, risk management, accounting, tax and treasury affairs for this renowned manufacturer of jeans and sportswear. At nearly $5 billion in sales, Levi Strauss & Company is the world's largest apparel company. Mr. James previously served as Executive Vice President and Group President of Crown Zellerbach Corporation, a leading paper, container, and distribution company and as a Vice President at Pepsico, Inc.

Charles Huggins
President, See's Candies

Founded in 1921, See's Candies is one of the nation's oldest and best known makers of fine candies. Charles Huggins has been with See's for more than forty years and has served as President since 1972, overseeing much of the company's expansion. He has guided the company through its development from a regional confectionery into a multinational model of manufacturing and retail operations. While limited in its geographic distribution, See's has earned a worldwide reputation as producing some of the finest and most desired chocolates anywhere.

Nancy E. Glaser
President, Golden Gate Chips

Before starting an innovative potato chip company, Golden Gate Chips, Nancy Glaser was a partner in U.S. Venture Partners, a venture capital firm well known for funding retail enterprises. When she joined the firm in 1985, Ms. Glaser had more than 15 years in retail management. She helped take The Gap Stores, Inc. from a 35-store chain to 350 stores in less than five years. She also served with Macy's, Lord & Taylor, and the Barton Candy Corporation. U.S. Venture Partners has helped develop leading retail enterprises, such as Ross Stores and Home Club. The firm is also active in technology and medical fields, with portfolio companies such as Sun Microsystems and Applied Biosystems.

Michael Damer

Community Affairs
New United Motor Manufacturing, Incorporated

New United Motor Manufacturing, Incorporated (NUMMI) is a joint venture between Toyota Motor Corporation and General Motors, designed to bring the benefits of the extremely efficient and cost-effective Toyota production system to the production of cars in the United States. Although located in Fremont, California, NUMMI's manufacturing plant is run entirely according to Japanese manufacturing principals and with Japanese management techniques. NUMMI began producing automobiles in 1984, and now manufactures both Chevrolet and Toyota cars and light trucks. Mr. Damer serves in the Community Affairs Department.

Acknowledgments

I would like to thank the many people who offered assistance and support during the course of the preparation of this book. In particular, I wish to acknowledge the help of these individuals:

Matthew Abergel, my editor and dear friend, who relentlessly pursued every "to be" verb; who greatly enhanced the quality of this book; and who understands the tyranny of working with words and provided many amusing diversions from them;

Eugene Kleiner, for his years of friendship and for serving as my personal business tutor; who first showed me what a good business plan should look like, and who continually shares with me his unequalled insight into the entrepreneurial process;

The expert "tipsters" who generously shared their expertise with me. They were, without exception, gracious, forthcoming, and insightful;

Charles Orr, for allowing me to adapt the basics of his company, Productivity Point International, into the fictional company ComputerEase;

Pamela Richards, owner of Computer Ease of San Rafael, California, for allowing me to borrow the name for the fictional company featured in this book;

Jennifer Arthur, Scott Belser, Marilyn Burns, Kate Ecker, Edgar Holton, Edward Pollock, Andy Schneit, and Lori Silver, for their professional advice on the specifics of accounting, marketing, financing, and law; and for their friendship;

Jay Leshner for helping create the fictional town of Vespucci, Indiana;

Rhoda Goldman and Raquel Newman for arranging introductions to two of my contributors (tipsters);

Authors Donna Levin Bernick and David Chanoff for their advice about writing and publishing, and Elaine Petrocelli, owner of Book Passage in Corte Madera, California, for her insight into the book industry;

Mark, Randy, Charlie, and the staff and sales representatives at Publisher's Group West for their support and commitment to this book;

Virginia Grosso, my editor, for the improvements she made to the book and for her patient disposition, and with whom I shared a year-long dialogue on content, tone, and grammar;

Emmett Ramey, for his openness and fairness, and for welcoming my participation in decision making on all aspects of this book;

Francie Marks, who introduced me to PSI, for her intelligence, creativity, and friendship; I remain appreciative of the opportunity to create this book, although she gave me fair warning of what it would take;

Cathy Dobbs Goldstein, my attorney and dear friend, who not only provided wise counsel and served as a continuing source of information but understood when I had to cancel plans to stay at the computer;

My sisters and brothers: Janice, Arnie, Mary, Karen, and Scott, for their support, encouragement, and indulgence over the years;

And finally, thanks to my dog Teddy, who not only introduced me to my first business plan client on a walk in Golden Gate Park years ago, but who every day while I was writing, energetically and persistently reminded me to go outside and take a break.

Table of Contents

Section III Putting the Plan to Work

Section IV Reference

Sample Plan

Worksheets in this Book

Worksheets in this Book (continued)

Worksheets in this Book (continued)

Illustrative Examples and Charts

How to Use this Book

The Successful Business Plan: Secrets & Strategies is an interactive tool for the action-oriented, busy entrepreneur. It helps you develop a comprehensive, effective business plan in a thoughtful, yet time-efficient manner.

As you work through this guide, you will find a number of features that make your business planning process easier, faster, and more thorough. By the time you have worked through this book in its entirety, you should have a completed, compelling business plan.

Tips from Experts

Throughout this book you'll find tips from successful entrepreneurs, venture capitalists, and other business leaders. In these quotes, the experts share their secrets and strategies about business plans, and what makes a business work, that they have garnered through their real-life experience. You will find their words a source of guidance, advice, and inspiration. (For more complete profiles of these experts, see "About the Contributors.")

How this Guide Is Organized

Three main sections lead you step by step through the process of preparing, writing, and sending out your business plan.

Beginning

Section I, "Starting the Process," shows how to organize your planning activities, clarify your business concept, and gather the data you need. The chapters in this section give you insight into the practical details that will make your plan more compelling to future readers, particularly potential funding sources.

The Parts of a Business Plan

Section II, "Business Plan Components," clarifies the standard sections comprising a business plan and provides you with detailed information on each. You do not need to work through this section in any particular order; however, you will most likely find it helpful to identify your target market (Chapter 7) and competition (Chapter 8) before describing your marketing strategy (Chapter 9).

After Your Plan Is Completed

Section III, "Putting the Plan to Work," describes how you can use your completed business plan to meet your particular needs. It provides advice for existing and large corporations on the use of the plan for internal purposes, and gives specialized information for retail, manufacturing, and service businesses. But perhaps most importantly, this section tells you how to organize and conduct your search for financing. If you are looking for money for your business, you will find this section particularly beneficial.

Reference Materials

Additional information is provided at the end of this book to give you greater resources and knowledge in your planning process. You will also find a glossary of commonly used business terms.

Worksheets and Forms

Four kinds of worksheets and forms, described below, are used throughout this guide.

General Worksheets

Use these worksheets to do your internal planning and gather and coordinate the information you will use in your completed plan. The information on these worksheets is not necessarily included in the plan itself.

Plan Preparation Forms

These forms help you outline the information you will include in your completed business plan document. To complete these forms, synthesize the information you have recorded on the general worksheets. If you already know all the basics of your business and need an extreme-ly quick planning guide, go straight to the Plan Preparation Forms in each chapter.

Flow-Through Financials

Recognizable by the dollar-sign logo in the top right-hand corner, the Flow-Through Financials are a quick, efficient way to organize your financial and budgetary information. Once you complete all these work-sheets, you will have the basis of almost all the formal financial reports to be submitted with your plan. A directory explaining how to use the data from each Flow-Through Financial is found in Chapter 13.

Standard Financial Forms

This book contains all the standard financial forms to be submitted along with your plan. These include Income Statements, Balance Sheets, and Cash-Flow Projections.

Sample Plan

At the conclusion of each chapter of Section II is an example of how the information conveyed in that chapter would translate into an actual completed plan. The Sample Plan illustrates how you can incorporate the information provided in the text into your own plan, and helps you understand the concepts discussed. Space limitations require the Sam-ple Plan to be in an abbreviated form; your own plan may be longer. The company featured in the Sample Plan is fictional and bears no relation to the real software training company, Computer Ease, head-quartered in San Rafael, California, which generously allowed the use of its name.

Foreword

In today's environment, a business plan is an entrepreneur's most crucial business document. No company can expect to articulate its goals or to secure financing without a well-conceived and well-presented business plan. Without a convincing business plan, no one will seriously consider your business idea.

This wasn't always the case. The first business plan I ever wrote as an entrepreneur was not a business plan at all; it was just a letter. Eight of us from Shockley Laboratories for various reasons wanted to start a semiconductor company on our own, and we needed the money to make it possible. We drafted a letter, perhaps four or five pages long, describing what we proposed to do and sent that letter along with our resumes to an investment banker.

Fortunately for us, that letter found its way to the desk of a young business school graduate named Arthur Rock who felt that we might have promise. As a result, we were able to get our funding, and Fairchild Semiconductor was born. From Fairchild, the eight of us branched out and went on to form or fund such companies as Intel, Tandem Computer, and many other leading Silicon Valley firms.

Today, our letter might never be completely read. Investors now are far more structured and expect a far higher level of expertise and preparation from the entrepreneurs they choose to fund. When examining a proposal, they want to see much more than just a good idea and a bright young man or woman; they want to see a business plan showing that the concept has been rigorously assessed and that the entrepreneur has carefully thought through the issues for steps necessary to take the idea and fashion it into a successful company.

At Kleiner, Perkins, Caufield, & Byers, the venture capital firm I co-founded in 1972, we had a diligent system of evaluating business plans. A plan had to stand up to the most exacting scrutiny and toughest standards. Most plans, of course, never made it past the initial screening phases. Only the most interesting and well-conceived plans warranted the allocation of resources necessary for a more thorough examination. From that group, we narrowed our selection down even further, spending a great deal of time investigating each plan's merits. Finally, before deciding to invest in a company, part of the staff would serve as "devil's advocate," suggesting all the pitfalls. Only the plans that made it through that process were considered for final funding.

In this book, Rhonda Abrams has given you the tools you need to create a successful business plan. Working with Rhonda over the years, I've developed a strong appreciation and respect for her grasp of the business planning process. We have had many sessions evaluating what it takes to make a successful company, and I've seen her take what I've shared with her about long-term and strategic planning and expand upon that knowledge, bringing to bear her own experience with clients and her intelligent, practical approach to the entrepreneurial process.

Eugene Kleiner

Introduction

If you don't know where you are going,
how will you know when you are lost?

Why Are You Developing a Business Plan?

Quite possibly, you are developing a business plan because someone else wants you to do so. Perhaps the bank is requiring a business plan before granting you a loan. Or an investor or venture capitalist needs one to decide whether to finance your business. Maybe your attorney or accountant said you must have one, or your company president requires a strategic plan for your new division.

Reasons enough. But entrepreneurs are self-motivated people, used to setting their own goals and determining their own tasks. They undertake endeavors not merely to please others, but because they understand the importance of an activity in reaching their overall objectives.

Creating a business plan only as a response to an external request makes the process seem like a burden instead of an opportunity.

What a Business Plan — and this Book — Can Do for You

As you start developing your business plan, keep in mind that the greatest beneficiary of this project is not your banker, investor, or accountant — it's you. A complete, thoughtful business plan is perhaps the best tool you can have to help you reach your own long-term goals.

"With the first edition of your plan, you shouldn't even think about getting money. Use the planning process to decide if the business is really as good as you think it is. Ask yourself if you really want to spend five years of your life doing this. Remember, that's about 10% of your active working life, so seriously examine whether the enterprise could really be worthwhile to you."

Eugene Kleiner
Venture Capitalist

"The intensity in football incorporates, in one season, what a corporation must have over five years or so. You deal with people under stress; performance is measured by the bottom line; success is what the group accomplishes. To succeed, you must set goals, define roles, recognize excellence, acknowledge failure, recover from disappointment, and stay abreast of the competition. You must always be evolving systematically, improving the mechanisms for developing progress, and bring along younger players."

Bill Walsh
Former Coach and
President, S.F. 49ers

Whether your business is large or small, a startup or long established, developing a business plan enables you to:

- Make the crucial business decisions that focus your activities and maximize your resources.
- Understand the financial aspects of your business, including cash flow and break-even requirements.
- Gather crucial industry and marketing information.
- Anticipate and avoid obstacles your business is likely to encounter.
- Set specific goals and measurements to assess progress over time.
- Expand in new and increasingly profitable directions.
- Be more persuasive to funding sources.

Remember that when you start or expand a business, more than your money and time are at stake; you risk your dreams as well. A good business plan helps you realize your dreams.

Insiders' Secrets

Wouldn't it be nice to have an opportunity to learn directly from those who deal with business plans professionally? Bankers, chief executive officers, and venture capitalists all review business plans frequently and know what goes into a strong and compelling plan.

To enable you to gain the benefit of these experts' knowledge, some of the most successful and well-respected business leaders were interviewed for this book. Their views on every aspect of business plans were sought, and they shared their insider views and advice.

They were asked for their secrets — how to create a business plan that stands out from the pack; and for their strategies — how to develop a business that is successful and profitable over time. You can now put these secrets and strategies to work for yourself.

What They'll Tell You

This book addresses your real-life concerns; it is far more than just a textbook description of what a business plan should be. You will learn from a venture capitalist whose firm funded companies such as Ross Stores and Avia Shoes what must go into a retail operation to make it a likely candidate for venture capital. The President of See's Candies tells how his company manages to keep costs down and quality up through constant inventory control.

Champion manager Bill Walsh shares his advice on how to deal with competition. And owners of smaller businesses let you know the steps they took to get their companies started. This is practical information that will make a difference in the quality of your business plan and the success of your business.

A Roadmap to Success

A business plan is essentially a map to your targeted destination. Ideally, it gets you from your starting point to your goal: from your basic business concept to a healthy, successful business. It gives you a clear idea of the obstacles that lie ahead, and points out alternate routes.

Many people view the business planning process as a chore; in fact, it is an opportunity. While creating your business plan, you have the chance to 1) Learn about your industry and market; 2) Gain control over your business; and 3) Obtain a competitive edge.

Learning Your Industry and Market

One of the major benefits you'll receive from developing a business plan is getting to know your industry and market thoroughly. Even a small amount of information in this area can make a difference.

For example, one new entrepreneur, in the course of developing a business plan for his print and frame shop, learned that his target customers, middle-class women in the age range of 28 to 45, preferred Impressionist paintings and the colors blue and mauve. As a result, he chose a well-known Impressionist work as his company logo, and he always keeps a blue or mauve print in his window. This entrepreneur learned about his market and acted on what he learned. Business is booming.

Getting Control of Your Business

The business plan process also helps you, as the person most responsible for the growth of your company, gain more control over both the short-term and long-term progress of your business.

While developing your business plan, you'll increase your understanding of the many forces that have an impact on your company's success, which in turn will give you a stronger sense of control. A business plan provides mechanisms to enhance your management in these areas:

- **Marketing.** By developing a marketing plan based on a well-defined target market and evaluation of your industry and competition.
- **Operations.** By evaluating and establishing the procedures, labor deployment, and work flow necessary to run your business from day to day.
- **Finances.** By realistically projecting cash flow, income and expense, break-even points, and by creating channels of information to keep you fully informed of your financial picture.
- **Long-Term Development.** By setting specific goals and objectives; identifying milestones; devising an exit plan, if appropriate; and determining how your company will be positioned to respond to both internal and external changes.

"Strategic planning is part of the ongoing management job. The plan itself is only a snapshot; planning should be going on all the time. And it's not enough to just have planning at the top; each division should have the resources to do its own planning."

George James
Sr. V.P. & CFO
Levi Strauss & Co.

"It's easy to sit in an office and think up a brilliant strategy, but you have to be able to execute it. The deciding factor of a plan is really whether it's able to be executed. We kept looking for what we could do, rather than what we wanted to do."

Larry Leigon
President, Ariel Vineyards

Obtaining a Competitive Edge

By evaluating and refining your business concept through the planning process, you will be far more effective when you attempt to convey your message to your target market. Your message will be clearer, and customers will be better able to distinguish your company from the competition. Evaluating your competition and your company's strengths and weaknesses provides you with a better sense of how to position your company in relation to competitors. Focus and consistency give you a competitive edge.

Why Preliminary Plans Don't Do the Job

It may be tempting to consider developing only a preliminary plan or "concept paper" to circulate to potential funding sources before making the effort to develop a complete business plan. The presumption is that through this abbreviated process, you can determine whether funders are likely to support your business concept and, if not, you can save the time it takes to create a full-fledged business plan.

This is not a good idea. Preliminary plans are not a realistic way to determine whether your business can succeed in securing financing, and they can hurt your subsequent efforts to obtain funding.

Sending a preliminary plan (which by its very nature is incomplete and raises unanswered questions) may leave the impression that you are not a careful planner and your business concept is flawed. It will most likely reduce your chances of having a subsequent complete plan examined fairly, if at all. The funder will just remember, "Oh yes, I looked at that. It had a lot of problems." Remember, you have only one chance to make a good first impression.

Moreover, the process of sending a plan, even a preliminary one, and receiving an answer takes a great deal of time; you may wait weeks, or even months, for a funder to respond. You may have to use valuable contacts to get your plan into the hands of the right investor, so you should ensure he or she will see you and your business in the best possible light.

A Good Business Plan Can Take You to the Top

A good business plan for a sound business concept helps you achieve your business goals. It saves you money and time by focusing your business activities, giving you more control over your finances, marketing, and daily operations, and helps you raise the capital you need.

Virtually no other endeavor propels you as far forward in your enterprise as building your business plan. The process is challenging, creative, and rewarding. It may even be fun!

Starting the Process

Section I

Chapter 1

The Successful Business

It is not enough merely to survive;
the goal is to succeed.

Factors of a Successful Business

The ultimate purpose of developing a business plan is to have a fully functioning, successful business. In the long run, it is fruitless to write a business plan that can raise the funds you want if the enterprise is so poorly conceived that it is bound to fail. So, as you create your plan, be certain to address the long-term needs of your business and devise strategies that will enhance both the overall performance of your company and your personal satisfaction.

These factors contribute most to securing business success and should predominate your planning process:

- The Business Concept
- Understanding the Market
- Industry Health
- Capable Management
- Financial Control
- Consistent Business Focus
- Anticipating Change

The Business Concept

Meeting needs is the basis of all business. You can devise a wonderful new machine, but if it doesn't address some real and important need or desire, people won't buy it, and your business will fail. Even Thomas

"Even if you have all the money you need, you still need a business plan. A plan shows how you'll run your business. Without a plan, you don't know where you're going, and you can't measure your progress. Sometimes, after writing a business plan, you may change your approach, or even decide not to go into a certain business at this time."

Eugene Kleiner
Venture Capitalist

Edison recognized this fact when he said, "Anything that won't sell, I don't want to invent."

Typically, entrepreneurs get their original business inspiration from one of four sources: 1) previous work experience; 2) education or training; 3) hobbies, talents, or other personal interests; or 4) recognition of an unanswered need. Occasionally, the impetus will come from the business experience of a relative or friend.

As you refine your business concept, keep in mind that successful businesses incorporate at least one of these elements:

- **Something New.** This could be a new product, service, feature, or technology. An example of something new was the fax machine.
- **Something Better.** The something-better element encompasses a better service, lower prices, greater reliability, or increased convenience. Disposable diapers were one such product.
- **An Underserved or New Market.** Most often this is an unaddressed niche market, an unserved location, or a market for which there is a greater demand than competitors can currently satisfy. Publishers of guidebooks for computer software recognized a niche market.
- **Increased Integration.** This situation occurs when a single product is both manufactured and sold by the same company, or when a company offers more services or products in one location. An example of increasing integration was the one-hour photo shop.

Your business should incorporate at least one of these factors — more than one if possible. Ideally, you can bring a new or better product or service to an identifiable but underserved market. For example, computer companies opened a new market of small businesses by utilizing technology to make less expensive, less complicated laser printers.

Evaluate the ways your business concept addresses the four elements described above. If your concept isn't strong in at least one of them, assess whether your company will truly be competitive. The Basic Business Concept worksheet on the opposite page helps you evaluate the strengths and weaknesses of your basic business idea.

Understanding the Market

It is not enough to have a great idea or new invention as the basis of your business; you must also have a market that is sufficiently large, accessible, and responsive. If you can't reach your market, or it isn't ready for you, your business will fail. Consider the automatic teller machine (ATM) now seen on virtually every street corner. It was invented more than 10 years before it became popular, but the company that initially marketed the ATM was unsuccessful — people weren't yet willing to trust their banking to machines.

Basic Business Concept

Using this worksheet as a guide, outline your business concept as you presently conceive it.

Is yours a retail, service, manufacturing, or distribution business? _____

_____

What industry does it belong to? _____

_____

What products or services do you sell? _____

_____

Who do you see as your potential customers? _____

_____

Describe your basic overall marketing and sales strategy: _____

_____

_____

_____

Which companies and types of companies do you consider to be your competition? _____

_____

_____

List your competitive advantages, if any, in each area listed below.

New Products/Services: _____

_____

_____

Improved Features/Services and Added Value: _____

_____

_____

New or Underserved Markets Reached: _____

_____

_____

Methods of Increased Integration: _____

_____

Market readiness is one of the most difficult and most unpredictable aspects to measure when examining your market. That is why companies spend substantial amounts of money on market research before launching a product.

Even if you are not creating an entirely new product or service, you should attempt to determine if your market is ready for you. For instance, if you are opening a flower shop in a neighborhood where none currently exists, what indications are there that the neighborhood residents are interested in buying flowers? Do they currently purchase flowers at a nearby supermarket? Does the national demographic data on flower purchasers coincide with neighborhood demographics? Perhaps you should conduct a survey of the neighborhood's residents, asking about their flower-buying habits and preferences.

You may not have the funds to undertake extensive market research, but even a small amount of analysis can help you gauge the receptivity of a particular market to your idea.

In addition to market readiness, key market factors such as demographics, size of market, and price points must be analyzed. As you develop your business plan, these factors will influence your choice of marketing strategy and help you make realistic financial projections. Methods of conducting market research and evaluation in a practical, economical fashion are discussed in chapters 2 and 7.

When gathering information for your business plan, spend considerable time learning about your market. The more thoroughly you understand the various factors that affect your market, the more likely you are to succeed.

Industry Health

Your business does not operate in a vacuum; generally, your company is subject to the same conditions that affect your overall industry. If consumer spending declines and retail industries as a whole suffer, there's a good chance your neighborhood boutique will also experience poor sales.

As you develop your plan, you need to respond to the industry-wide factors that will affect your own company's performance. While it is certainly possible to make money in an industry that is experiencing hard times, you can only do so if you make a conscious effort to position your company appropriately. For example, if you are in the construction business and the number of new-home starts is down, you may want to target the remodeling market rather than the new-home construction market.

It is also harder to raise money to start or expand businesses in troubled industries. Even though opportunities exist in such fields, investors and bankers are concerned about the increased risk a new enterprise faces in entering an unhealthy industry. Conversely, if your business is in a healthy and expanding industry, investors are likely to be more receptive.

If you are seeking outside funds, your business plan must reassure investors or bankers that you understand the industry factors affecting your company's health and that you have taken those factors into consideration when developing your business strategy.

Capable Management

Perhaps more than any other factor, competent management stands out as the most important ingredient in business success. The people you place in key positions are crucial in determining the health and viability of your business. Moreover, their apparent experience and skills often determine whether your business plan is acted upon favorably by investors or banks.

Because of the significance of management to business success, many venture capital firms place the single greatest emphasis on this factor when deciding on their investments, and they review the management section of a business plan with special scrutiny. Your business plan must inspire confidence in the capabilities of your management.

Before submitting your business plan to investors, conduct your own analysis of your management team. Evaluate each individual (and yourself) to see if he or she fits the profile of a successful manager. Some of the traits shared by successful managers are:

- **Experience.** They have a long work history in their company's industry and/or they have a solid management background that translates well to the specifics of any business in which they become involved.

- **Realism.** They understand the many needs and challenges of their business and honestly assess their own limitations. They recognize the need for careful planning and hard work.

- **Flexibility.** They know things go wrong or change over time, and they are able to adapt without losing focus.

- **Ability to Work Well with People.** They are leaders and motivators with the patience necessary to deal with a variety of people. They may be demanding, but they are fair.

In developing your own business plan, determine whether key members of your management team possess these characteristics. If not, perhaps you can increase training, add staff, or take other measures to enhance your management's effectiveness. For instance, if you have little or no experience in your chosen field, perhaps you should first take a job with an existing company in that field before opening your own business.

"Before planning my own restaurant, I went to work at my friend's restaurant. I learned about inventory control, personnel, and financial management. It's invaluable to get real-life experience before starting your own business."

Martha Johnson
Owner, Suppers
Restaurant

Financial Control

Key to any business is how it handles money. Not fully anticipating start-up costs can immediately place impossible pressures on a new business. Inadequate cash-flow management can bring down even a seemingly thriving business.

As you develop your business plan, make sure you have the information to understand your financial picture on an ongoing basis. What does it take to open your doors each month? Where is your real profit center? How much expansion do you need to maintain growth? What are the hidden costs of marketing your company? What are the consequences of your credit policies?

Build in mechanisms to keep you continually informed as your business develops. It is easier to establish good financial procedures right from the start than to wait until you face a financial crisis. How frequently will you do your billing? What kind of credit policies will your business follow? How will you keep informed on inventory?

Make certain you receive detailed financial statements at least monthly and that you understand them thoroughly. Examine financial reports for any deviations from your plan or any indications of impending cash-flow problems.

Controlling and understanding your finances makes decisions easier. And you'll sleep better at night.

Consistent Business Focus

An often overlooked but crucial factor for a successful business is the necessity of developing a clear, consistent focus. All too often, businesses fail because management loses sight of the central character of the enterprise.

Understanding the basic goals and nature of your company will enable you to maximize the use of your resources, motivate your employees, and develop a competitive edge.

To clarify your company's focus, as part of the business plan process you should define a Statement of Mission (or Mission Statement). This Mission Statement should guide your company's short-term activities and long-term strategy, position your marketing, and influence your internal policies. Such a Mission Statement, however, cannot be developed until you have conducted your basic industry and market research.

Distinguishing Yourself from Your Competition

In putting together your Statement of Mission (a worksheet to help you do this is included in Chapter 5, "Company Description"), keep in mind the overall goal of your company. Different companies may be selling a similar product, but each may have a very different sense of what its business is really all about.

For example, suppose four companies are making jeans. Company A defines itself as selling work clothes; Company B sees itself as a sportswear manufacturer; and Company C defines itself as being in the business of selling youth and sex appeal. But Company D has never clarified its mission — it just sells jeans.

These different self-concepts will greatly affect the way each company markets itself, what subsequent products it develops, even the employees it hires. The first three companies may succeed and rarely be in competition with one another. But Company D, which misses the big picture, is almost certain to fail over time, as it flounders in its attempts to compete with all of the other, more focused companies.

Developing a Company Style

The second aspect of company focus is the development of a company style or corporate culture; you should give serious consideration to your company's style as you develop your business plan. By creating a consistent style that permeates every aspect of your enterprise, from the design of your stationery to personnel policies, you give your customers and employees a sense of trust in your company.

Imagine two different restaurants on the same street, both with basically the same business mission: providing good, fast food, priced at only a few dollars a meal.

The first restaurant is a national burger chain. Its style is characterized by consistency, cleanliness, and impersonal friendliness. A strong corporate image is important, which is reinforced through the restaurant's decor, the food's packaging, and the employees' uniforms. The meals are prepared by standardized routines, and every customer is given the same greeting.

The second restaurant is a diner. Management characterizes its corporate culture as that of a friendly neighbor. To help make sure that employees know customers' names and food preferences, management aims to retain employees for many years. A bulletin board features notices of local events. This restaurant's target market is the neighborhood regulars who know they will feel at home there.

With a strong company style, each restaurant clearly distinguishes itself from its competitors and gives its target customers a clear understanding of what to expect.

Every business, even a nonretail company, needs to consider its style as it relates to the company's overall mission, and then infuse that style into virtually all aspects of its undertakings.

"Each year we select a 'theme' for the year and a slogan suggested by team members. Once a year, we hold an annual meeting of the entire company, all team members. At this meeting, the president and senior managers articulate the goals and objectives for the year. The entire plant is shut down while we hold this meeting. We have seven areas in which we define each year's goals and objectives: 1) quality; 2) cost reduction; 3) human resources; 4) corporate citizenship; 5) communication; 6) quantity; and 7) material management.

**Michael Damer
New United Motor
Manufacturing Inc.**

Anticipating Change

Change is inevitable, and the rate of change gets ever faster. As you develop your business plan, anticipate that changes will occur affecting your company and consider how you can respond appropriately. A company caught off guard by changing conditions is likely to fail.

In planning for change, keep in mind the kinds of conditions that can affect your business future. They include:

- **Technological Changes.** It's impossible to predict the exact technological developments that will affect your industry, but you can be sure that you will be faced by such changes. Even if you are making old-fashioned, home-baked cookies, advancements in oven design or food storage will place competitive pressures on your business.
- **Sociological Changes.** Demographic and lifestyle trends should be evaluated in light of their potential influence on your business. In the cookie business, for example, new information on nutrition may influence the number and kind of cookies you sell. What sociological factors make your company most vulnerable? Don't build a business dependent on passing fads.
- **Competitive Changes.** New businesses start every day. How hard is it for a new competitor to enter the market, and what are the barriers to entry? Can you capture and hold sufficient market share to withstand new competition?

When developing your business plan, consider how your company deals with these outside changes. Also anticipate major internal changes, such as growth, the arrival or departure of key personnel, and new product or service development.

No business is static. Planning a company responsive to change will make the inevitable changes easier.

Personal Satisfaction: The Four C's

For start-up businesses, smaller enterprises, or businesses that are heavily influenced by one or two key members of management, issues of personal satisfaction can be a central element in influencing long-term success.

Thus, you must evaluate and consider your personal goals when deciding upon the course of your business development. For most entrepreneurs, these goals can be summed up by the Four C's: Control, Challenge, Creativity, and Cash.

Control

How much control you need to exercise on a day-to-day basis helps determine how large your company can be. If you are unwilling to delegate or share authority, your business should be designed to stay small. Likewise, if you need a great deal of control over your time (because of family or personal demands), a smaller business without rapid expansion is more appropriate.

If your company is large, put mechanisms in place and structure management reporting systems to ensure that as the company grows, you continue to have sufficient direction over developments to give you personal satisfaction. Understand the nature of control your funders will have and be certain you are comfortable with these arrangements.

Challenge

If you are starting or expanding a business, you are likely to be a problem-solver and risk-taker, enjoying the task of figuring out solutions to problems or devising new projects.

It is important to recognize the extent of your need for new challenges and develop positive means to meet this need; otherwise, you may find yourself continually starting new projects that divert attention from your company's overall goals. As you plan your company, establish personal goals that not only provide you with sufficient stimulation but advance the growth of your business.

Creativity

Entrepreneurs want to leave their mark. Their companies are not only a means of making a living, but a way of creating something that bears their stamp. That's why many businesses carry the founder's name.

As you develop your company, make certain it reflects your larger values. You'll want to shape your business so it is not just an instrument for earning an income but a mechanism for maintaining creative stimulation and making a larger contribution to society. But don't overpersonalize your company, especially if it is large. Allow room for others, particularly partners and key personnel, to share in the creative process.

Cash

Understand how your personal financial goals have an impact on your business plan. For instance, if you need substantial current income, you may need investors so that you have sufficient cash to carry you through the lean start-up time. You will most likely have to share equity, and the business must be devised for substantial profit potential to reward those investors appropriately.

If your current income needs are less exacting, but you want larger long-term financial rewards, you may be able to forego giving up a piece of your company to investors and instead look for loans of smaller amounts.

"Writing a business plan forces you into disciplined thinking if you do an intellectually honest job. An idea may sound great in your own mind, but when you put down the details and numbers, it may fall apart."

Eugene Kleiner
Venture Capitalist

Chapter Summary

A successful business plan is one that not only ensures you achieve your short-term objectives, but one that helps secure the long-term viability of your business. When developing your plan, keep in mind the underlying factors that affect business success and personal satisfaction. Make sure your business concept is clear and focused, your market well-defined, and that you have responsive, disciplined management procedures.

Chapter 2

The Business Plan Process

*You only find easy answers
by asking tough questions.*

Five Steps to a Great Business Plan

Once you determine a business plan is a necessary tool for your company, you may wonder, "Where do I start?" Because a plan requires detailed information on almost every aspect of your business, including industry, market, operations, and personnel, the process can seem overwhelming.

The business plan process entails five fundamental steps:

1. Laying out your basic business concept.
2. Gathering data on the feasibility and specifics of your concept.
3. Focusing and refining the concept based on the data you compile.
4. Outlining the specifics of your business.
5. Putting your plan in compelling form.

The first step is to lay out your basic business concept. In the last chapter, you were provided a worksheet on which to delineate the various components of your business. With an existing operation, it may be tempting to skip over this step, but if you wish to develop strategies for future success you must first examine the assumptions underlying your current efforts.

Before you tackle the body of your business plan, you need information. So your next task is to gather reliable data relating to the different aspects of your business. Solid information gives you a realistic picture

"You must have ongoing contingency plans to allow for miscalculations, disappointments, and bad luck. It's assumed that if you're a leader, you don't make mistakes. But it's not so; if you're decisive, you'll sometimes miscalculate, and sometimes just be unlucky. You need to openly discuss the possibility of mistakes, so people are prepared and aren't crestfallen when they occur. You need to rehearse your contingency plans."

**Bill Walsh
Former Coach and
President, S.F. 49ers**

of what happens in businesses similar to yours, as well as a better understanding of your own company.

In this chapter, you will learn how to find and interpret the data you need. You can then evaluate and refocus your concept in light of your newly acquired information; a worksheet provided at the end of this chapter will help you with this evaluation.

Only after you have compiled sufficient information and re-evaluated your business concept should you begin to actually write your plan. Follow the subsequent chapters of this book and complete the Plan Preparation Forms to shape your plan into a compelling document.

Developing a business plan is much more of a business project than a writing assignment. The process itself, as well as the document produced, can positively affect the success of your business. During the everyday operation of your business, you do not have time to think through the issues you examine while putting together your business plan; the preparation process gives you a rare opportunity to enhance your knowledge of how your company, market, and industry work.

Gathering Information

Knowledge is power. With accurate information at your fingertips, you can make a persuasive presentation of your plan when meeting with a banker, potential investor, or divisional president.

For example, after two partners thoroughly researched their plan for a new flower shop, they presented their plan to a bank officer and were initially viewed with doubt. But the two entrepreneurs had solid data proving their numbers were right in line with national averages. They turned skepticism into support and received their loan.

Take time to do your homework. Sufficient research prevents you from including inaccurate information in your plan — a mistake that can keep you from getting funded — and enables you to make informed decisions.

To begin your information-gathering efforts, start by checking the reference materials listed later in this chapter for general information about each of the areas you've identified in your Basic Business Concept worksheet from Chapter 1. As you progress, focus your research on more specific issues, compiling the information necessary to make operational and financial decisions. Chapters 5 through 13 outline the data you need to complete each section of your business plan, and in some cases include suggestions of possible sources of such information.

How Much Information Is Enough?

Once you begin to gather the material you need, it is natural to feel either overwhelmed with too much information or frustrated because some data is proprietary and unavailable.

Don't try to be exhaustive in your research efforts; it's not necessary or possible. You are merely looking for information that will answer basic questions about your business. At the same time, your research must be thorough enough to give you, and those reading your plan, confidence that the answers are accurate and from reliable sources.

For example, if you are manufacturing dolls, you might identify your target market as girls between the ages of four and ten. One of the questions you need to address in your plan is "How large is the market?" For this, you may have to consult only one source, the U.S. Census Bureau, to find a reliable answer. However, other questions that arise, such as "What are the trends in doll-buying habits?", may require consulting three or four industry sources or undertaking your own market research to compile information you can trust.

Start Your Research by Asking Questions

Start your research process by making a general statement that is the basis of your business (or one portion of your business). For example, if you are planning on opening a dry cleaning establishment, the statement might be, "There is a substantial need for a new dry cleaner to serve the Laurelwood neighborhood."

Next, make a list of questions that logically follow from and challenge that statement. Here are some questions you might then ask:

- How many dry cleaners now serve the neighborhood?
- How profitable are the current dry cleaners in the neighborhood?
- Are residents generally satisfied with the current dry cleaners?
- Is there more business than current dry cleaners can handle?
- What are the trends in the dry cleaning industry nationally?
- What are the demographic trends in Laurelwood?
- How do Laurelwood demographics relate to national dry cleaning trends and statistics?

After formulating this list of questions, look for answers. You will find some of your answers by consulting reference material and trade associations identified through a library or business development center. Others will come through information from government agencies. To get some answers, you will have to conduct your own market research by talking to local merchants and residents, and watching foot traffic at existing dry cleaners.

As you start the business plan process, use the Research Questions worksheet on the next page to record the general questions you have at this point and the issues you will investigate.

How much information you gather will be, to a large extent, a result of your resources, both of time and money. If you are working on a business

"In our planning, we try to get away from just arithmetic projections, and try to get to the underlying issues. Planning is more than just a numbers game."

George James
Sr. V.P. & CFO
Levi Strauss & Co.

Research Questions

List the questions you will examine in each area of your business, using the categories below as guidelines.

Industry/Sector: _____

_____

_____

_____

Products/Services: _____

_____

_____

_____

Target Market: _____

_____

_____

_____

Competition: _____

_____

_____

_____

Marketing & Sales Strategy: _____

_____

_____

_____

Basics of Operations: _____

_____

_____

_____

Long-Term Considerations: _____

_____

_____

_____

plan for a one-person business while concurrently holding down a full-time job, you don't need to compile the same amount of information appropriate for a large corporation with a market research budget and staff.

Sources of Information

If this is your first time conducting business research, you may be surprised at just how much information exists. Mountains of statistics and bookshelves of studies are available concerning virtually every endeavor and activity of American life. Without difficulty, you can find data revealing the average purchase in a fast-food restaurant, how many photocopying machines were sold last year, and the likely number of new housing units that will be built in your community in the coming year.

You can locate most of the general information you require from government sources, business publications, and trade associations. To find more specific information relative to your particular business or industry, you may have to undertake some market research.

In a limited number of cases, either when you lack the time to do the research yourself, or are involved in a new industry or one in which data is mostly proprietary, you may have to utilize paid sources of information.

Main sources of general information are listed on the next page. Sources of more particular information relating to costs, equipment, or other specific areas of your business are listed in the appropriate chapters of this book.

Local Libraries

The best place to start your research is at the library. Ideally, you will want to go to a library that is a depository of U.S. government documents. Most large urban and university libraries serve as such depositories, and each Congressional District has at least two depository libraries.

Choose the largest library convenient to you; the larger the library, the more likely it is to have the business and industry publications you need. Don't be surprised if it takes you a full day at the library just to begin your research.

Review articles about your industry from business and trade publications, read any appropriate studies from trade organizations, and examine government statistics that relate to your business. A large library will have many of the articles and most of the government statistics you need, but you will probably have to contact trade associations directly to order their publications and studies.

"You need a detective-like mentality to gather information. You have to know how to track down experts, find key sources. Eighty percent of the information is available from computerized, on-line sources, but the rest takes old-fashioned leg work."

Christine Maxwell
President
Research on Demand

"Every major newspaper has a research department. This department may have information about shopping centers, such as attendance and demographic makeup of shoppers. The state Board of Equalization has information on taxable retail sales by location."

Charles Huggins
President, See's Candies

Research Sources

U.S. Government	*American Statistics Index (ASI)*	
	U.S. Department of Commerce & U.S. Department of Labor	
	U.S. Census Bureau	
	Other government departments appropriate to your industry	
State Government	Sales Tax	Planning Departments
	Franchise Business Tax	New Business Licenses
	City and County Governments	
Quasi-Governmental Sources	Regional Planning Associations	
Industry & General Business	Trade Associations	Corporate Annual Reports
	Trade Publications	Thomas Register
	General Business Publications	
Community Services	Chambers of Commerce	Newspaper Libraries
	Merchants Associations	Real Estate Agents
	Banks	*Yellow Pages*
	Universities	
Computer Databases	Business and Trade Information	
	Individualized Research Services	
	Cendata (U.S. Government Statistics)	
Market Research Sources	Customers	
	Suppliers	
	Distributors	
	Independent Sales Representatives	
	Managers of Related Businesses	
	Loan officers/Factors/Venture Capitalists	
	Competitors	
Paid Services	Industry-Related Research firms	
	Survey/Polling Firms	
	Market Research Consultants	
Internal Data	For existing businesses	

U.S. Government Sources

The U.S. government is a voracious compiler of statistics, and you can reap the benefits of its relentless appetite for numbers.

The single best source for locating government statistics is the *American Statistics Index (ASI)*, which is published annually by the Congressional Information Service of Bethesda, MD, with monthly supplements. The *ASI* provides an index to all the statistical publications of the U.S. government in one handy location. It lists documents from the U.S. Census Bureau, *Current Industrial Reports (CIR)*, the U.S. Bureau of Labor Statistics, and special studies by governmental agencies.

You will find the *ASI* particularly helpful, not only because it contains an index, but because its second volume, *ASI Abstracts*, briefly summarizes the actual reports listed in *ASI*. Thus, you can avoid wasting time trying to locate a document that may not contain information useful to you.

U.S. Department of Commerce

The *U.S. Industrial Outlook*, published annually each January by the U.S. Department of Commerce, provides a general economic outlook by forecasting growth rates for the coming year and reporting on production in the past year. You may find it a useful reference for anticipating trends in your industry.

U.S. Census Bureau

The U.S. Census Bureau publishes more than 100 *Current Industrial Reports* on 5,000 manufactured products, accounting for 40% of all goods manufactured in the United States. *CIRs* provide information on production, shipping, inventories, consumption, and the number of firms manufacturing each product. The U.S. Census Bureau also publishes *Economic Censuses* and *Related Statistics* for a variety of industries, such as retail trade, service, transportation, and manufacturing. These publications report on monthly sales figures and trends, and information on sales by geographic area, zip code, and merchandise line. The U.S. Census Bureau also offers an on-line database called "Cendata."

A source of industry information analyzed by geography, the U.S. Census Bureau's *County Business Patterns* is useful in evaluating the performance and trends of your industry in your target location. The printed version of *County Business Patterns* includes listings for each industry having more than 50 employees in an area, and a computerized version has listings of every Standard Industrial Classification (SIC) category with at least one employee.

"To begin, I started by talking to people. I went to stores to see what products were already out there. I went to the Fancy Food Show and looked around for products similar to mine. I called the city Health Department to get names of commercial kitchens, so I could talk to people who made food products locally. From these kitchens, I got a lot of information about what I would need, as well as leads for production facilities."

Deborah Mullis
Founder
D.A.M.E.'S Foods

Most federal government publications can be ordered from:

Superintendent of Documents
U.S. Government Printing Office
Washington, D.C. 20402
(202) 783-3238
(202) 275-0019 (fax)

To gain access to government statistics by computer, contact:

Data User Services Division
Bureau of the Census
Washington, D.C. 20233
(301) 763-4100
(301) 763-4794 (fax)

In addition to the agencies listed above, check your state and local agencies; these can be good sources of information specific to your geographic market or regional industry. State sales tax receipts are a good indicator of the health of your local economy. Local planning department information regarding building permits indicates population growth or stagnation.

Trade and Industry Sources

If you have a small business, you can locate many of the trade references you need in the *Small Business Sourcebook*, published by Gale Research of Detroit, MI. Although the *Small Business Sourcebook* is limited to a relatively few types of businesses, with a strong orientation towards retail trade, if your business happens to be included, you'll find substantial information, well-organized for easy accessibility. The book lists trade publications, industry associations, trade shows and conventions, even venture capital firms and consultants active in each business.

For bigger businesses or those not listed in the *Small Business Sourcebook*, try Gale Research's *Encyclopedia of Business Information Sources*. Arranged by industry, this guide lists trade associations and major sources of statistical information, including databases, directories, and major publications in the field.

If you still need help finding information on your industry's sources, consult *Gale's Encyclopedia of Associations* or the *National Trade and Professional Associations of the United States,* published by Columbia Books of Washington, D.C. These two publications offer information on more than 30,000 trade associations and also list the major publications of such associations.

General Business Sources

The publications discussed in this section are available from most libraries.

Standard & Poor's Industry Surveys, while designed for investors, can be a source of insight about your overall industry and major competitors. The "Basic Analysis" section gives overviews of trends and issues in the industry. The remaining sections define some basic industry terms, report the latest revenues and earnings of more than 1,000 companies, and occasionally list major reference books and trade associations. When using *Standard & Poor's*, consider the broad industry category under which your business falls, for instance, "Retail" or "Textiles" for an apparel or home furnishings store.

Predicasts F&S Forecasts provides an index to articles from more than 750 business and trade magazines, newspapers, financial publications, and special reports. This index helps you find interesting and useful stories about new developments and products, mergers and acquisitions, and general sociological and political issues that may affect your business.

Predicasts is divided into two sections: "Industries and Products" and "Companies." "Industries and Products" is arranged by Standard Industrial Classification (SIC), the number the government has assigned to identify each industry. You will find an alphabetical list of industries with their SICs at the beginning of the book, and it will be useful for you to know the SIC number of your business when referring to other documents.

When consulting *Predicasts'* "Industries and Products" section, look for citations for articles about your industry, product, sales, and market demand. The front of this section includes an index of general economic subjects, including information about the economy, wages, population, and other sociological factors. The "Companies" section will help you find articles about competitors or possible business customers.

Business Periodicals Index, published by H.W. Wilson Co. of Bronx, NY, is an index to articles in major business publications. It is arranged alphabetically and is easier to use than *Predicasts*, but the articles it refers you to are likely to contain fewer details.

Consumer's Index, published by Pierian Press of Ann Arbor, MI, lists articles evaluating products and services. This can help you in assessing your competitive position, as the articles report what consumers are saying about the products they use.

The *Thomas Register,* published by Thomas Publishing Company of New York, NY, may be an invaluable source of information as you develop your business. It's a good place to identify suppliers, distributors, potential customers, or competitors. There are three sections to the *Thomas Register*: "Products and Services," which lists companies according to their products; "Company Profile," an alphabetical listing of companies and their products; and "Catalog File," which has copies

> *"When starting on a new project, we always keep the negatives in mind. We don't try to sell ourselves."*
>
> **Charles Huggins**
> **President, See's Candies**

of company catalogs. The *Thomas Register* is particularly useful as you develop the marketing and operations sections of your business plan.

For nongovernmental statistics, refer to the *Statistical Reference Index (SRI),* published by Congressional Information Service of Bethesda, MD. *SRI* indexes reports and statistical studies from major organizations and trade associations. A second volume, *SRI Abstracts,* provides brief summaries of the information included in these reports.

One often overlooked source of business information is the *Yellow Pages* of your local telephone directory. The *Yellow Pages* can give you insight about the nature and scope of your local competition and potential suppliers.

Computer Databases

You can locate a great deal of the information you need to develop your business plan by using computerized on-line database services. Major public libraries have linkups to these databases; if you are equipped with a modem and have an ongoing need for specialized information, you can subscribe to such services yourself. More convenient and economical if you are conducting a limited amount of research are services, such as Research On Demand or NEXIS EXPRESS (see below), which you can reach by telephone, even without a computer.

Libraries are most likely to have Dialog (1-800-3-DIALOG), one of the oldest services to supply access to computerized information. Dialog incorporates more than 300 different databases, including Dun & Bradstreet and Standard & Poor's. Dialog contains "Findex," which catalogs and describes industry and market research studies that are available commercially. "Business Dateline" indexes articles, itemized by industry, from regional business publications.

NEXIS (1-800-227-4908) is one of the most popular on-line databases, featuring a wide variety of useful information. In addition to indexing most newspapers, this service includes "Investext," which lists industry reports from more than 100 brokerage houses; corporate filings with the Securities and Exchange Commission; international news; legislative-bill tracking; public relations and advertising information; medical and pharmaceutical information; and, through its LEXIS service, legal documents. Of particular interest is NEXIS' thorough listing of trademarks and patents.

NEXIS EXPRESS (1-800-843-6476) allows you to reach the NEXIS service without subscribing, even if you do not own a computer. You simply telephone with a question to find a statistic or to check a state law, and a researcher conducts the search for you. This service is relatively inexpensive, and you can obtain a cost estimate before beginning a search. The search can be charged to a credit card, and the information will be delivered to you by phone, mail, fax, or computer. These costs add up when you ask for many printed pages. NEXIS EXPRESS cannot check legal documents for you because the law prohibits the service from acting as an attorney. However, you can check trademarks and patents with NEXIS EXPRESS by telephone at a competitive price.

Maxwell Online (1-800-955-0906) operates two databases: BRS for business, social sciences, medical, and pharmaceutical information; and Orbit Search Service for patents, chemistry, electronics, and other scientific information.

Maxwell also operates two services you can reach with or without a computer. Information on Demand (1-800-999-4-IOD) will retrieve a specific document for you if you know the citation. Research on Demand (1-800-227-0750 or 1-415-841-1145) will, like NEXIS EXPRESS, conduct a search for you. Unlike the NEXIS service, however, Research on Demand has a minimum fee, but it will quote you a price before beginning a search. Maxwell also operates Maxwell Business Information Services which provides you with information on European industries and companies.

The Dow Jones News Retrieval Service (1-800-522-3567), which encompasses 50 databases supplying information on business, financial, corporate, and leisure news, is another well-known database service, though it is generally more expensive than others.

Paid Research Services

In some cases, you will want to use a private research firm as a source of data. Private firms gather information (sometimes from confidential sources), provide more detailed competitor-sales estimates, and undertake market research projects. These firms are all relatively expensive, so you should use them only when your time is very limited, when undertaking an unusually large or expensive enterprise, or when the information you are seeking is hard to find, proprietary, or has never been compiled.

Check with your industry trade associations for research firms that are particularly knowledgeable about your industry. Each firm provides different services, and costs vary dramatically. Sometimes these firms have reports or surveys they prepared for private corporate clients which, after a few months, they are able to sell to the general public. The reports may be a good source of information and a relative bargain.

> *"Time costs money. When considering whether to use a paid research service, ask yourself if you have the time to look up information yourself. Put a value on your time. The kind of information we gather can be very time consuming to the entrepreneur. For instance, we had an international client interested in the sewing machine market—market size, trends, market share distribution, distribution systems, names of importers and wholesalers, prices, warranty standards, habits of the home-sewing market. The budget for that in 1990 was $750."*
>
> **Christine Maxwell**
> **President**
> **Research on Demand**

Historical Performance of Your Company

If yours is an ongoing business (not newly established), you also need to gather historical data about your own company. In particular, you should examine your past internal financial records. Here is some of the information you may need to locate:

- Past sales records, broken down by product line, time period, store, region, or salesperson.
- Past trends in costs of sales.
- Overhead expense patterns.
- Profit margins on product lines.
- Variations from budget projections.

If you cannot gather this information easily, change your reporting system so that in the future you will be able to have the data you need for adequate planning.

How to Conduct Your Own Market Research

Some of the most important information you need will not be available from any published source, particularly information that is quite specific to your market or new product. To obtain this data, you will have to undertake your own research. For most businesses, even very large businesses, this research needn't be expensive or prohibitively time-consuming.

Personal Observation Is an Easy Method

One fundamental way to gather information — and also one of the easiest — is through personal observation. Watching what goes on in other businesses or the way people shop gives you insight into factors affecting your own business. You can observe auto and foot-traffic patterns near a selected location, how customers behave when shopping in businesses similar to yours or for similar products, and how competitors market or merchandise their products or services. Personal observation is a vital tool in your planning process and applicable for almost every business.

Informational Interviews Can Be Structured or Informal

The second principal method of market research is informational interviewing. Since the amount of information you can garner from personal observation is limited and colored by your own perceptions, you should talk with as many people as possible who can provide you with information relating to your business.

Some of these interviews may be highly structured. For instance, you might make personal appointments with those you want to interview

"We taste-tested our product in all the places we wanted to sell it eventually: hotels, restaurants. We wanted to see what our potential consumers wanted and spent an enormous amount of time talking to them. We tested at supermarkets, parties, polo matches. We watched how people reacted physically as well as what they told us. We changed the product a dozen times in the first couple years in response to consumers. You have to be willing to make radical changes."

Larry Leigon
President, Ariel Vineyards

and have a prepared list of questions. In other cases, such as when you go into a competitor's store and chat with a salesperson, your questions will appear to be more casual.

Surveys Help You Spot Trends

If you decide you need information from a large number of people, you may want to conduct a survey, either by phone or by mail. Surveys are a good way to spot trends and are particularly useful in assessing customer satisfaction and desires. Mail surveys have a notoriously low response rate, so if you conduct one, it is a good idea to include some kind of incentive, such as discounts or free gifts to encourage people to respond. But don't depend on a mail survey alone to provide you with information.

Focus Groups Offer Candid Opinions

A popular form of market research is the focus group, a small group of people brought together to discuss a product, business concern, or service in great detail. For example, a few joggers might be brought in to examine and evaluate a new pair of running shoes. Focus group participants are often paid a small fee.

Market research firms conduct focus groups for businesses, bringing together the participants and leading the group discussion in a room with a one-way mirror, so that the businessperson involved can observe. However, if you do not have the funds to hire a market research firm, you might still consider assembling a focus group of your own, perhaps a group of potential consumers. Try, however, to find focus group participants you do not know personally.

"Vendors are a good source of information and even professional advice. We had a lot of help on kitchen design from our vendors."

Martha Johnson
Owner, Suppers
Restaurant

Accessible Sources for Market Research

Here are some sources to consider for your market research:

- Potential customers, both end-users and buyers or distributors, if you are in a wholesale business.
- Potential suppliers.
- Businesses related geographically or by product line.
- Similar businesses serving different cities.
- Banks, real estate agents, universities, local or regional chambers of commerce, merchant groups, or others observing the local economy.
- Your competitors.

Suppliers, distributors, and independent sales representatives can give you a great deal of information about industry trends and what your competition is doing without violating confidentiality. Because they are in touch with the market, these individuals know which products and services are in demand.

Learn from Other Businesses

Likewise, those in related businesses often know about conditions affecting your company. For example, if you are considering locating a retail store in a mall, managers of other mall shops can give you a realistic idea of foot traffic, slow periods, and shopper demographics.

Try talking to people who are in the same type of business as yours in a different city; they are an excellent source of information, especially for retail or service enterprises. If you are starting an office machine repair company in San Antonio, Texas, you might arrange to meet with a similar company in Houston. Since you will not be competing with Houston businesses, they may be very helpful in providing information not only on marketing but on operations and financial considerations.

In addition, large banks and universities frequently maintain information about the health of the local economy and particular industries. They are a good and reasonably reliable source of future-growth forecasts. Don't overlook real estate agents. They often have more up-to-date information about neighborhood trends than any other source.

Talk to Your Competition

Sometimes you can even talk to your competitors. In certain professions and in those instances where there is more work than the market can handle, your competitors may be willing to talk with you directly and openly. In other cases, you need to use less direct ways of approaching them.

However, be careful not to use illegal or unethical methods of dealing with your competitors; not only is it wrong, but you'd be surprised at how such activities can come back to haunt you. Today's competitor may one day be a source of referrals, and possibly, in a merger or acquisition, it could end up owning your company.

Evaluating the Data You've Collected

Once you start compiling information, you might feel you have more facts than you know what to do with. Here are a few tips to keep in mind about the information you gather:

- Use the most recent data you can find; printed information is often two years old and a lot can change in two years.

- Translate data into units rather than dollars whenever possible. Due to inflation, dollars may not give you consistent information from year to year.

- Give the most reliable source the most credence. Generally, the larger the group sampled for information, or the more respected the organization that conducted the research, the more trustworthy the numbers you collect.

- Integrate data from one source to another in order to draw conclusions. However, make sure the information is from the same time period and is consistent; small variations can lead to vastly inaccurate results.

- Use the most conservative figures. Naturally, you'll be tempted to paint the brightest picture possible, but such information often leads to bad business decisions.

Bringing Your Business Concept into Focus

Once you complete your initial research efforts, but before you lay out the specific components of your plan, re-examine your business concept. In light of the information you now have, check to see if your idea, as originally conceived, needs to be modified or refocused.

The business planning process is a learning process; it is appropriate for you to adapt your business in response to your increased knowledge.

Now is the time to ask yourself some hard questions, such as:

- Can the business be viable?
- Does a real market exist?
- Is there too much competition already?
- How does the financial picture look?

The Evaluating Your Business Concept worksheet on the next two pages helps you answer these and other crucial questions. Be sure to complete it after finishing your initial research.

Chapter Summary

The business planning process offers you an outstanding opportunity to better understand your business, market, and industry. Keep in mind that this process is a business activity, not a writing assignment.

Steps in the process include laying out your concept, gathering information, assessing that information and, finally, refocusing your business idea. A thorough planning process gives you ammunition to use when looking for money to fund your business, and an honest examination of your business concept increases your chances of success.

Evaluating Your Business Concept

This worksheet, which should be completed after conducting your initial research, helps you further refine your focus and determine whether your business idea is viable. In answering the questions, be honest, and be tough.

Your Business Industry

How economically healthy is your business industry or sector? _____

_____

Explain how your industry/sector is sensitive to economic fluctuations. _____

_____

Yes No
☐ ☐ Are the forecasts for your industry or sector positive?

Your Product/Service

Yes No
☐ ☐ Is your product or service viable?

☐ ☐ Can it be developed in a reasonable period of time?

☐ ☐ Are the costs of development prohibitive?

☐ ☐ Are necessary supply and support systems established?

Your Market

Yes No
☐ ☐ Is your market clearly identifiable?

☐ ☐ Is your market large enough to support your business?

☐ ☐ Is your market too large, and the costs to reach it prohibitive?

☐ ☐ Is your market growing, shrinking, or remaining stable?

☐ ☐ Is your market ready?

☐ ☐ Is your product/service too new for customers?

☐ ☐ Do customers have strong loyalty to existing companies?

☐ ☐ Is it costly for customers to convert to your product or service?

☐ ☐ Does your product/service integrate easily with existing products or services?

Your Competition

How formidable is your competition? _____

Yes No
☐ ☐ Do one or two competitors dominate the market?

☐ ☐ Is market share widely distributed, making it easier to get a foothold?

☐ ☐ Is there a competitor with "deep pockets" who can drive you out?

What barriers to market entry will your future competitors face? _____

_____

Your Suppliers/Distributors

How close are you to sources of supplies? _____

How reliable are your suppliers and distributors? _____

Yes No

☐ ☐ Are you dependent on one or two suppliers or distributors?

☐ ☐ Are your suppliers/distributors well-established and dependable?

Your Operations Concerns

Yes No

☐ ☐ Does your business entail unusually difficult operational problems? If so, describe them. _____

_____

☐ ☐ Will personnel be hard to find, retain, or train?

☐ ☐ Is manufacturing particularly complex?

☐ ☐ Must you make substantial initial capital expenditures?

☐ ☐ Will you need to maintain large, expensive inventories?

☐ ☐ Does new technology exist that will help you reduce costs?

Your Insurance Concerns

Yes No

☐ ☐ Are you able to secure the necessary insurance?

☐ ☐ Is there a significant liability issue?

☐ ☐ Will you have to carry heavy insurance premiums?

Your Financial Concerns

Describe any financial problems you anticipate: _____

_____

_____

Yes No

☐ ☐ Is overhead unusually high, thus putting extra pressure on cash flow?

☐ ☐ Will credit be hard to establish?

☐ ☐ Are profit margins narrow, making the business vulnerable?

☐ ☐ Will you have to carry a large amount of debt?

☐ ☐ Do the principals have the expertise necessary?

☐ ☐ Will ongoing training be required?

☐ ☐ Will it be costly to retain additional experts?

☐ ☐ Is the industry or market changing rapidly?

☐ ☐ Are there demographic or sociological factors likely to affect the market?

☐ ☐ Are there rapid technological changes that will affect costs and competitiveness?

"If you're truly creating something new, it doesn't show up in trends."

Larry Leigon
President
Ariel Vineyards

Chapter 3

Making Your Plan Compelling

People don't read.

Five Crucial Minutes

Time is valuable for businessmen and businesswomen. Rarely can they give any one matter the attention it deserves. This is especially true of bankers, venture capitalists, and other investors, who are inundated with business plans and proposals; a typical venture capitalist can expect to see more than 1,000 business plans a year.

Although you may spend five months preparing your plan, the cold, hard fact is that an investor or lender can dismiss it in less than five minutes. If you don't make a positive impression in those critical first five minutes, your plan will be rejected. Only if it passes that first cursory look will your plan be examined in greater detail.

It is, of course, possible to secure more attention for your plan through such methods as those discussed in Chapter 19, "Sending Out Your Plan & Looking for Money." But there is no escaping the fact that the written document itself must make a strong, positive first impression.

The most important aspects of your plan must jump out at even the most casual reader. Even if your plan is intended for internal company use only, it will be more effective if it is presented in a compelling, vivid form. Once you have developed your plan, you will want to refer to key points on a regular basis, but it is unlikely you will ever take the time to reread the plan in its entirety. Highlighting specific goals and conclusions will make it easier to use your plan as a true working document.

How Your Business Plan Is Read

When evaluating a business plan, experienced business plan readers generally spend the first five minutes reviewing it in this order: first, the Executive Summary; second, the Financials; third, the Management section; and next, the exit plan and/or terms of the deal, if applicable.

The Most-Asked Questions

Funding sources primarily look for answers to these questions concerned with the heart of the plan:

- Is the business idea solid?
- Is there a sufficient market for the product or service?
- Are the financial projections healthy, realistic, and in line with the investor's or lender's funding patterns?
- Is key management described in the plan experienced and capable?
- Does the plan clearly describe how the investors or lenders will get their money back?

Within the first five minutes of reading your business plan, readers must perceive that the answers to all these questions are favorable.

Increasing the Reader's Interest

Three sections — the Executive Summary, the Financials, and the Management description — must spark enough interest and inspire sufficient confidence to make the reader decide it is worthwhile to spend additional time reading other sections of your plan. You may have done a bang-up job of describing how your company will operate, but it is unlikely the Operations section will even be read if your Executive Summary and Financials aren't enticing to the reader.

Some venture capitalists and investors have specific areas of interest, or are known for giving certain aspects of a plan more weight than others. If you know this information, highlight those areas that are consistent with the particular investor's funding patterns when sending out your plan; do this in the Executive Summary and in your cover letter.

For instance, if you know a venture capital firm is especially interested in new technology, emphasize any patents you have secured and the aspects of your company that represent ground-breaking technological developments. Or, if a member of your management team (or one of the Board of Directors) is known and respected by a particular investor, you may want to discuss management near the beginning of your Executive Summary.

If you are preparing your business plan on a computer, you can tailor the order of the Executive Summary, even the entire plan, for individual

"I certainly don't go from page one to the end when first reviewing a plan. I skip around to the various sections, perhaps only reading the Executive Summary completely. I don't need 10 reasons to turn down a plan — I only need one. So the first thing I look at, after the Summary, is whatever aspect seems weakest. Then, if I cannot find a solution to the problem, I don't have to read the rest."

Eugene Kleiner
Venture Capitalist

recipients. Information about how to research your intended funding sources is discussed in Chapter 19.

Length of the Plan

How long should the perfect business plan be? No magic number exists, but here are some guidelines:

- Limit the plan itself (not including the Financials and appendices) to 15 to 35 pages; 20 pages are enough for nearly any business.

- Only a plan for a complicated business or product should be more than 30 pages (not including the appendices). If you need 40 pages or more, your plan had better be intended for a very motivated, sophisticated reader, or for use solely as an internal document.

- If you have an uncomplicated small business, you may not need 15 pages, but anything fewer than 10 pages will seem somewhat unsubstantial to the reader.

- Limit appendices to no more than the length of your plan. While they are a good way to present additional information, appendices should not be so long as to make the entire document appear burdensome.

- Make sure your business plan fits easily and comfortably into a briefcase; you don't want your plan to be the one left behind when an investor goes on a business trip. After all, it will receive uninterrupted attention if reviewed on a plane.

These guidelines apply to most business plans. But if you are confident that your business requires a different configuration, go ahead!

What Period of Time Should Your Plan Cover?

Most plans should project three to five years into the future, or until you have reached your anticipated exit strategy, whichever is earlier. However, you need only include monthly financials for the first year or two, depending on development time. For the second and third years, quarterly financials are usually adequate; annual projections suffice for the fourth and fifth years.

Similar time guidelines apply to how much detail you should include when describing your business operations. Quite thorough information should be provided for the first year or two; for subsequent years, a more general Operations description is acceptable.

Plans for existing businesses and in-house corporate use should include historical performance information for the past five years, or the duration of your business, if less than five years. If your business is longstanding, you may want to examine trends over the life of the business, or the last 10 years; this gives you insight into cyclical patterns and helps you anticipate events that are likely to recur.

"If I have a stack of business plans to go through, I'll pick the thin ones first. After all, I'll feel I've accomplished more if I get through five thin ones instead of just one thick one."

Ann Winblad
Venture Capitalist

"I don't like a plan that's too long. To avoid that, put detailed plans in the appendices so that people can refer to them only if they want to. A well-written plan should be no more than 25 pages, 100 pages total or less with appendices. If an investor is interested, they'll ask for more details."

Eugene Kleiner
Venture Capitalist

> *"I want to see detailed month-to-month reports for the first year, and quarterly projections for the next two to three years. After three years, the numbers become less significant."*
>
> **Eugene Kleiner**
> **Venture Capitalist**

> *"The important thing about a business plan is believability. I want to see a simple logic to the whole plan. The more a plan relies on leaps of faith, the less believable it is."*
>
> **Robert Mahoney**
> **Executive Director**
> **New England Corporate**
> **Banking, Bank of Boston**

Use Language to Convey Success

The language you use in your plan can give the impression you are thoughtful, knowledgeable, and prudent, or, conversely, it can make you seem naive and inexperienced. Your fundamental goal is to convey realistic optimism and businesslike enthusiasm about your prospects.

Use a straightforward, even understated, tone. Let the information you convey, rather than your language, inescapably lead to the conclusion that your business will succeed. Avoid formal, stilted language. Instead be natural, as if you were speaking to the reader in person; however, avoid slang and don't be "chatty." Always be professional.

Listed below are some other pointers to keep in mind when writing your business plan.

Be Careful with Superlatives

Readers are naturally skeptical of over-reaching self-promotion. Avoid using words such as "best," "terrific," "wonderful," or even "unmatched." They reduce credibility. Rather, use factual descriptions and specific information to make positive impressions.

Instead of saying "Our widget will be the best on the market, clearly superior to all others," say "Our widget will not only handle all the functions of existing widgets, but will also add features x, y, and z, and sell for $3 less than our closest competitor's widget. No competitor of ours offers these features at any price."

When trying to get additional financing for your restaurant, don't tell the reader that the food and atmosphere are "terrific." Instead provide specific information that proves you are doing something right: "Due to the restaurant's popularity, there is an average 45-minute wait for a table on Friday and Saturday nights, and a wait of 15 to 30 minutes on other evenings."

The only exception to this rule is when you use superlatives as part of your goal in a Statement of Mission. Then it is appropriate to state, "We intend to make a dog food unmatched in quality by any national brand." Even then, however, it is important to include the specifics of what you mean by such a goal.

Avoid Purely Subjective Comments

Everyone expects you to think your product or service is outstanding; thus, your own comments are meaningless. Instead, use outside sources to give the reader confidence in your competitiveness. Eliminate comments such as "We believe this will be the best dog food on the market," or "Adeena's fashions are equal to those made by top designers." Such statements use up valuable space in your business plan, and a reader is likely to tune out when encountering such hyperbole. However, the same comment, when made by an authority, becomes quite powerful: "*Women's Wear Daily* states that Adeena's fashions equal those of the top designers," or "The newspaper's annual survey rated our restaurant among the top 10 in its price category."

You don't even have to quote a well-known authority; anyone with credible related experience will do, as this example shows: "The breeder of the winner of last year's Tri-County Dog Show tested our dog food and concluded, 'This will be the best dog food on the market, superior to any national brand.'"

Use Business Terms

Although it is certainly not necessary to be a business school graduate to develop a business plan, you should know and use appropriate basic business terms. You don't want to be discredited or misunderstood by using words improperly. If business is new to you, familiarize yourself with the Business Terms Glossary at the back of this book.

Also, become familiar with the basic terms of your industry and use those words when appropriate in your plan. If you don't know these already, you should be able to pick many of them up while doing background work for the Industry Analysis section of your plan. However, do not fill your plan with a lot of technical jargon in the hope of sounding impressive; there is a good chance that someone totally unfamiliar with your industry will be reading it, especially if you are seeking outside funding.

Points of Style

In addition to using the most beneficial and appropriate language in your plan, you should pay attention to the elements of style discussed below.

Use Numbers for Impact

People tend to put great faith in numbers, and using numbers to support your plan can add significant credibility. If the figures come from a reputable source, they have even more power.

One particularly good technique you can use to make your plan stronger is to make a statement such as "Our _____ is supported by . . . . ," followed by specific figures relating to demographics, growth of market, information from other businesses, or market research. For example: "Our foot-traffic projections are supported by figures that show neighboring stores average 22 customers an hour on weekdays and 43 customers an hour on Saturdays."

"*The business plan had 15 pages of text. We also included an opening budget, cash-flow projections, a summary of return on investment, a furnishings and equipment list, a map of the area, and a site analysis based on Planning Department information on new and renovated housing in the vicinity. In the business plan for our next restaurant, we also included publicity the current restaurant had received.*"

**Martha Johnson
Owner, Suppers
Restaurant**

Another good example is: "Our choice of the young adult market is supported by U.S. Bureau of Census figures projecting a growth of 32% in that age category over the next five years."

It is vital to bring data from your Financials into the text of your plan to indicate specifically why you will be able to achieve certain goals. For instance, state: "The new production method we utilize will reduce each unit cost by 43% (currently projected savings: $1.57 per unit), thus allowing us to offer additional features at a competitive price while still maintaining our profit margin." Do not expect the reader to pick out these kinds of specifics just from looking at your Financials; the information must be incorporated into the text.

Know How and When to Be Redundant

Writing a business plan gives you the rarely granted right to repeat yourself. People do not read a plan from start to finish; they turn first to the sections that most interest them and then skip around. For this reason, it may be beneficial to refer in one section to conclusions you have reached in another.

For instance, when addressing the issue of staff training in your Operations section, you can refer to the importance of high-quality service to your target market, and underscore the wisdom of choosing this market by restating information provided earlier in your plan: "Surveys indicate high-quality service is demanded by our target market — women ages 35 to 49 — who, as shown in the market analysis, spend the most per capita on our product."

Two cautions about repetition, however: 1) Only repeat information that is important and impressive; and 2) Don't repeat information within the same section.

Use Bullet Points

Bullets are symbols that precede information offset from the text (such as the small boxes before the three sentences below). Bullets:

- Draw attention to specific information.
- Make long material more inviting to read.
- Eliminate the need to write whole sentences.

Bullet points are an excellent way to convey information, and they make writing your plan somewhat easier. Because they are read faster than text and quickly get the reader's attention, use bullet points only with information you particularly want the reader to notice.

Be careful not to clutter a plan with too many bullets; use them selectively. Bullets seem to work better with short items than with long ones. Also, each list of bulleted items must be presented in a consistent manner, such as starting with a verb or being a complete sentence.

Keep in mind that lists can be as few as one item or as many as ten, but a long list weakens effectiveness.

Using Visuals in Your Plan

In the case of your business plan, a picture may be worth more than a thousand words. A thousand words, after all, most likely will not be read, but a picture will definitely be looked at. Graphs, charts, and illustrations also are visually appealing; they catch the reader's attention, forcefully explain concepts, and break up the monotony of the text. Enhance your business plan by using visuals.

Photographs and Illustrations

Photographs can be extremely effective, especially if your company is producing a product that is unusual or difficult to understand. You can include pictures of your location, specialized equipment, or packaging but not of yourself or individual members of your management team. Photographs should be placed in the appendix only.

Illustrations help present information about products or marketing materials still in development. While generally placed in the appendix, a small illustration can be inserted directly into the text. If an illustration is not of good quality, don't use it; a business plan is not the place for exhibiting amateur art.

Graphs and Charts

Graphs and charts are excellent tools for communicating important or impressive information, and you should find ways of including at least one or two graphs or charts in your plan, if appropriate. Place charts, particularly of half-page size or less, in the text rather than in the appendix; this will engage the reader with your plan, and many readers pay minimal attention to the appendix.

A number of inexpensive computer software programs are available for generating graphs and charts, or you can have them produced by desktop publishing services (found in the *Yellow Pages*). Do not draw charts and graphs by hand. The four examples on the next page help you identify various types of charts and judge when each would most appropriately be used in your business plan.

Layout, Design, and Presentation

Because you must limit the total number of pages in your business plan, you may be tempted to fill each page from top to bottom. Resist this urge. A page crammed with too much information intimidates and

"The physical appearance of a plan (layout, binder, etc.) isn't significant in making the investment decision. But it sets your mind in a certain frame if it is well done. And it is certainly a negative if it's done wrong or poorly."

Eugene Kleiner
Venture Capitalist

Examples of Charts to Use in Your Business Plan

Here are some different types of charts you can use to help convey specific information.

Bar charts work especially well when making comparisons:

Line charts are useful when demonstrating trends or drawing comparisons:

Pie charts are ideal for showing the specific breakdowns of products sold, markets, etc:

Flow charts illustrate development patterns and organization of authority.

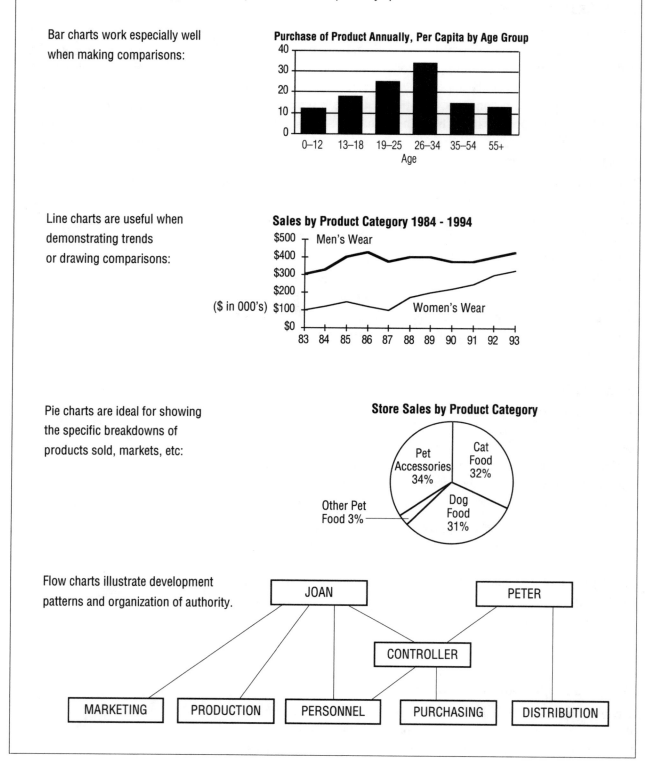

may even annoy the reader. (People make up their minds about how difficult a page is to read before they actually start reading it.)

Therefore, leave sufficient "white space" (unused, blank space) on the pages of your plan to make the text appear inviting to the reader.

"Frame" your text by leaving a border around it. Generally, leave about a 1" margin on the top and right side, with a little more (such as 1$\frac{1}{4}$") on the bottom and left side (to allow for binding).

Single-space your text, but leave double spaces between paragraphs. Keep your paragraphs short. Use either underlined or bold-print headers (such as the one directly below this paragraph) to begin each section or show a change of topic.

Desktop Publishing

Most business plans are produced using desktop publishing computer software and a laser printer (or ink-jet), which give a more polished, professional look than a plain typewriter. Typewritten plans are acceptable though less desirable. However, do not submit a business plan produced with anything less than true letter-quality print (in other words, avoid most dot matrix printers).

If you do not have desktop publishing capabilities yourself, such services are readily available and inexpensive in most cities (see "Desktop Publishing," "Printers," or "Computer Services" in the *Yellow Pages*, or check computer or copy centers near a college or university).

Choosing a Typeface

Desktop publishing offers many choices of serif and sans-serif typefaces. A serif typeface is a more traditional style having small fine lines or "feet" which make words and lines of type easier to read; this is especially effective when a document has a lot of text, as in the case of a business plan.

More modern looking, sans-serif type has no fine lines. Use it for headings, lists, and other places where there is a limited amount to read.

Shown below, in their actual form, are a few of the more commonly used serif typefaces:

- Times or Times Roman (used in main text of this book)
- Garamond (used in text of Sample Plan in this book)
- New Century Schoolbook
- Palatino

Here are some examples of sans-serif typefaces:

- Helvetica Condensed (used in worksheets in this book)

> *"We fund software companies. So if they're not using a word processor and desktop publishing when putting together their plan, it shows they're behind the technology. I can't imagine a typewritten plan getting funded by us."*
>
> **Ann Winblad**
> **Venture Capitalist**

- Avant Garde
- Univers
- **Helvetica Bold (used in Sample Plan subheads)**

When selecting type for your business plan, follow these guidelines:

- Choose type that is easy to read and businesslike in appearance.
- Use no more than two plain and one italic typeface in your plan.
- Use a serif for the text, and serif or sans-serif type for headlines.

Type size is measured in "points." For text, 10-point type is recommended; smaller than 9 points is a strain to read. (You are now reading 11-point type.) Section headings and titles generally can be set in 12- to 14-point type.

Binding and Report Covers

Binding your business plan, while not necessary, gives it a more polished, complete look. Professional binding (with a process such as Velobind) is provided at most copy centers for just a few dollars.

Choose quality report covers in a professional color such as black, deep blue, or burgundy. Use a clear cover, with a title page, or a label on the front. Make sure the reader can see the name of your business without having to open the plan.

The Final Step: Editing Your Plan

Once you finish your plan, go through it again thoroughly. Find ways to make your sentences shorter and easier to understand.

Eliminate unnecessary words. Change passive verbs and jargon to clear, active language. For example, instead of saying "Profitability will have been reached by Teddy's Dog Togs in its third year of operation," be more direct with a sentence like this: "Teddy's Dog Togs will show a profit by year three."

A business plan must inspire trust. Misspellings, typographical errors, and improper grammar undermine trust. Proofread your plan for such mistakes and have at least one other person proofread it as well.

Chapter Summary

When preparing your plan, remember that your most impressive information must be grasped in less than five minutes. You can help ensure this result by using language that is believable, professional, and authoritative. Your plan should be visually interesting and attractive; use bullet points, charts, and other devices to create this effect.

Keep your plan uncluttered and easy to read, make no mistakes, and edit, edit, edit!

"Automatic turnoffs for a business plan? Writing on both sides of the paper. Typing mistakes. Not knowing how to present financials. Always use straightforward financials; don't get imaginative. Avoid fancy covers; use black or clear binders. Get it professionally typed, or better, desktop published. Looks count a lot."

Robert Mahoney
Executive Director
New England Corporate
Banking, Bank of Boston

Business Plan Components

Section II

Chapter 4

The Executive Summary

*If they don't understand it at first,
they won't understand it at all.*

The Executive Summary Is Crucial

Without a doubt, the single most important portion of your business plan is the Executive Summary. If you can't prepare a clear, concise, and compelling condensation of your business right up front, no one will spend time wading through the rest of your plan. No matter how beneficial your product, how lucrative your market, or how innovative your manufacturing techniques, it is your Executive Summary alone that persuades a reader to spend the time to find out about your product, market, and techniques.

Write Your Summary Last

Because of this, it is imperative that you prepare the Executive Summary last. Although it appears first in your completed document, the Summary reflects the results of all your planning and should be crafted only after careful consideration of all other aspects of your business.

The Executive Summary is so important, in fact, that some venture capitalists prefer to receive just a Summary and Financials before reviewing an entire plan. If you want to send out only a "concept paper" to gauge investor interest before submitting a complete business plan, the Executive Summary should serve as that document. As important as the financial considerations are to investors and bankers, it is the Executive Summary that first convinces them that yours is a well-conceived and potentially successful business strategy.

"A good Executive Summary gives me a sense of why this is an interesting venture. I look for a very clear statement of their long-term mission, an overview of the people, the technology, and the fit to market. Answer these questions: 'What is it? Who's going to build it? Why will anyone buy it?' To paraphrase the movie Field of Dreams, *we want to know, 'If we fund it, will they (buyers) come?"*

Ann Winblad
Venture Capitalist

Even if your business plan is for internal use only, the Executive Summary is still crucial. The Summary is the place where you bring all your thoughts and planning together, where you make a whole out of the disparate parts of your business, and where you "sum up" all that you propose. So, if you have not yet completed the other sections of your plan, proceed to the next chapter and return to the Executive Summary when you have finished the rest of your plan.

What to Convey in Your Executive Summary

The Executive Summary gives the reader a chance to understand the basic concept and highlights of your business quickly, and to decide whether to commit more time to reading the entire plan. Therefore, your goal in the Executive Summary is to motivate and entice the reader.

To do so, you want to convey your own sense of optimism about your business. This does not mean using "hype"; it simply means using a positive, confident tone and demonstrating that you are well-positioned to exploit a compelling market opportunity.

In a short space, you must let the reader know that:

- Your basic business concept makes sense.
- Your business itself has been thoroughly planned.
- The management is capable.
- A clear-cut market exists.
- Your business incorporates significant competitive advantages.
- Your financial projections are realistic.
- Investors or lenders have an excellent chance to get their money back.

If someone reading your Executive Summary concludes that all the elements above exist in your business, that person will almost certainly commit to reading the rest of your business plan.

Targeting the Summary

Ask yourself: "Who will be reading my business plan?" You can improve your chances for a positive reception if you know the answer to that question before you prepare your Executive Summary. Since the Summary is what the reader reads first (and perhaps is the only portion read at all), try to find out what "buttons" to push. Is the bank mostly interested in managers who have had previous business successes? Is the venture capital firm particularly interested in patentable new technology? Does the division president like to see new markets for existing products?

Do a little homework on your potential recipients (see Chapter 19, "Sending Out Your Plan & Looking for Money") and then organize your Executive Summary so that the issues most important to each recipient are given precedence.

Be careful, however, not to tailor the Executive Summary for just one person at a bank or venture capital firm; your plan is likely to end up in the hands of someone else. Target your Summary to address institutional concerns rather than individual preferences.

The Two Types of Executive Summary

Depending on the nature of your business and the capability of the writer, you can approach the Executive Summary in one of two ways: the synopsis Summary or the narrative Summary.

The Synopsis Summary

A synopsis Summary is the more straightforward of the two: It simply relates, in abbreviated fashion, the conclusions of each section of the completed business plan. Its advantage is that it is relatively easy to prepare and less dependent on a talented writer. The only disadvantage is that the tone of a "synopsis" Summary tends to be rather dry.

The synopsis-style Executive Summary covers all aspects of your business plan and treats each of them relatively equally, although briefly. In addition, it tells the reader what you are asking for in the way of financing — which you also state in your cover letter.

The Narrative Summary

The narrative Summary is more like telling the reader a story; it can convey greater drama and excitement in presenting your business. However, it takes a capable writer to prepare a narrative Summary that communicates the necessary information, engenders enthusiasm, and yet does not cross over the line into hyperbole.

A narrative Executive Summary is useful for businesses that break new ground, either with a new product, new market, or new operational techniques which require considerable explanation. It is also more appropriate for businesses that have one dominant element — such as holding an important patent or the participation of a well-known entrepreneur — that can be highlighted. Finally, the narrative Executive Summary works well for companies with interesting or impressive backgrounds or histories.

A narrative-style Executive Summary has fewer sections than the synopsis Summary. Greater emphasis is placed on the business' concept and distinctive features, and less attention given to operational details.

With a narrative Summary, you want to get the reader excited about your company; you do this by taking the one or two most impressive

"You need a business plan so you have a Bible of what you're going to do in your business, a clear statement of your company's mission. The important thing in a business plan is to tell the truth. If there's a problem, we (the venture capitalists) are going to learn it anyway, so it's better if you don't try to hide it."

Ann Winblad
Venture Capitalist

features of your company and giving the reader an understanding of how those features will lead to business success.

A narrative Summary may do more "scene-setting" — recounting the sociological or technological changes that have led to the development of your company's products or services. It may be more personal, telling how the founders' relevant experiences motivated them to start the company.

You may place the topics of a narrative Summary in any order that best showcases your company. The topics do not have to be covered equally; the business concept may be described in three paragraphs and the management team in only one or two sentences. Printing topic headings is not necessary, although you may do so if you wish.

Do not feel it is necessary, however, to use a narrative Summary. Most businesses are well served by a synopsis Summary, especially if the business concept is easily understood and the marketing and operations relatively standard. A synopsis is a very businesslike approach, and experienced business plan readers are comfortable reviewing such straightforward Executive Summaries.

Writing the Summary

Clear, strong writing can pay off in the Executive Summary more than in any other section of your business plan. A dynamic, logical writing style can make the difference between a plan being considered or being discarded.

If you are unsure about your own writing ability, consider hiring a professional writer for the Summary or asking help from a friend or family member who is a good writer. Writing style is less important in a synopsis than in the narrative approach to an Executive Summary, and if your writing ability is limited, use the synopsis form for your Summary.

Length and Design of the Summary

The great advantage to the reader of the Executive Summary is that it is short. A busy funder must be able to read your Summary in five minutes or less. Thus, an Executive Summary should be no more than two to three pages in length. A one-page Summary is perfectly acceptable.

Refer to Chapter 3, "Making Your Plan Compelling," for tips on page layout. Remember to use white space to make the page less intimidating. Bullet points can also be used effectively in the Summary. Since you are limited to so few pages, it may seem frustrating to have to give up space for visual considerations, but these techniques make your plan more inviting to the reader.

Use the Plan Preparation Forms on the next few pages to develop your Executive Summary; there is one for the synopsis type of Summary and one for the narrative type. A Sample Plan of each kind of Executive Summary is also provided.

Chapter Summary

Your Executive Summary is the single most important part of your business plan; it must motivate the reader to consider your plan as a whole. Target your Summary for particular readers and use the style of Summary, either synopsis or narrative, best suited for your business and writing ability. Prepare your Executive Summary last, only after your entire plan is completed.

Synopsis Executive Summary Plan Preparation Form

Take the highlights from each section of your completed plan and address the areas listed below. Remember, you must be brief and clear. Cover each topic in no more than one to three sentences. Describe only the most important and impressive features of your business. After the first two topics, "Company Description" and "Statement of Mission," place the remaining sections in any order that gives the best impression of your business to your target reader. For the reader's quick comprehension, print topic headings at the beginning of each paragraph (see the Sample Plan at the end of this chapter). If you'd like a Summary that seems less like a list, omit the headings. Feel free to combine related topics, such as "Target Market" and "Marketing Strategy," to create a more fluid document.

Company Description. *List the company name, type of business, location, and legal status, e.g., corporation, sole proprietorship, partnership.* _____

_____

_____

Statement of Mission. *Write the concise statement of company purpose you developed in Chapter 5, "Company Description."* _____

_____

_____

Stage of Development. *State whether your company is a startup or continuing business, when it was founded, how far along the product or service is in its creation, and if you've already made sales or started shipping.*

_____

_____

Products and Services. *List the products or services your company sells or plans to sell; this can be generic for a company with many products, e.g., women's sportswear, or specific for a company with just a few.* _____

_____

_____

Target Market(s). *List the markets you intend to reach and why you chose them; indicate the results of any market analysis or market research.* _____

_____

_____

Marketing and Sales Strategy. *Briefly describe how you intend to reach your target market(s), and the advertising, direct mail, trade shows, and other methods you will use to secure sales.* _____

_____

_____

Competitors and Market Distribution. *Indicate the nature of your competition and how the market is currently divided.* _____

_____
_____

Competitive Advantages and Distinctions. *Show why your company will be able to compete successfully; list any important distinctions, such as patents, major contracts, or letters-of-intent.* _____

_____
_____
_____

Management. *Briefly describe the histories and capabilities of your management team, particularly those of company founders.* _____

_____
_____
_____
_____

Operations. *Outline your key operational features, such as locations, crucial distributors or suppliers, cost-saving production techniques, etc.* _____

_____
_____
_____

Financials. *Indicate your company's expected revenues and profits for years one through three.* _____

_____
_____
_____

Long-Term Goals. *Describe the expected status, e.g., sales, number of employees, number of locations, market share of your company five years from now.* _____

_____
_____
_____
_____

Funds Sought and Exit Strategy. *Indicate how much money you are seeking, how many investors you plan to have, how the funds raised will be used, and how investors or lenders will get their money out.* _____

_____
_____
_____

Use this information as the basis of your plan's synopsis Executive Summary.

Narrative Executive Summary Plan Preparation Form

This form provides you an opportunity to outline the Executive Summary portion of your business plan if you choose to write a narrative type of Summary.

The Company. *Describe how your company is organized, its stage of development, stage of product creation, legal status, location, and company mission.* _____

_____

_____

_____

_____

_____

_____

_____

The Concept. *Explain the background of your company, how the product came about, how the market opportunity was recognized, the products and services.* _____

_____

_____

_____

_____

_____

_____

_____

Market Opportunity. *Describe your target market, market trends that exist, why there was a need for the company, the results of market research, the competition, and market openings.* _____

_____

_____

_____

_____

_____

_____

Competitive Advantages and Distinctions. *Indicate why your company can compete successfully; list any important distinctions such as patents, major contracts, and letters-of-intent; specify the barriers-to-entry for new competitors.* _____

_____

_____

_____

_____

Management Team. *Describe the background and capabilities of your key managers, and relate past successful business experiences.* _____

_____
_____
_____
_____
_____
_____
_____
_____
_____

Milestones. *List the milestones by which you will measure success and at what date you expect to reach them; these might include specific revenue or profit levels, the percentage of market share reached, shipments of first product, and the number of employees or locations.* _____

_____
_____
_____
_____
_____
_____
_____
_____
_____

Financials. *Specify the amount of funds sought, the number of likely investors, the use of funds secured, and how investors or lenders will get their money back — through an exit plan (acquisition, public offering, merger) or security (collateral) for a loan.* _____

_____
_____
_____
_____
_____
_____
_____
_____
_____
_____
_____
_____
_____

Use this information as the basis of your plan's narrative Executive Summary.

SAMPLE PLAN: Synopsis Executive Summary

Executive Summary

The Company

ComputerEase, Incorporated, is an Indiana-based company providing computer software training services to corporations in the greater Vespucci, Indiana, area. Technology-related business services are among the fastest growing and healthiest areas of the economy, and ComputerEase intends to capitalize on the opportunities in that area. The company's stock is currently held by President Scott E. Connors and Vice President Susan Alexander.

The Company's Mission

ComputerEase views its mission as increasing the corporate community's productivity by helping them realize the maximum benefit from their personnel and computers through software training. ComputerEase is dedicated to building long-term relationships with customers through quality training and support, and to being known as the premiere software training company in the greater Vespucci area. The goal is steady expansion, becoming profitable by the third year of operations.

Products and Services

The company provides software training seminars targeted to the corporate market. Classes are conducted either at the customer's place of business or at ComputerEase's training center. Additionally, weekend classes are offered to the general public. Training is offered for all leading software programs or ComputerEase will devise custom programs at corporate customers' requests.

Marketing and Sales Strategy

ComputerEase differentiates itself in the market by aiming to satisfy not only students in the training classes, but the actual customers: the corporate clients. The company does this by emphasizing training that increases productivity and by providing comprehensive ongoing service and followup to the corporate customer. Sales are secured predominantly through face-to-face solicitation.

The Competition

No market leaders have yet emerged in the corporate software training field, and competition is diverse and uneven, creating substantial market opportunities. ComputerEase maintains the following advantages over existing competition: ongoing local support to clients, a strong marketing emphasis on increasing customers' productivity, a coordinated marketing program, professional image, authorization from software publishers, qualified management, consistent quality of training, and the availability of the ComputerEase training center.

Target Market
ComputerEase operates in the greater Vespucci area, targeting large and medium-sized businesses with high computer use. Vespucci is the 16th largest city in the United States, with a diverse and healthy economy. Reliable sources estimate that more than 10,000 companies and institutions with more than 50 employees are located in the area.

Management
President and Founder Scott E. Connors brings significant technology-related management experience to his position and previously co-owned his own computer retail outlet. Immediately before starting ComputerEase, Mr. Connors served as Regional Vice-President for Chanoff's Computer Emporium, a large computer hardware retail chain. Earlier, he was a sales representative for IBM. Vice President Susan Alexander brings direct experience in marketing to, and contacts with, the target market from her prior position as Assistant Marketing Director for AlwaysHere Health Care Plan and sales experience as Sales Representative for SpeakUp Dictation Equipment.

Emphasizes past business ownership and directly related experience.

Operations
On August 1, 1993, ComputerEase opened its first corporate training center with 10 personal computer stations. The company offers corporate training sessions at this center as well as at the customer's place of business. It plans to open a second training center by January 1, 1994. ComputerEase utilizes the excess capacity of the training center by offering Saturday classes to the non-corporate community. All training equipment is leased, and training materials are produced by the "just-on-time" method to reduce costs.

Stage of Development
ComputerEase began operations in January 1993, and opened its first Software training center classroom in August 1993.

Financials
The financial strategy of ComputerEase emphasizes reinvestment of income for growth during the first few years of operation, with the company reaching profitability by year three. Annual revenue projections for the current year are $233,000; for 1994, $493,875; and for 1995, $818,615.

Tells investors there is no return on capital for at least three years.

Funds Sought and Utilization
The company is currently seeking $80,000 in investment financing in return for 20% of the stock and a seat on the Board of Directors. These funds will be used for expansion activities, including the opening of an additional training center, hiring of new staff, and increasing marketing activities. Long-term plans call for the company to either develop a franchise operation or expand to become a regional chain, adding at least one training location annually.

Uses specific numbers and uses for funds.

SAMPLE PLAN: Narrative Executive Summary

Executive Summary

The Concept

Provides a sense of the health and opportunities of industry.

Technology-related business services are among the fastest growing industries in the United States. The explosion of the use of computers in virtually every business setting has provided unprecedented opportunities to companies providing support and services for computer equipment. Because the field is relatively new, market leaders have not yet emerged, and customer loyalty has not yet been established. This enables a well-conceived and well-executed company to secure a leading position in the field.

Background

Gives history of motivation for business.

Scott E. Connors, President and Founder of ComputerEase, Incorporated, recognized this opportunity when, as Regional Vice President for Chanoff's Computer Emporium, he conducted a study of the potential market for corporate software training in the Indiana, Ohio, and Illinois areas. As a result of this study, he realized that a professionally managed software training company could quickly become the region's market leader.

The Company

Tells developmental stage, products and services, long-term goals, legal status, and ownership.

ComputerEase is positioned to become the premiere provider of corporate software training targeted to the corporate market. The company began operation in January 1993, and was quickly able to secure corporate clients with software training programs offered at the customer's location.

The client base expanded when ComputerEase opened its first Training Center in August 1993, with 10 personal computer stations, allowing corporations to send their employees off-site for computer instruction. ComputerEase offers software training for all leading software programs, as well as custom programs at corporate customers' request. Additionally, the company offers Saturday classes to the general public.

ComputerEase is incorporated in the state of Indiana and stock is currently held by Mr. Connors and Vice President Susan Alexander.

The Market

The company targeted large corporations in the greater Vespucci, Indiana, area as the base of its initial operations. As the 16th largest city in the United States, Vespucci offers a diverse and healthy economy. More than 10,000 companies employ more than 50 employees.

Competitive Position

Currently corporate software training programs are offered in the Vespucci area by small, local, underfunded, and generally poorly managed companies and through national programs providing no local support or sales. Market research indicates an extremely high level of dissatisfaction with current providers among current customers of software training. ComputerEase's coordinated marketing program to the corporate community, professional image, outstanding training, emphasis on training for business productivity, and its ongoing customer support sets the company apart from its competition.

Management Team

The current management of President Scott E. Connors and Vice President of Marketing Susan Alexander gives ComputerEase an excellent team with which to begin operations. Mr. Connors brings extensive technology-related management and sales experience from his years with Chanoff's Computer Emporium and IBM. Connors successfully managed his own business as a co-owner of Chanoff's downtown Vespucci retail store. He sold his interest in that store to finance the founding of ComputerEase.

In her position as Assistant Marketing Director for AlwaysHere Health Plan, Ms. Alexander gained significant experience in sales and marketing to ComputerEase's target market: corporate human resource directors. Her personal connections with this target audience are extensive, giving ComputerEase immediate access to the potentially most lucrative clients.

Emphasizes previous business ownership and related experience.

The Future

Long-term development calls for the company to progress in one of two directions. One, the company may become a franchise operation, selling franchise licenses, materials, and training for independent operations under the ComputerEase name. Two, ComputerEase may expand its own company-owned and -operated training centers throughout the Midwest region, becoming the dominant regional software training provider.

Provides investors with a sense of growth opportunities.

Financials

The company projects rapid growth, with sales revenues of $233,000 in 1991, $493,875 in 1992, and $818,615 in 1993. It emphasizes the reinvestment of income for expansion rather than profit taking, funding growth internally rather than through additional investment beyond that currently sought.

Funds Sought

The company anticipates only one round of financing (unless franchising is later undertaken) with $80,000 being sought from one investor in return for 20% of the equity and a seat on the Board of Directors. These funds will be utilized to add a new training center, hire staff, and expand marketing activities.

Gives specific numbers and uses of funds.

"It's very difficult to create a new market, even if there's a need. Developing a new market takes years, even if you're 100% right about the need and the product. The best market to look for is a market that already exists, that is already being served, but being served in a marginal fashion."

Eugene Kleiner
Venture Capitalist

Chapter 5

Company Description

The reason most businesses fail is because
they don't understand the business they are in.

Conveying the Basics of Your Business

Before you can discuss the more complex aspects of your business
and the meatier sections of your business plan, such as marketing
strategy or new technology, you must first inform the reader of the
basic details of your business.

Primarily straightforward information, the Company Description section of your plan will probably take you the least amount of time to
prepare. If you've already thought through issues such as your company name and legal form, you'll have most of the information you
need right at your fingertips.

Only one aspect of the Company Description is likely to require additional preparation, but it is an important one. Seemingly simple, your
Statement of Mission, or Mission Statement, should concisely
describe the goals, objectives, and underlying principles of your company. This statement can be placed at the beginning of your Company
Description to set the tone for your entire business plan, or it can be
located near the end of this section.

The topics that follow should be addressed in the Company Description
of your business plan.

"We ask each division to define its own Mission, as well as having an overall corporate Mission Statement. The statement is only a few paragraphs and is descriptive of what we're trying to accomplish. It's reviewed each year, but we discourage minor changes in the mission statement. The corporate mission statement hasn't been changed for five or six years now."

George James
Sr. V.P. & CFO
Levi Strauss & Co.

"Our concept, a club with a membership fee, gives our customers a sense of ownership, of belonging. It's a little like a speakeasy: Our stores are located where they are not obvious, you have to be a member to get in, and you're in on something special."

Robert Price
Chairman of the Board
The Price Club

Company's Objectives/Statement of Mission

Many, if not most, successful large companies describe the main goal of their internal planning process as articulating and clarifying their "philosophy" or "mission." All other aspects of a business should be aimed at achieving the overall company purpose.

You should be able to sum up the basic objectives of your company in just a few sentences. One statement should encapsulate the nature of your business, your business philosophy, your financial goals, your "corporate culture," and how you expect to have your company viewed in the marketplace.

A Statement of Mission provides focus for your company and should be the guiding principle of your business for at least the next few years. It should be the result of a meaningful examination of the foundations of your company, and virtually every word should be important.

A finished Statement might be: "AAA, Inc., is a spunky, imaginative food products and service company aimed at offering high-quality, moderately priced, occasionally unusual foods using only natural ingredients. We view ourselves as partners with our customers, our employees, our community, and our environment. We aim to become a regionally recognized brand name, capitalizing on the sustained interest in Southwestern and Mexican food. Our goal is moderate growth, annual profitability, and maintaining our sense of humor."

The Statement of Mission worksheet on the opposite page helps you outline your company's objectives.

The Company Description Plan Preparation Form at the end of the chapter asks you to describe your business in detail. The main aspects of such a description are detailed on the next several pages.

Company Name

In many cases, the company's name is not the same as the name(s) it uses in doing business with the public. A company might have a dba (doing business as) name under which it operates. It's also quite common for one company to own a number of brand or trade names.

A fictitious business name is a made-up name, rather than the name of a real person, that the company uses as either its legal or corporate name or its dba.

In your business plan, include the legal name of your company and any brand or trade names, dba's, or subsidiary company names.

For instance, a company might list its legal name as AAA, Incorporated, doing business as Arnie's Diner, operating the subsidiary business, Rosie's Catering Service, and selling products under the trade name Arnie's Atomic for its line of food products.

Statement of Mission

Describe your company's philosophy in terms of the areas listed below.

Range/Nature of Products/Services Offered: _____

_____

_____

_____

_____

_____

_____

_____

Quality: _____

_____

_____

_____

_____

Price: _____

_____

_____

_____

Service: _____

_____

_____

_____

_____

Overall Relationship to Customer: _____

_____

_____

_____

_____

Management Style/Relationship to Employees: _____

_____

_____

_____

Continued on next page

Statement of Mission (continued)

Nature of Work Environment: _____

_____

_____

_____

_____

Relationship to Rest of Industry: _____

_____

_____

_____

_____

Incorporation of New Technology/Other New Developments: _____

_____

_____

_____

_____

Growth/Profitability Goals: _____

_____

_____

_____

_____

Relationship to Community/Environment/Other Social Goals: _____

_____

_____

_____

_____

Other Personal/Management Goals: _____

_____

_____

_____

_____

_____

If yours is a new business and you have not yet chosen a name, consider selecting a name that will give you maximum flexibility over the years. A person's name or one that is too narrowly descriptive may limit your ability to grow, change focus, or sell the company. Hill's Airplane Repair is more confining than Take-off Aviation Services, or even Take-Off Transportation Services.

Legal Form of Business

You must indicate the legal form of your company. Is it a corporation, an "S" corporation, general or limited partnership, or sole proprietorship? In what state is it incorporated? Who owns the company, and if a corporation does, how many shares are outstanding and who are the major shareholders?

Here is an example of how to handle the legal description of a business: "AAA, Inc., is incorporated in the state of California, licensed to do business in Jackson County, California. The three shareholders — Arnie Matthews, Brendan Muir, and Aaron Joshua — each own 331/3% of the total shares in the company." If you need more information about the various ways to legally structure a business and the regulations likely to apply to your company, consult your state's edition of The Oasis Press' *Starting and Operating a Business* series.

Management/Leadership

Next, include the name of the chairman/woman of the board of directors, president, and/or chief executive officer. If there are other key members of management, especially those that might be known to potential investors, list their names here. Also, if you have a board of directors, advisory board, or other governing entity, indicate how many people serve on that body and how frequently it meets. If the membership of these bodies is particularly impressive, include their names, otherwise it is not necessary to do so.

Business Location

List the location of your company's headquarters, main place of business (if different), and any branch locations. If you have more than one or two branches, you can list just the total number (although you might want to include a complete list in your plan's appendix). Also, it is very important to describe the geographical area your company serves.

For instance, state: "The corporate offices of AAA, Inc., are located at 123 Amelia Earhart Drive, Jackson, California. Arnie's Diner is located at 456 Lincoln Street in Jackson. Rosie's Catering Services operates from the diner and serves the entire Jackson County area. Arnie's Atomic food products will be sold in five Southwestern states."

> "Kaizen *is the cornerstone of the company. This is a philosophy of continuous pursuit of improvement. We believe small, continuous improvements create greater value than anticipating major leaps. We can never stand still. We have a program of employee suggestions and rewards. In 1990 about 90% of our employees submitted suggestions; we receive over 10,000 suggestions per year. The challenge to managers is to get a higher percentage of employees making workable suggestions. In Toyota's plants in Japan, on average, every employee submits a suggestion per month."*
>
> **Michael Damer**
> **New United Motor Manufacturing Inc.**

Development Stage

Someone reading your business plan should be able to get a clear sense of how far along your company is in its development and what progress you have made in building the company.

Begin by stating when the company was founded. Next, indicate what kinds of milestones have been reached and the company's immediate development goals.

Indicate your phase of development: a seed company (without a product or service even finalized); a startup (in early stages of operation); expansion (adding new product, services, or branches); retrenchment (consolidating or repositioning product lines); or established (maintaining market share and product positioning).

Indicate how far along your plans have progessed. Has the product been developed or tested? Have orders been placed, the product shipped? Are leases signed? Have suppliers been secured? Have branch offices been opened? Has packaging been designed, market surveys undertaken? What have been the past milestones and successes of current operations?

Using the above example of AAA, Inc., this section might read: "Arnie's Diner opened in 1986, and the company began packaging food products used in the restaurant in 1988. These were sold in grocery stores on a local basis beginning in 1990. A distributor has been secured to sell these products to grocery and specialty stores in five Southwestern states. The first orders have been received, placed, and renewed, and the company now plans to expand its production facilities to accommodate increased sales and develop new products."

Financial Status

You also want to give a brief idea of the status of your company in financial and personnel terms. For example, how you have been funded to date and any major financial obligations. If seeking funding, briefly indicate how much money is sought and for what purpose. You will expand on your financial obligations and use of funds sought in the Financials section of your plan.

Thus, this section might read: "AAA, Inc., has maintained overall profitability through slow, careful expansion of its component companies. Total income for the previous year was approximately $991,000.

"Rosie's Catering is presently the most profitable, last year showing a profit of $128,000 on sales of $525,000; Arnie's Diner showed a profit of $81,000 on sales of $385,000; Arnie's Atomic Foods projects a current year loss of $27,000 on sales of $81,000. Currently the total work force is five full-time employees and seven part-time employees.

> *"Some potential milestones a business plan could indicate include product completion, product testing, first customer shipment, unit volume goals, company infrastructure developments, core agreements reached, and second product shipping."*
>
> **Ann Winblad**
> *Venture Capitalist*

"We are now seeking to expand the production facilities, add employees, and increase our sales and marketing efforts. To do so, we are seeking an additional $250,000 in capital."

Products and Services

You can include this next portion either in the Company Description section of your business plan, or you can list it separately, as a section of its own. If your product or service is particularly technical or revolutionary, it is advisable to treat this as a separate section.

Here, you want to clearly identify the nature of your business and the products or services you provide. You should be fairly specific, but if you have a large line of products or services, you do not need to list each and every one, as long as you indicate the general categories.

You want to also indicate future products or services planned by your company and when you expect to introduce them.

Once again using the fictional AAA, Inc., this section might read: "Arnie's Diner is a full-service restaurant specializing in Mexican and Southwestern cuisine. Rosie's Catering Services provides catering for both business and personal occasions, offering a diverse menu, not limited to Southwestern cuisine.

"The Arnie's Atomic food line currently consists of seven shelf-stable chili and salsa products. We anticipate releasing a line of four packaged Southwestern spice mixtures in the next six months. In the second year of this plan, we anticipate introducing a line of tortilla chips."

Patents and Licenses

Next, indicate the trademarks, patents, licenses, or copyrights your business has secured or has pending. If you have quite a few, merely indicate the number and type. Thus, "AAA, Inc., has trademarks to the name Arnie's Atomic Foods, which is used on its food product line, and to the Triple A Shooting Star logo."

Chapter Summary

Your plan's Company Description communicates the basic aspects of your business in a brief form. From the Description, a reader gets a clear idea of what your company is about, how far along you have developed, and what you plan to do. The Statement of Mission shows that you understand the focus of your company and can articulate your objectives concisely.

"I worked on a shelf-stable product for eight months, but at the last minute I changed it to a fresh, refrigerated sauce. Everyone told me the down sides of such a product: harder to get shelf space, shorter shelf life, more retailer resistance. But I didn't love the product in its shelf-stable form. People kept saying not to fall in love with your product, but I had to love what I sold. And I found I didn't end up facing nearly as many problems as they warned me I would."

Deborah Mullis
Founder
D.A.M.E.'S Foods

Company Description Plan Preparation Form

List facts about your business according to the categories below.

Names

Legal/Corporate Name: _____

Doing Business As: _____

Brand/Trade Names: _____

Subsidiary Companies: _____

Legal Form

Legal Form of Business: _____

State Incorporated (if incorporated): _____

County in Which Business is Licensed: _____

Owner(s) of Company or Major Shareholders: _____

Management/Leadership

Chairman/woman of the Board: _____

President: _____

Chief Executive Officer: _____

Other Key Management Members: _____

_____

_____

Governing/Advisory Bodies: _____

_____

Number of Members: _____

Location

Company Headquarters: _____

Place of Business: _____

Branches: _____

Geographic Area Served: _____

Developmental Stage

When Company was Founded: _____

Stage of Formation or Immediate Goals: _____

_____

When Product or Service was Introduced: _____

Progress of Current Plans and Milestones Reached: _____

_____

Past Milestones and Successes: _____

_____

Other Developmental Indicators: _____

_____

Financial Status

Last year's Total Sales: _____

Last year's Pretax Profit: _____

Sales and Profitability by Division or Product Line: _____

_____

Current Number of Employees: _____

Amount of Funds Sought: _____

Basic Use of Funds Sought: _____

Previous Funding and Major Financial Obligations: _____

_____

Products and Services

General Product/Service Description: _____

_____

Number and Type of Lines: _____

_____

Number of Products or Services in Each Line: _____

Patents and Licenses

Patents Held/Pending: _____

Trademarks Held/Pending: _____

Licenses Held/Pending: _____

SAMPLE PLAN: Company Description

Company Description

Tells company basics: incorporation, location, services.

ComputerEase, Incorporated is an Indiana-based company providing computer software training services to businesses in the greater Vespucci, Indiana, area. Corporate headquarters and the software training center are located at 987 South Main Street, Vespucci, Indiana.

States how the company intends to distinguish itself to customers.

The Company's Mission

Our goal is to increase the customers' business productivity by helping them realize the maximum benefit from their personnel and computers. We do this by offering training programs of consistently high quality with an unequalled staff, and backing our programs with ongoing support. We are a service company, dedicated to long-term relationships with our customers. We aim to be known as the premiere software training company in the greater Vespucci area. Our development goals are for steady expansion, with profitability by the third year.

Services

The company offers software training seminars for all leading business software programs, as well as devises custom training programs. These classes are targeted to the corporate market, and training is conducted at the customer's place of business or at the training center. Saturday classes are offered at the training center for the general public.

Shows how the company has grown and established revenues.

Prior to opening the training center, the company was limited in the services it could offer potential clients. The most lucrative business, continuing corporate contracts, was severely restricted, and no public seminars could be offered. Nevertheless, in the first nine months of operation, the company conducted 21 on-site training programs and three Saturday public training programs, and secured continuing training contracts with three of the primary target corporate customers. This produced revenues of $85,500 through August 1993.

Provides specific financial development data.

The company projects deficits for the first two years of operation, with income reinvested for expansion. We anticipate that the company will be profitable by the third year. In these three years, our goal is to become the premiere software training company in the greater Vespucci area. Trends in training, however, are toward nationally-known and marketed providers, so the company anticipates either joining or starting a national franchise or training association by year three.

The company owns the trademark to the name ComputerEase, under which it does business, and to the slogan "We Speak Your Language."

Development to Date

Founded in January 1993 by Scott E. Connors, ComputerEase began operation by providing software training at customers' sites. In August 1993, the company opened its first software training center, at its present location. In March 1993, Susan Alexander became Vice President for Marketing. Ms. Alexander immediately began an extensive marketing program, targeting 200 large companies in the Vespucci area.

Legal Status and Ownership

ComputerEase is incorporated under the laws of the state of Indiana. Ten thousand shares in the company have been issued: 6,000 are owned by President and CEO Scott E. Connors; 1,000 are owned by Vice President of Marketing, Susan Alexander; and 3,000 shares are retained by the company for future distribution.

Funding of the company to date has come from the personal savings of Mr. Connors — a $15,000 loan from Connors' family members — and from the income generated by sales. The company is now seeking $80,000 from outside investors in return for 20% equity ownership. These funds will be used to add a classroom, hire payroll trainers and additional staff, and expand marketing activities.

Gives clear picture of current ownership and equity available.

*"Acknowledgment —
praise — is absolutely
vital to get the job done.
But acknowledgment
must be sincere. Even
acknowleding someone
in private, in quiet ways,
is very important. In
recognizing achieve-
ment, stay away from
sophomoric platitudes.
Don't just throw compli-
ments around, or they
mean nothing."*

**Bill Walsh
Former Coach and
President
San Francisco 49ers**

Chapter 6

Industry Analysis

*A company must know both how it is
like, and how it is unlike, other businesses.*

Your Business and the Industry

No company operates in a vacuum. Every business is part of a larger, overall industry; the forces that affect your industry as a whole will inevitably affect your business as well. Evaluating your industry increases your own knowledge of the factors that contribute to your company's success and shows potential investors that you understand external business conditions.

An industry consists of all companies supplying a similar product or service, other businesses closely related to that product or service, and supply and distribution systems supporting such companies. For example, the apparel industry comprises companies making finished clothing, including the fabric and notion suppliers, independent sales representatives and clothing marts, trade publications, and retail outlets.

What this Chapter Does for You

In this chapter, you are given the tools to examine your industry. Most of the forms are for your internal planning use, and once you complete them, you will have the information necessary to compile your Industry Analysis. In your plan, you want to focus on:

- A description of your industry.
- Current trends in your industry.
- Strategic opportunities that exist in your industry.

"Doing an industry analysis reinforced our initial business premise. The analysis showed restaurants with limited menus, such as the one we planned, were the most rapidly growing segment of the industry. Looking at industry surveys, we saw the trends in eating at that time were towards smaller portions and less formal dining, particularly among the demographic group we intended to serve. So we knew we were on target."

**Martha Johnson
Owner, Suppers
Restaurants**

Naturally, you will need to do some research to get this information. For guidance in your research endeavors, see Chapter 2.

Your Economic Sector

Your economic sector is the broad category into which your industry or business falls; the four general sectors are 1) service; 2) manufacturing, 3) retail; and 4) distribution. Your business may belong to more than one sector; for example, you could both manufacture products for resale by others and sell them yourself at the retail level.

Economic sectors experience trends, and it's useful to note your sector's patterns. Because an economic sector is large and diverse, your business can vary dramatically from overall sector performance and trends. It is unnecessary to do a detailed analysis of your sector, but you should understand its past performance and growth projections. Study articles in business publications, then fill in the worksheet below.

Past and Future Growth of Your Business Sector		
Business Sector	**Past Growth** (Low, Med., High)	**Future Growth** (Low, Med., High)
1. _____	_____	_____
2. _____	_____	_____
3. _____	_____	_____

Your Industry

Your business may intersect two or more industries. For instance, you may produce electronic devices utilized in new and used automobiles. Thus, you are part of three industries: electronics, new automobiles, and the automobile after-market. (The used car industry has many different issues than the new car industry.) If your business falls in more than one industry, research each of the applicable industries, giving particular weight to issues most relevant to your business. Below list the industry or industries in which your company operates.

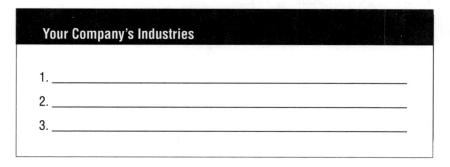

Your Company's Industries
1. _____
2. _____
3. _____

Size and Growth Rate of Your Industry

Pay particular attention to the rate at which your industry is expanding; this gives you insight into the opportunities available for your business.

How does the growth rate for your industry compare with the growth of the gross national product (GNP), which measures the national economy? This comparison will give you an idea of the current health of your industry.

For example, if your industry is growing at 2% a year, and the GNP at 5% a year, your industry is losing ground and opportunities will be few. However, if your industry is growing at 15% a year, while the GNP is at 5%, you are in an industry with far greater potential.

If information for your overall industry is difficult to find, you may be able to estimate its approximate size and growth by evaluating the largest companies in your field. Get copies of their annual reports or analyses from stock brokerages and read articles about them in trade and business publications.

After obtaining these basic facts about your industry, fill in the worksheet below, indicating the industry's past and future growth.

Of course, your own company's development may differ greatly from industry averages — statistics may show that on a national scale, fewer people are dining out, yet your restaurant could be booming.

"Look at annual reports of companies engaged in similar businesses and see what they're doing in the way of financials. Your numbers, of course, won't be the same, but the ratios should be similar. If your plan shows you doing much better than these big companies (in areas like profit margins), you won't be believable.

Eugene Kleiner
Venture Capitalist

Past and Future Growth of Your Industry

Factor	2 Years Ago	Past Year	This Year	Next Year	Next 5 Yrs (Avg.)
Total Revenue					
Total Units Sold/Volume					
Total Employment					
Industry Growth Rate					
GNP Growth Rate					
Rate Compared to GNP (+ or %)					

"The big wineries aren't willing to spend the time and money on something that looks too small. They want to see a large number of cases sold before they move in. So we figured we had a healthy niche for a while. But as the market gets bigger, we have to either sell out to one of the big guys or we have to bring in additional financing in return for equity."

Larry Leigon
President, Ariel Vineyards

If your business plan's figures are far out of line with industry averages, you need to explain in your plan how you account for the variation.

Industry Maturity

Industries don't remain static; they may change dramatically over time. Generally, the life cycle of an industry comprises four phases 1) new; 2) expanding; 3) stable; and 4) declining. The last phase, decline, is not inevitable; many long-standing, stable industries show no sign of decline.

Industries have distinct attributes in different stages of maturity. Even industries that seem closely related are quite dissimilar based on development stage. For instance, the soft drink industry is relatively stable, and a few major companies dominate the field. Little room exists for newcomers, and it would be extremely expensive to try to compete. On the other hand, bottled waters are in a developing industry with lots of competition and variation.

The Industry Maturity Chart on the opposite page describes characteristics of industries in the four different stages. Examine the chart and the descriptions of the growth stages, then list the maturity characteristics of your industry and the opportunities and risks they represent on the worksheet below.

Maturity Characteristics of Your Industry and Associated Opportunities/Risks

Growth Rate: _____

Opportunities/Risks: _____

Competition: _____

Opportunities/Risks: _____

Market Leaders/Standards: _____

Opportunities/Risks: _____

Marketing Goals: _____

Opportunities/Risks: _____

Market Share Strategy: _____

Opportunities/Risks: _____

Product Range: _____

Opportunities/Risks: _____

Customer Loyalty: _____

Opportunities/Risks: _____

Industry Maturity Chart

Characteristic	Development Stage			
	New	**Expanding**	**Stable**	**Declining**
Growth Rate	Very High	Very High	Plateau	Minimal/None
Competition	Increasing	Shake-Out	Entrenched	Decreasing
Market Leaders/ Standards	None	In Flux/Emerging	Fixed	Contracting
Marketing Goals	Exposure and Credibility	Differentiate from Competition	Industry Leadership	Survive
Market Share Strategy	Gain Foothold	Build Market Share	Maintain Share	Cannibalize Weakened Competitors
Product Range	Limited	Expanding	Wide	Reduced
Customer Loyalty	None	Hardening	Strong	Weakening

The four stages of an industry's life cycle are described below.

New industries provide excellent entrepreneurial opportunities. Smaller companies are well-suited to respond to rapid changes, and larger companies have not yet recognized the field's potential. The market, however, is limited because customers are not yet comfortable with the product or service.

Expanding industries enjoy rapidly growing markets as customers begin to recognize the need for the product or service. Competition is brisk as well-funded companies begin to enter the field. All companies are vulnerable, even those that looked strong when the industry was new.

Stable industries have arrived at a plateau with markets leveled off at a reasonably high level. The rate of growth is slow, and customers maintain strong brand loyalty. It is relatively difficult to enter these industries.

Declining industries result from technological, demographic, and sociological changes, and from overwhelming foreign competition. Corporations leave the field or go bankrupt, and the few major companies fight to survive by stealing remaining customers from weakened competitors.

Sensitivity to Economic Cycles

Some industries are heavily dependent on strong economies, either nationally or internationally, and it is crucial to understand how vulnerable your industry is to economic downturns.

Construction, large consumer items (autos, furniture, etc.), and tourism all suffer substantially when the economy is in recession. Industries dependent on new business formation or business expansion, such as office and technical equipment, also suffer in poorer times.

Industries such as discount department stores and used-car dealerships are counter-cyclical, doing relatively better in poor economies than in strong ones. And some industries, such as personal care products and low-cost entertainment, are relatively immune to economic cycles.

If your business is located in a smaller community that is heavily dependent on one industry or one major employer, consider the effect of the economy on that industry or company and thus, your own business.

Considering the economic conditions or cycles that affect your business helps you anticipate and plan for difficult times. On the worksheet below, describe the effect, if any, of each of the listed factors on your industry.

"With a $100 million company, it is vital that I'm tuned in to what's happening in our industry and with national and global economic trends, so I can take steps both in marketing and pricing that will lead my competitors. I look at least six months ahead. To deal with economic downturns, you must be less aggressive with pricing. You plan for these times by marshalling your resources and building up liquidity to take care of the rainy day. The trick is to accurately predict what is happening out there, and to decide whether to scale back on capital expenditures or new acquisitions. Knowing when to pull back differentiates the successes from the potential disasters. And when you can see the bottom of the downturn, resume a more aggressive approach."

Andre Tatibouet
President, Aston Hotels

Effects of Economic Conditions and Cycles on Your Industry & Business

Low Business Expansion/Formation: _____

_____

_____

Growing Unemployment/Low Consumer Confidence: _____

_____

_____

High Interest Rates: _____

_____

_____

High Inflation: _____

_____

_____

Weak Dollar/Cheaper Imports: _____

_____

_____

Seasonality

For many industries, certain times of the year produce higher revenues than others. For example, toy companies are dependent on Christmas sales, while summer is the big season for bathing suit manufacturers.

But many other industries also fluctuate throughout the year. Most retail businesses and consumer products are affected by the Christmas season, which may account for one-third to one-half of all sales.

Spring is an important season for any wedding-associated industry. Tourism-related businesses may depend heavily on the summer. And nonessential products and services may actually suffer during the Christmas season, as consumers reduce nongift expenses.

When preparing your financial forms, particularly cash-flow projections, it is imperative that you understand and account for the seasonal factors that have an impact on your income and expenses. Your product may be sold in December, but you may have to pay for raw materials in June.

On the worksheet below, describe the impact, if any, that the various seasons have on the economic health of your industry. Also describe any additional seasonal factors.

How Seasonal Factors Affect Your Industry
Christmas/Holiday: _____
_____
_____
_____
Summer: _____
_____
_____
_____
Winter: _____
_____
_____
_____
Other: _____
_____
_____
_____

"Forty-seven to forty-eight percent of our volume occurs around Christmas. We keep historical records of our sales volume and timing, so we know what the sales pattern is likely to be, both in the stores and when mail order and quantity orders will be placed. If Christmas is on a Tuesday this year, we go back and look at the last time it fell on a Tuesday, to see sales volume by day of the week, so we'll know what to expect the Friday before Christmas. We put together a 'game plan,' a complete schedule, so we can keep fresh product churning."

Charles Huggins
President, See's Candies

Technological Change

In today's society, technological advances affect every industry. Technology changes the way products are made, how information is managed, and how costs are reduced. Technological developments change manufacturing processes, the way inventory is tracked, communications with customers, and the way paperwork and billing is handled.

It is, of course, impossible to imagine all the technological developments that may affect your industry in the next five years. But it is useful to take note of the trends of the last five or ten years. If yours is an industry in which technology changes rapidly, assume that you will need to be positioned to respond to change, and indicate in your business plan your strategy to do so and the financing it will take for new equipment.

Some technological developments may provide you with strategic opportunities that you want to emphasize when writing your plan. Also, if you have to purchase new equipment periodically, be certain to keep this information in mind when preparing the Financials section of your plan.

On the checklist below, indicate the rate of technological change each area of your industry has experienced over the last five years.

Technological Change in Your Industry Over the Last Five Years

Product/Service Features	High	Moderate	Low	None
Manufacturing/Production	☐	☐	☐	☐
Billing/Administration	☐	☐	☐	☐
Information Retrieval	☐	☐	☐	☐
Inventory Control	☐	☐	☐	☐
Delivery Time/Method	☐	☐	☐	☐
Marketing/Communication	☐	☐	☐	☐
Other: _____	☐	☐	☐	☐
_____	☐	☐	☐	☐
_____	☐	☐	☐	☐

Regulation/Certification

Certain industries are particularly affected by the actions of governmental authorities. While all businesses are influenced by regulation to some degree, regulation, licensing, and certification in some cases can dictate in large part how an industry conducts its business. Take time to think about how, if at all, your business and industry are influenced by governmental regulations.

Consider the actions of governmental entities at all levels — national, state, county, and municipal — as well as special regional bodies, when analyzing the regulatory trends in your industry. Some regulatory measures actually create strategic opportunities. In the environmental field, for instance, increased governmental regulation over pollution has led to whole new industries dealing with waste management and energy conservation.

You may also find your business is subject to certification, either by a governmental body or an industry association. You may be required to take state tests to qualify to conduct your business. If your company benefits from regulatory actions, in your plan emphasize how you intend to capitalize on these opportunities.

Indicate your industry's sensitivity to regulation and certification on the checklist below.

How Sensitive Is Your Industry to Government Regulation?

Area of Sensitivity	High	Moderate	Low	None
Environment	☐	☐	☐	☐
Health and Safety	☐	☐	☐	☐
International Trade	☐	☐	☐	☐
Performance Standards	☐	☐	☐	☐
Licensing/Certification	☐	☐	☐	☐
Fair Trade/Deregulation	☐	☐	☐	☐
Product Claims	☐	☐	☐	☐
Other: _____	☐	☐	☐	☐
_____	☐	☐	☐	☐

"We started with the technology; we didn't really know what we were going to make. We could have used our process to produce low-alcohol wine, nonalcoholic wine, bottled water, or a soft drink. In taste tests, we got a very high response to the soft drink, but it would have been beyond our resources to get distribution for a soft drink. We had contacts and experience in distribution in the wine industry, and an excellent response to our nonalcoholic wine, so we went with the plan we could execute. I would hate to start a product in a distribution system I didn't know."

Larry Leigon
President, Ariel Vineyards

Supply and Distribution Channels

The supply and distribution channels in your industry can be crucial in determining your company's success. In some industries it is notoriously difficult to gain access to distribution, and in others there are few reliable sources of supply. In industries with a large number of suppliers and distributors, costs remain lower and entry is relatively easy.

Be cautious when entering industries with extremely limited supply or distribution systems. Imagine, for instance, that you are considering starting a new magazine. While the lines of supply present little or no problem (many sources of paper, printing plants, writers), distribution may be problematic. One or two companies may control all magazine newsstand distribution in your area, making costs extremely high, if they are willing to carry your magazine at all.

In some industries or businesses, the company itself can control its supply or distribution channels. Below indicate the relative numbers of supply and distribution channels in your industry.

"This is a capital-intensive industry; inventories are expensive to maintain. You get a low asset turnover because your inventory has to sit around in barrels for a long time. Profit margins are not good. You must determine what are the key ratios in the business, even if the formal financials don't follow for six months. Stay on top of the payables and receivables turnover, the gross profit margin, the inventory turnover ratio."

Larry Leigon
President, Ariel Vineyards

Supply and Distribution Channels in Your Industry

Number of Channels	High	Medium	Low	Self-Control
Supply	☐	☐	☐	☐
Distribution	☐	☐	☐	☐

Financial Characteristics

No area of your Industry Analysis is more important than an evaluation of the financial patterns characterizing your industry, especially if you are new to the field. Knowing the standards of such aspects as markups, commissions, and returns on sales will substantially help your own budgeting process.

Much of this information may seem difficult to locate if you are just entering the industry. Perhaps the best way to get this information is to interview those already in the industry, especially those who are not your direct competitors. Just make certain the information is industry-specific; knowing the retail markup on apparel won't tell you the markup on food, consumer electronics, or fashion accessories.

The Financial Patterns worksheet on the opposite page lets you keep crucial financial specifics handy when preparing budgets. Established businesses should complete this worksheet with actual company data.

Financial Patterns $ ▶ $$ ▶ $$$

Fill in this worksheet with figures representative of the financial standards in your industry.

Normal Retail Markup of Goods: _____

_____

_____

Normal Distributor Markup of Goods: _____

_____

_____

Typical Sales Commission Percentage: _____

_____

_____

Standard Credit Terms: _____

_____

_____

Days of Inventory Maintained: _____

_____

_____

Average Percentage of Return on Sales: _____

_____

_____

Other Financial Patterns of Note: _____

_____

_____

Percentage of Merchandise Price due to:

Cost of Labor: _____   Fixed Costs: _____

Cost of Materials: _____   Shipping: _____

Energy: _____   Other: _____

Preparing the Industry Analysis for Your Business Plan

Once you have analyzed your industry for your internal planning purposes, coordinate that information and incorporate the highlights in the Plan Preparation Form on the opposite page. This form, when completed, will contain the information that will serve as the basis for the Industry Analysis segment of your business plan.

Chapter Summary

Evaluating the standards, trends, and characteristics of your industry helps you ensure your own company's success and assists in planning your budgets. Although each company is unique, no business completely escapes the realities and constraints of the industry in which it operates. You need to understand the larger environment before you can successfully differentiate your own business.

Industry Analysis Plan Preparation Form

Using this form as a guide, summarize the main points you wish to convey in your Industry Analysis.

Industry Description: _____
_____
_____
_____
_____
_____
_____
_____
_____
_____

Industry Trends: _____
_____
_____
_____
_____
_____
_____
_____
_____
_____
_____
_____
_____

Strategic Opportunities: _____
_____
_____
_____
_____
_____
_____
_____
_____
_____
_____
_____

Use this information as the basis of your plan's Industry Analysis.

SAMPLE PLAN: Industry Analysis

Industry Analysis

ComputerEase is well-positioned to take advantage of the significant opportunities presented by the rapidly expanding industry of computer-related business services.

Computer-Related Services on the Rise

Cites statistics, showing real knowledge of industry.

Service industries represent the fastest growing sector of the national economy, and computer-related business services reflect that continued growth. These services as a whole grew in excess of 125% over the five years from 1985–89, compared to an overall GNP of approximately 29.5% during that period.

Newly Developing Industry

Shows market opportunity.

Computer software training is a relatively new industry, an outgrowth of the phenomenal expansion of computer use. The industry is still in a state of flux, with no market leaders, nationally known providers, or widely recognized accreditation programs. Individual software manufacturers do offer certification as trainers for their products, but this certification is yet to be standardized, and such certification is not yet a key issue for consumers.

Open Competitive Environment

Currently, the level of service is broadly uneven, and providers enter and leave the field rapidly. Some training is marketed through direct mail by national companies generally offering one- or two-day sessions by traveling trainers. These companies do not maintain an ongoing local profile or relationship with customers. Other software training is offered by individual consultants. Generally, these are not presented or marketed in any continuing, professional manner. They are not perceived in the marketplace as "businesses," and quality and pricing are widely uneven.

Barriers to Entry

Indicates limits to new competition.

The high costs of purchasing current computer equipment and continually updating expensive training materials (software is revised approximately every six months) makes it difficult for undercapitalized companies to enter or stay in the software training field. Moreover, software providers are becoming more selective about which companies they will allow to serve as "authorized training companies." These relationships are crucial to the training company in terms of receiving advanced copies of software updates, purchasing training copies of software below cost, and co-sponsoring product introduction events.

Long-Term Opportunities

Thus, the long-term outlook for the industry is to develop regionally or nationally known companies, as is currently the case with other business services, such as accounting or employment services. These companies will be able to develop revenues and market share sufficient to sustain the high overhead. National franchises or affiliations will make it possible to share training materials and other resources.

ComputerEase Can Develop Strong Position in Region

The current lack of industry leaders represents an exceptional opportunity for ComputerEase to develop a dominant presence in the software training field in the greater Vespucci area. The company will then be well-situated to take advantage of national affiliations, either with franchisors, national associations, or software providers.

"People won't accept a new product if they think it's something totally new. So, you have to present it as something they already know, only somewhat better. Change needs to be incremental."

Larry Leigon
President, Ariel Vineyards

Chapter 7

Target Market

*It's easier to get a piece of an existing market
than it is to create a new one.*

Know Your Customers

Essential to business success is a thorough understanding of your customers. After all, if you don't know who your customers are, how will you be able to assess whether you are meeting their needs? Since success depends on your being able to meet customers' needs and desires, you must know who your customers are, what they want, where they live, and what they can afford.

Is Your Company Market Driven?

Moreover, if you are using your business plan to secure financing, defining the nature and size of your market is critical. Many investors look for companies that are market driven. In other words, they seek to fund companies whose orientation is shaped by the demands and trends of the marketplace rather than the inherent characteristics of a particular product or service.

Being attuned to your market may cause you to make changes in your advertising, packaging, location, sales structure, even the features and character of the product or service itself. In the long run, a market analysis will save you money. When deciding which marketing vehicles to use (advertising, trade shows, etc.), you can choose approaches based on whether they reach your specific target market.

"You have to be market driven. Who will buy it? What do they feel about it? Do they think it's a luxury or commodity? Do they need a big bottle or a small bottle? Particularly with a brand new product, you have to understand your market."

**Larry Leigon
President, Ariel Vineyards**

"Be willing to look at different market segments instead of just the obvious or largest market to secure some degree of market penetration. Take, for instance, the credit-card electronic key for hotels. Even though these keys represented substantial savings, established hotels at first were reluctant to make the change-over from traditional locks. Instead, new hotels were the first to put in this type of lock, and existing hotels followed later, once the benefits were well-known."

Eugene Kleiner
Venture Capitalist

A market analysis differs from a marketing plan. An analysis enables you to identify and understand your customers; a marketing plan tells how you are going to reach your customers. Laying out a marketing plan is covered in Chapter 9.

If you do not sell your product or service directly to the end-user but rather to retail outlets, distributors, etc., you have two markets and you should define both of them — the ultimate consumer and the intermediary who is your actual customer. These two markets may have different concerns which you need to understand.

To gather information for this chapter, use the methods discussed in Chapter 2.

Defining Your Target Market

You may be tempted to describe your market in the broadest possible terms, choosing to include all those who might potentially use your product or service. Doing so gives you the comforting sense that you have a huge market to exploit.

Unfortunately, this gives you little genuine information on which to base your business decisions. You could end up defining the market for furniture as everyone who lives indoors, hardly helpful if you're trying to come up with a marketing plan for your furniture store.

Instead you need to identify the particular market segments you wish to reach. These segments describe distinct, meaningful components of the overall market and give you a set of specific characteristics by which to identify your target market.

Let's say you are considering opening a discount dry cleaning establishment. You plan your service to be less expensive and faster, but also of slightly less quality than the dry cleaner now serving the area.

Thus, you might define your target market in these terms: "Employed women in white-collar jobs, price and time sensitive, commute by car, ages 25 to 50, household incomes of $20,000–$50,000 per year, children living at home, reside in the Laurelwood neighborhood."

You then need to determine whether the neighborhood has enough consumers who fit this profile to support your business.

To be a useful planning tool, the definition of your target market must meet these criteria:

- **Definable.** It should have specific characteristics identifying what the potential customers have in common.
- **Meaningful.** The characteristics must meaningfully relate to the decision to purchase.
- **Sizable.** It must be large enough to profitably sustain your business.

- **Reachable.** Both the definition and size must lead to affordable and effective ways to market to your potential customers.

Once you have defined your market, you should then assess its size and trends, evaluate your competitors for that particular market, and probe the market for strategic opportunities.

Demographic Description

Begin describing your market by the most basic, objective aspects of the customer base. These details are the specific and observable traits that define your target market.

Demographic information is particularly useful when devising your marketing plan. Many marketing vehicles, such as publications, mailing lists, radio, and TV, accumulate this kind of data about the market they reach. Thus, you are better able to judge whether such vehicles are appropriate for your company.

Remember, you want to define those characteristics of your target market that meaningfully relate to the interest, need, and ability of the customer to purchase your product or service.

In the previous definition of the target market for the Laurelwood dry cleaner, for instance, the definition "white-collar jobs" directly relates to the need for regular dry cleaning; "women" relates to the fact that most dry cleaning nationally is purchased by women; "commute by car" is important because the location is not near public transportation; and "$20,000–$50,000" relates to the customer's ability to pay for dry cleaning while being less likely to afford the more expensive cleaners.

On the Demographic Description worksheet on the next page, describe the demographic details of your target market, whether you are marketing to consumers or businesses.

Geographic Description

Perhaps the easiest aspect of your target market to define is the geographic area you intend to serve.

This definition should be as concrete as possible, indicating whether your business serves a particular neighborhood, entire city, regional area, state, national region, complete nation, or portion of the international market.

Also, look at the density of the area — whether urban, suburban, or rural, and whether the location is in a mall, strip center, business district, or industrial area, or will be a stand-alone facility. Some businesses define their geographic market by climate, serving only cold-weather or hot-weather locations.

"Customers can be categorized in several ways, by income level or by lifestyle issues. The income levels can fall into one or more of the following categories: luxury, upscale, upper moderate, moderate, and budget. Lifestyle issues are more subjective. The target customer is less dependent on income level and more on her attitude about how she spends her disposable income."

Nancy Glaser
President, Golden
Gate Chips

Demographic Description

This worksheet helps you chart a demographic profile of your target market.

Consumer

Age Range: _____
_____
_____

Income Range: _____
_____
_____

Sex: _____
_____
_____

Occupation: _____
_____
_____

Marital Status: _____
_____
_____

Family Size: _____
_____
_____

Ethnic Group: _____
_____
_____

Level of Education: _____
_____
_____

Home Ownership: _____
_____
_____
_____

Other: _____
_____
_____

Business

Industries: _____
_____
_____

Sector: _____
_____
_____

Years in Business: _____
_____
_____

Company Revenues: _____
_____
_____

Number of Employees: _____
_____
_____

Number of Branches: _____
_____
_____

Square Footage: _____
_____
_____

Company Ownership: _____
_____
_____

Other: _____
_____
_____
_____
_____

On the worksheet below, describe the geographic details of your target customers, whether consumers or businesses.

Geographic Description

Area Served (city, region, nation, etc.): _____

_____

_____

Density (urban, rural, suburban, etc.): _____

_____

_____

Nature of Location (mall, strip center, business district, etc.): _____

_____

_____

Climate Conditions: _____

_____

"The decision to locate in Napa was a marketing decision. We could have made our product anywhere, but Napa is associated with premium wines. We wanted Napa on the label."

**Larry Leigon,
President, Ariel Vineyards**

Lifestyle/Business-Style Description

In the Target Market section of your plan, convey a sense of the concerns and interests of your customers. How do they spend their time? What issues are they facing in their lives or businesses? With whom do they associate? How do they relate to their employees and community?

Your natural instincts and experience with customers gives you some sense of what your customers are interested in. It's logical, for instance, to assume that receptive targets for your expensive specialty food product are fairly likely to subscribe to *Gourmet* or other food magazines and might belong to local food and wine organizations. Or, if the market for your business service is law firms, you would naturally assume they belong to the local Bar Association.

A little research can help you identify other aspects of your target market's lifestyle or business style. Observe customers in places where they shop or live. What other products or services do they buy? What kinds of cars do they drive? What kinds of clothes do they wear?

Review the publications you think target customers subscribe to. What other companies are advertising? What are the articles about? Survey your customers, either in person, by mail, or on the phone, and ask them about some of their activities.

"I had a strong sense of my target market from the beginning. I clearly defined the user profile: 30 years and up, $35,000-plus income, urban, sophisticated palate, leisure travel, exposure to foreign foods, subscribe to a food magazine, busy. Then I looked at retail outlets that I thought served that profile end-user. My customer is really the retail outlet, and I had to focus on them as well. There's a tendency to look only at the end-user and neglect your real customer. But ultimately, to serve the retailer, you have to make a product that sells."

Deborah Mullis
Founder
D.A.M.E.'S Foods

What kind of people or businesses need or want your product or service? Do they go to the movies, watch TV, or rent videos? Do they entertain at home? If so, for whom? What other kinds of products or services would be used in the same setting with yours?

Develop a mental picture of your customer's entire week. Be creative, but logical and realistic. You want to relate to your customer as a whole, which makes you more responsive to their needs and gives you ideas for marketing vehicles and approaches. The worksheet on the opposite page helps you achieve this.

Pyschographic Description

In addition to the observable, objective characteristics of your market, less tangible but equally important psychological factors also influence your targeted customer's purchasing decisions. These are aspects of self-image: how customers see, or want to see, themselves. Some of these are fairly self-conscious attributes, for example, a homemaker priding himself or herself on being a smart shopper. Some are less conscious, perhaps being status-seeking or gadget-happy.

Business customers as well as consumers can be described in psychographic terms. Some companies view themselves as being on the cutting edge of technology, others as fiscally responsible, and others as socially responsible. These distinctions can help in determining marketing efforts and in positioning your product or service. Apple Computer, Inc., for example, has generally been viewed by consumers as the computer of choice for "hip" companies, while IBM appeals to those who "don't take chances." On the checklist below, check off each of the psychographic traits that characterize your target customer.

Psychographic Description

Consumer	Business
☐ Technically Adept	☐ Technically Advanced
☐ Status Seeking	☐ Industry Leader
☐ Trend-Setting	☐ Innovative
☐ Conservative/Responsible	☐ Conservative/Responsible
☐ Socially Responsible	☐ Socially Responsible
☐ Environmentally Conscious	☐ Environmentally Conscious
☐ Smart Shopper	☐ Smart Business Operator
☐ Family-Oriented	☐ Fiscally Prudent
☐ Fun-Seeking	☐ Good Manager of Employees
☐ Good Housekeeper	☐ Influenced by Leading Companies
☐ Other: _____	☐ Other: _____

Lifestyle/Business-Style Description

Complete this worksheet to describe the lifestyle/business-style of your target customers.

Consumer

Family Stage: _____

_____

_____

Hobbies: _____

_____

_____

Sports: _____

_____

_____

Television Shows Watched: _____

_____

_____

Other Forms of Entertainment: _____

_____

_____

Publication Subscriptions: _____

_____

_____

Organizations/Affiliations: _____

_____

_____

Political Affiliation: _____

_____

_____

Other: _____

_____

_____

_____

Business

Business Stage: _____

_____

_____

Employee Relations: _____

_____

_____

Trade Association Memberships: _____

_____

_____

Business Products & Services Used: _____

_____

_____

Workforce Type: _____

_____

_____

Publication Subscriptions: _____

_____

_____

Community Activities: _____

_____

_____

Management Style: _____

_____

_____

Other: _____

_____

_____

_____

Purchasing Patterns Description

In planning, it's particularly important to understand the buying patterns of your customers. For instance, if Fortune 500 companies are your target market, you must recognize that these large companies have slow decision-making processes and, due to their size, resist change even when presented with compelling facts. You must keep these realistic constraints in mind when forecasting your sales to this market.

Complete the worksheet below to describe the likely purchasing patterns of your target customers, whether consumers or businesses.

Purchasing Patterns Description

Reason/occasion for first purchase: _____

Number of times they'll purchase: _____

Interval between purchases: _____

Amount of product/service purchased: _____

Motivation for continued use: _____

How long to make decision to purchase: _____

Where customer first learned about product/service: _____

Place where customer purchases product/service: _____

Where customer uses product: _____

How customer uses product: _____

Method of payment: _____

Special needs: _____

Other: _____

_____

Buying Sensitivities Description

What factors are of greatest importance to your customer when deciding to buy? Of course, all customers would say that they want the highest quality, best service, and greatest convenience, at the lowest price.

But in reality, customers know they have to make tradeoffs: paying a little more for extra features, driving farther to get a lower price. What aspects are your customers least willing to give up? What are the areas of their greatest sensitivity?

The checklist on the opposite page helps you indicate how sensitive your customers (consumers or businesses) are to various factors.

Buying Sensitivity Description

	High	Medium	Low	Not at All
Price	☐	☐	☐	☐
Quality	☐	☐	☐	☐
Brand Name	☐	☐	☐	☐
Product Features	☐	☐	☐	☐
Salesperson	☐	☐	☐	☐
Sales/Special Offers	☐	☐	☐	☐
Advertising	☐	☐	☐	☐
Packaging	☐	☐	☐	☐
Convenience of Use	☐	☐	☐	☐
Convenience of Purchase	☐	☐	☐	☐
Location	☐	☐	☐	☐
Store Decor/Environment	☐	☐	☐	☐
Customer Service	☐	☐	☐	☐
Return Policy	☐	☐	☐	☐
Credit Availability	☐	☐	☐	☐
Maintenance Program	☐	☐	☐	☐
Warranty	☐	☐	☐	☐
Nature of Existing Customers	☐	☐	☐	☐
Other: _____	☐	☐	☐	☐

"We want to understand what our customers are buying and how they are buying our product. We analyze our sales by distribution channel, by customer type. We see how many of our goods are sold off-price. It's not enough to just know how many sales you have; you also need to know what kind of sales you are making."

George James
Sr. V.P. & CFO
Levi Strauss & Co.

Market Size and Trends

Once you have defined the characteristics of your target market, you must then assess the size of this market and evaluate the trends likely to influence both market size and customer behavior in the near future.

Size

You want to make sure your customer base is large enough to sustain your business and, if seeking funding, to convince potential investors that your company can grow to a size that will make their investment profitable.

Surprisingly, you don't want your target market to be either too small or too large. Markets that are too small are obviously in trouble from the start, as you won't have enough customers. (Niche markets may be quite small, serving a limited number of customers with a very specific need, but can still be lucrative and able to support a well-defined business.) Very large markets, however, invite numerous well-financed competitors, require expensive marketing vehicles, and soften the focus of marketing efforts.

For many businesses, particularly smaller retail operations, determining whether your market is sufficiently sizable will be mostly a matter of intuition and observation. You needn't do a scientific study. But if you are unsure about your market, or need to convince investors, you should gather data to support your plan.

When assessing the size of the market, you will find demographic and geographic information easiest to locate. Much of this data is available from U.S. Census Bureau reports, local governmental agencies, real estate brokerages, chambers of commerce, and business directories.

Information about other characteristics of your market can be gleaned from existing market research studies about the general population or from trade associations. You may want to conduct your own market research, much of which is rather simple; include pertinent highlights of such research in your business plan.

Trends

Equally as important as estimating the size of your current market is evaluating the trends that may affect the market in the coming years. Doing so will give you a sense of your company's continuing viability, the strategic opportunities the market presents, and how the company must plan to respond to changing behavior of customers.

Preparing for change is not so much a matter of predicting the future as analyzing the recent past. Much of your analysis can be based on observable changes in demographics and customer behavior. For instance, let's say your product is designed to appeal to retired individuals in the American Southwest.

You can analyze increased population figures for that age group in particular states and membership trends in organizations such as the American Association of Retired People (AARP). This will provide you with a sense of how the market size is changing. Studies of new hobbies, disposable income growth, and altered buying habits for the age group will give you indicators of the issues and opportunities facing your company in the near future.

Use the worksheet on the opposite page to describe your market size and the trends likely to affect customer behavior in the next few years.

Market Size and Trends

What is the current approximate size of your target market? _____

What is the rate of growth of the target market? _____

What changes are occurring in the makeup of the market? _____

What changes are affecting ability to afford the product/service? _____

What changes are affecting the need for the product/service? _____

How are customers changing the use of the product/service? _____

What changes in social values and concerns are affecting the product/service? _____

Preparing the Target Market Section of Your Plan

Based on what you have learned by analyzing your potential market, you are now ready to prepare the Target Market section of your written business plan.

Using the Plan Preparation Form on the next page as a guide, focus primarily on these three areas:

- Description
- Trends
- Strategic Opportunities

This section of your plan particularly lends itself to the use of bullet points, which makes writing easier.

Chapter Summary

A concise description and thorough understanding of your target market will give you focus when developing your product or service, designing your marketing plan, and forecasting sales and expenses. Potential investors want reassurance that your market is sizable and that you comprehend the opportunities and limitations of the market. You need to make certain your target market is definable and reachable.

"We didn't do a lot of market research. We were lucky. Our idea seemed to coincide with a big increase in the number of small, independent businesses—our target market. In some instances, we targeted the wrong kind of businesses. For instance, we first stocked a lot of hardware and houseware products in multi-packs for resale at small, independent hardware stores. What we didn't realize is that these kind of stores don't really exist much anymore."

Robert Price
Chairman of the Board
The Price Club

Target Market Plan Preparation Form

Outline the Target Market portion of your plan on this form. More detailed descriptions of your market and results of market research can be included in your plan's Appendix.

Market Description: _____

_____

_____

_____

_____

_____

_____

_____

_____

Market Size and Trends: _____

_____

_____

_____

_____

_____

_____

_____

_____

_____

_____

_____

Strategic Opportunities: _____

_____

_____

_____

_____

_____

_____

_____

_____

Use this information as the basis of your plan's Target Market section.

SAMPLE PLAN: Target Market

Target Market

Market Description

ComputerEase operates in the greater Vespucci, Indiana, area, targeting those large- and medium-sized businesses with high computer use. The geographic area includes the incorporated cities of:

- Vespucci
- Abergel Peak
- Newman City

and the suburban communities (with business centers) of:

- Karen's Springs
- Gaspar
- Lake Arthur

Market Size and Trends

Vespucci, with its surrounding communities, is a large and economically healthy area. The city of Vespucci has a population of approximately 675,000, according to 1992 census figures, making it the 16th largest city in the U.S. The Vespucci Metropolitan Statistical Area (MSA) has an overall population approaching 1,500,000.

The business climate has been consistently strong and less affected by downturns in the national economy due to its diverse economic base. The Vespucci MSA includes three county seats and is the home to numerous government offices. Also located in the greater Vespucci area are:

- An international airport.
- The regional processing centers for three national insurance companies.
- The data processing center for the state's highway patrol.
- A state university and six other colleges and universities.
- A major medical center.

The economic base has been expanding, and recently a national research institute with 280 employees announced its intention to relocate to Vespucci. A survey for the local newspaper, *The Vespucci Explorer*, showed that 43% of larger companies intended to add employees in the next 24 months.

Indicates specific geographic market.

Relates health and diversity of target market.

SAMPLE PLAN: Target Market (continued)

The breakdown of employment by industry is approximately:

- 25% retail and wholesale sales
- 25% government
- 25% manufacturing
- 25% education, health, and services.

Target Customers

Clearly identifies characteristics of target customers.

The businesses ComputerEase targets for its services have these characteristics:

Business attributes:

- Over 50 employees
- High computer use (data processing and retrieval, financials)
- Relatively high employee turnover; expanding number of employees

Industries:

- Government
- Insurance
- Financial/Banking
- Accounting
- Colleges and Universities
- Engineering
- Hospitals and Other Medical Facilities
- Airlines

The Vespucci Chamber of Commerce estimates that of the more than 10,000 companies and institutions with more than 50 employees in the area, at least 2,500 are in the industries listed above.

Indicates self-image and sensitivities of potential customer.

Management personnel in these industries generally view themselves as responsible and professional. They prefer to deal with service companies that present a stable, conservative image. They are generally more sensitive to quality than price, and can be considerably influenced by the fact that similar companies already use the service provider.

Market Readiness

ComputerEase's Vice President for Marketing conducted a market research survey with a selection of targeted companies. This survey indicated the particular patterns of these companies in relation to computer training need:

- 97% indicated a need for employees trained in computer use.
- 83% indicated some need for company-provided computer training.
- 67% indicated a need for occasional or specialized training.
- 41% indicated a need for continuing training programs.

The survey also revealed that such companies currently spend funds on computer training. Specific data indicates:

- 42% of these companies have a "training" amount allotted in their current year's budget.
- 18% specifically have "computer or software training" budgeted for the current year.
- 34% have purchased software training services in the last year.
- 66% indicated they would purchase more training than at present if better-quality, more reliable training were available.

Fully 74% of those using computer training said they were either highly unsatisfied or somewhat unsatisfied with their current training arrangements. This level of dissatisfaction is substantially higher than the satisfaction level with other business services (27% average dissatisfaction level with services such as accounting and legal).

Strategic Opportunities

Computer training services in these companies are overwhelmingly purchased, recommended, or approved by the Human Resources/Personnel Director (83%), providing a clear target for marketing efforts.

National surveys show an increasing percentage of businesses relying on computers to maintain, analyze, and retrieve information. A high percentage of businesses in the Vespucci area are in fields with significant dependence on computerized information.

Clearly, there is a real need for ComputerEase's services in the Vespucci area, an expanding and healthy market, a highly dissatisfied market, and an identifiable way to reach the market. This provides a substantial opportunity for ComputerEase to fill a void in the provision of software training services.

Shows real market exists.

"You must position your product or services so there is a significant reason for people to switch to your company. It's not enough to say there is room for one more player in the market, because by the time you catch up with the competition, they can lower their prices and squeeze you out. You have to be able to leapfrog the competition."

Eugene Kleiner
Venture Capitalist

Chapter 8

The Competition

*It is not enough just to build a better mousetrap;
you have to build a better mousetrap company.*

Know What You're Up Against

Famed baseball player Satchel Paige used to say, "Don't look back; someone may be gaining on you." But in business it is imperative to see who's gaining on you. It is far better to know what you're up against than to be surprised when your sales suddenly disappear to an unexpected competitor.

Every business has competition. Those currently operating a company are all too aware of the many competitors for a customer's dollar. But many people new to business — excited about their concept and motivated by a perceived opening in the market — tend to underestimate the actual extent of competition and fail to properly assess the impact of that competition on their business.

One of the very worst statements you can make in a business plan is "We have no competition." A knowledgeable investor will immediately disregard a plan with such a statement because it indicates that either: 1) You have not fully examined the realities of your business; or 2) There is no market for your concept.

You can see this by looking at the example of the photocopier. When the first one was invented, no competition existed from other makers of photocopiers, of course. But competition still came from many sources, including suppliers of carbon paper and mimeograph machines. And if the copier worked and the market was receptive,

"Don't allow yourself to be awed by an opponent, or, on the other hand, to have contempt for them. Don't allow the extremes of your emotions to dictate your assessment of the competition. Never overreact to a great deal of success or failure, either your own or the competition's."

Bill Walsh
Former Coach and
President, S.F. 49ers

future competition could realistically be projected. If no competition truly existed at the time it was invented — if people weren't duplicating documents by some means — it would have meant no market for photocopiers existed.

Honestly evaluating your competition will help you better understand your own product or service better and give investors a reassuring sense of your company's strengths. It enables you to know how best to distinguish your company in the customer's eyes, and it points to opportunities in the market.

Learn from your competition. The basic concept of competition is responsiveness to customers, and watching your competitors can help you understand what customers want.

As you begin your competitive assessment, keep in mind that you need to evaluate only those competitors aiming for the same target market. If you own a fine French restaurant in midtown Manhattan, you don't have to include the McDonald's next door in your competitive evaluation: You're not aiming for the same customer at the same time. On the other hand, if you are thinking of opening the first sports memorabilia shop in Alaska, you have to look far afield, at any such retail stores in Seattle or Vancouver and mail-order dealers from all over the country, as that is where your potential customers shop now.

When preparing the competitive analysis portion of your business plan, focus on identifying:

- Who your major competitors are.
- On what basis you compete.
- How you compare.
- Potential future competitors.
- Barriers to entry for new competitors.

Competitive Position

It is tempting to want to judge your competition solely on the basis of whether your product or service is better than theirs. If you have invented a clearly superior widget, it is comforting to imagine that widget customers will naturally buy your product instead of the competitors' and the money will roll in.

Unfortunately, many other factors will determine your success in comparison to other manufacturers of widgets. Perhaps their brand name is already well-known. Perhaps their widgets are much cheaper. Perhaps their distribution system makes it easier for them to get placement in stores. Or maybe customers just like the color of your competitors' packages better.

> *"Visit and observe successful stores. Analyse their strengths and weaknesses. Shop your competition."*
>
> **Nancy Glaser**
> **President, Golden Gate Chips**

> *"Competitors sales have helped me, as my sales have helped them. With a new product, you have to show there's a market. Stores are more willing to carry my product if there's a similar product already selling well."*
>
> **Deborah Mullis**
> **Founder**
> **D.A.M.E.'S Foods**

The objective features of your product or service may be a relatively small part of the competitive picture. In fact, all the components of customer preference, including price, service, and location, are only half of the competitive analysis.

The other half of the equation is examining the internal strength of your competitors' companies. In the long run, companies with significant financial resources, highly motivated or creative personnel, and other operational assets will prove to be tough, enduring competition.

Thoroughly Evaluate Your Competition

Two Competitive Analysis worksheets in this chapter help you evaluate your competitive position both in terms of customer preference and internal operational strengths.

The worksheets enable you to give greater or lesser importance to each competitive factor, depending on the significance of those particular aspects. To complete each worksheet, give each factor listed a maximum possible number of points, ranging from 1 to 10, with 1 being least important to your overall target market and 10 being the most important. Place the maximum number for each factor in the Maximum Points column.

For instance, on the Competitive Analysis: Customer Perception Factors worksheet, let's say your target market is extremely price sensitive but willing to travel a long way to get a bargain. The purchase price factor might be given a maximum of 10 points and the location factor a maximum of 2.

Once you have finished numbering the factors for your company and competitors, you will see how this weighting system gives you a better picture of the actual strength of your competitors as opposed to your own.

Keep in mind that you can also allot negative numbers. If, for example, your target market is interested only in items perceived as luxuries, having too low a price may be a liability. If your market is particularly socially conscious, the fact that your competitor conducts tests on animals may be a negative for the social image factor in their evaluation, giving you a competitive edge.

In your analyses, look at both specific competitors, those particular companies you compete against, and at the overall type of competition. In the example of the Alaskan sports memorabilia store, for instance, the Competitive Analysis might have four competitors listed: each of the two specific retail stores in Seattle and Vancouver, and mail-order dealers and traveling trade shows as categories.

If desired, you can include these completed worksheets in the Appendix of your plan, as well as use them for internal planning purposes.

"Price is not sufficient as a marketing strategy; you need to be in touch with the kind of market you're really focusing on. For us, we're targeting a clientele who own their own businesses. The merchandise we sell is oriented to products needed for the customer's business and the better quality product wanted by a higher income person. We don't just offer low price, we provide the combination of extraordinary value with unique, quality items."

Robert Price
Chairman of the Board
The Price Club

Customer Perception Factors

When doing your analysis, consider these customer perception factors:

- **Product/Service Features.** Specific inherent attributes of the product or service itself; if key features are particularly important, list separately.

- **Indirect/Peripheral Costs**. Costs other than the actual purchase price, such as installation or additional equipment required.

- **Quality.** Inherent merit of the product or service at the time it is provided.

- **Durability/Maintenance.** Quality of the product/service over time; ease of maintenance and service.

- **Image/Style/Perceived Value.** Added values derived from design features, attractive packaging or presentation, and other intangibles.

- **Customer Relationships.** Established customer base and customer loyalty; relationships of sales personnel to customers.

- **Social Image.** Perception of the company, product, or service relative to issues such as environment, civic involvement, etc.

Internal Operational Factors

Some internal operational factors that increase competitiveness include:

- **Financial Resources.** Ability of the company to withstand financial setbacks, and to fund product development and improvements.

- **Marketing Program/Budget.** Amount and effectiveness of advertising and other promotional activities.

- **Economies of Scale**. Ability to reduce per-unit costs due to large volume.

- **Operational Efficiencies.** Production or delivery methods that reduce costs and time.

- **Product Line Breadth.** Ability to increase revenues by selling related products; ability for customers to purchase needed items from one provider.

- **Strategic Partnerships.** Relationships with other companies for purposes of development, promotion, or add-on sales.

- **Company Morale/Personnel.** Motivation, commitment, and productivity of the employees.

Market Share Distribution

Some competitors are more important than others, due entirely to the fact that they command a large percentage of the market sales. Although these companies may not necessarily provide the best product or service at the best price, they nevertheless represent a crucial component in evaluating your competitive position.

Competitive Analysis: Customer Perception Factors

Following the directions on page 101, allocate points for each of the factors listed below for both your company and your competitors.

Factor	Maximum Points (1-10)	Your Company	Competitor:	Competitor:	Competitor:	Competitor:
Product/Service Features						
Purchase Price						
Indirect/Peripheral Costs						
Quality						
Durability/Maintenance						
Image/Style						
Perceived Value						
Name Recognition						
Customer Relationships						
Location						
Delivery Time						
Convenience of Use						
Credit Policies						
Customer Service						
Social Image						
Other:						
Other:						
Total Points						
Comments:						

Competitive Analysis: Internal Operational Factors

Following the directions on page 101, allocate points for each of the factors listed below for both your company and your competitors.

Factor	Maximum Points (1-10)	Your Company	Competitor:	Competitor:	Competitor:	Competitor:
Financial Resources						
Marketing Budget/Program						
Technological Competence						
Access to Distribution						
Access to Suppliers						
Economies of Scale						
Operational Efficiencies						
Sales Structure/Competence						
Product Line Breadth						
Strategic Partnerships						
Company Morale/Personnel						
Certification/Regulation						
Patents/Trademarks						
Other:						
Other:						
Other:						
Other:						
Total Points						
Comments:						

Companies that generate a significant portion of all sales to the target market must be carefully considered because they:

- Generally define the standard features of the product or service.
- Substantially influence the perception of the product or service by customers.
- Usually devote considerable resources to maintaining their market share.

Take time to understand the companies that dominate the market, if only to better distinguish yourself from them. Of course, if your company is fortunate enough to control a major share of the market, then you gain the advantage of defining the product or service in the marketplace; you are the proverbial "400-pound gorilla." Even so, you cannot be complacent, but must plan on committing the resources necessary to preserve or expand your share.

How Will You Obtain Sufficient Market Share?

Unless your industry is relatively new, a market already controlled by a few major players is generally more difficult and expensive to enter than one with many diverse competitors. If you are preparing a business plan for financing purposes, you will have to demonstrate to potential funding sources through your marketing plan how your company can realistically gain and maintain a reasonable market share.

Complete the Market Share Distribution worksheet on the next page to outline how sales are distributed among the competition, both by total sales revenues and by unit volume. (Some companies make fewer but higher-priced sales by targeting the most lucrative customers; others sell greater volume at lower per-unit prices.) Once again, look at competitors both by individual companies or by categories of competition, as they apply to your situation.

You will probably have to estimate the figures required by the worksheet on the next page, based on information gleaned from trade associations, annual reports, business publications, and independent industry research firms. Definitive information on sales is notoriously difficult to locate.

Future Competition

Finally, in your competitive analysis you have to do a little fortune-telling. You must make a few reasonable predictions of what the competition is going to look like in the future. New competitors enter markets all the time, and sometimes current competitors drop out. Who are your new competitors likely to be? If you are introducing a new product or service, how long will you have the field to yourself before other competitors jump in?

"When it comes to competition for a technology-based company, in the early stages, I'm more worried about the small operator than the large company. With the large well-known companies, you generally know what they're working on. Also, they have large overhead. But the small competitor can come in and compete against you head on, especially if the technology is low enough to allow easy entry to the market."

Eugene Kleiner
Venture Capitalist

Market Share Distribution

List below the current market leaders and the approximate percentage of the market each one commands.

Competitor	% of Total Revenues	% of Total Units Sold	Trend of Market Share (increasing or decreasing?)
1.			
2.			
3.			
4.			
5.			

Which competitor(s), if any, have historically been the market leader(s)? _____

_____

Which competitors have increased market share substantially in the last three years? _____

_____

Is overall competition increasing, stable, or decreasing? _____

Briefly describe the most important characteristics of the market leader(s):

Competitor #1: _____

Competitor #2: _____

Competitor #3: _____

Divide the pie charts below to indicate market distribution. (These charts can be included in your written plan for visual interest.)

Market Share By Revenues
(estimate)

Market Share By Volume
(estimate)

Forecasting the competitive situation over the next five years or so, based on logical conclusions from concrete evidence, such as current product lines, gives you and potential investors a better sense of the long-term viability of your business.

One of the most important factors to examine is barriers to entry: those conditions that make it difficult or impossible for new competitors to enter the market. Every company can gain a sense of how best to prepare for future competition by examining the barriers to entry.

If your company's competitive position depends on new technology, new manufacturing techniques, or access to new markets, outlining the barriers to entry is essential. This will be one of the first areas judged by potential funding sources.

Barriers to Entry

Some common barriers to entry for new competition are:

- Patents, which provide a measure of protection for new products or processes.
- High start-up costs, which effectively protect against small competitors entering the field.
- Substantial expertise required or manufacturing and engineering difficulties, which make it difficult for competitors to have the knowledge to compete.
- Market saturation, which reduces the possibility of competitors gaining a meaningful foothold.

Realistically, few barriers to entry last very long, particularly in newer industries. Even patents do not provide nearly as much protection as is generally assumed. Thus, you need to realistically project the period of time by which new competitors will breach these barriers.

Complete the worksheet on the next page, indicating future competition and barriers to entry.

Preparing the Competition Segment of Your Plan

To prepare the Competition portion of your business plan document, synthesize the information from the worksheets in this chapter into a brief synopsis. In particular, you want to provide:

- Description of Competition
- Market Share Distribution
- Competitive Positions
- Barriers to Entry
- Strategic Opportunities

Use the Plan Preparation Form near the end of this chapter to outline the Competition section of your business plan. Don't be afraid to use

"As a barrier to entry, it should take significant money and significant skill to enter the business. Patents, while desirable, are not sufficient to protect against new competition, although they help the entrepreneur in raising money because they show the product is unique. Service businesses have a harder time securing venture capital funds because competitors can enter the field easily, and investors are wary. You need barriers to entry to protect your market."

Eugene Kleiner
Venture Capitalist

Future Competition and Barriers to Entry

Potential future competitors include: _____

_____

_____

_____

Current competitors likely to expand efforts: _____

_____

_____

_____

Current competitors potentially leaving the field: _____

_____

_____

_____

_____

Indicate below how strong the following barriers to entry are and how much time (check the How Long Effective column) it will take before new competition overcomes each barrier.

Type of Barrier to Entry	Extent of Effectiveness Factor				How Long Effective
	High	Medium	Low	None	
Patents					
High Start-up Costs					
Substantial Expertise Required					
Engineering, Manufacturing Problems					
Lack of Suppliers or Distributors					
Restrictive Licensing, Regulation					
Market Saturation					
Trademarks					
Other:					

bullet-point lists and charts (see Chapter 3 for suggested usages) in this section. Also, include pertinent information from market research, particularly customer surveys.

Chapter Summary

You have to understand your competition if you're going to be an effective competitor yourself. Develop a strong sense of your competitive position — your strengths and weaknesses in terms of customer perception and your internal company resources; this will be vital when preparing your marketing strategy. Always assume competition will get more intense and be prepared for new competitors to enter the market.

"Quality means continuing to improve on your competitors."

Michael Damer
New United Motor
Manufacturing Inc.

Competition Plan Preparation Form

Using this form as a guide, summarize the main points you wish to make in the Competition section of your business plan.

Description of Competition: _____

_____

_____

_____

_____

Market Share Distribution: _____

_____

_____

_____

_____

Competitive Positions: _____

_____

_____

_____

_____

Barriers to Entry: _____

_____

_____

_____

_____

Strategic Opportunities: _____

_____

_____

_____

_____

Use this information as the basis of your plan's Competition section.

SAMPLE PLAN: The Competition

The Competition

Competing with ComputerEase to supply software training services to the target market (businesses with substantial use of computers, more than 50 employees) are these categories of software training providers:

- Individual independent training consultants.
- Local software training companies.
- National training companies (periodic traveling workshops).
- Software developers.
- Community college classes.
- Trainers from within the targeted companies themselves.

ComputerEase does not intend to compete with training provided by software developers. Such software is usually highly specialized and training is included in the cost of the software itself. Community college classes are generally not competitive in the marketplace; classes are held during the evenings and are at least 10 weeks in duration, conditions that do not meet the business customers' needs.

Local Competitors

Eight local businesses and four individuals listed in the current *Yellow Pages* under the classification "Computer Software, Services" indicate they provide training. An unknown number of additional individual consultants provide such training but are not listed in the phone directory. Since the publication of the directory, two of the eight companies have ceased operation.

Only one local company has developed a substantial presence with the target market: JMT Training. JMT has operated for more than six years and is the single largest local software training company.

The individual independent consultants generally provide training for merely one or two software programs, and only one consultant, Seth Rose, has a meaningful client base for his highly regarded spreadsheet training programs.

Other Competition

Three major national software training companies periodically conduct workshops in hotels in the Vespucci area. Lesser known national companies also occasionally provide such services, generally targeting recent purchasers of particular software.

Lists categories of competitors.

Indicates specific competitors.

SAMPLE PLAN: The Competition (continued)

In-house training taught by employees of the targeted companies varies widely in content, form, and quality. Very few companies have "trainers"; most training is provided on an *ad hoc* basis from supervisors and fellow workers. A conservative interpretation of ComputerEase survey results would indicate at least one-fifth of such training would be contracted out if satisfactory training could be obtained.

Market Share Distribution
In response to a ComputerEase survey, target companies currently conducting software training utilize providers as indicated by the pie chart below:

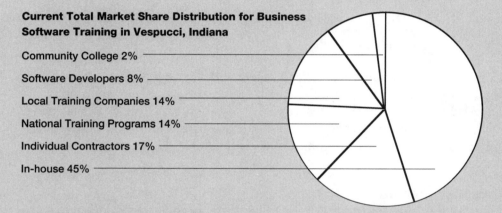

Current Total Market Share Distribution for Business Software Training in Vespucci, Indiana

Community College 2%

Software Developers 8%

Local Training Companies 14%

National Training Programs 14%

Individual Contractors 17%

In-house 45%

Advantages Over Competition
A chart outlining ComputerEase's competitive position is included in the Appendix. Generally, the advantages ComputerEase has in relation to its competitors are:

- Local, as opposed to national, provider.

- Ongoing support and repeat training at no or low cost, as opposed to those with no support services or added expense.

- Add-on "high productivity" training for customers to realize maximum potential from employees and computers; rarely offered by competitors.

- Coordinated, consistent marketing and sales programs.

- A professional, business-oriented image.

- Status as "Authorized Training Centers" for software publishers (two such relationships secured, six others to be approved within six to eighteen months) giving credibility, joint programs, and prerelease and steeply discounted software.

- Business-oriented, rather than computer-oriented, management.
- High-quality, professional trainers on staff, rather than contract workers.
- Availability of downtown training center with new computers.
- Consistent, highest-quality training.

Competitive Positions

This is how ComputerEase ranks the strength of its competitors:

1. JMT Training
2. Seth Rose, independent
3. In-house trainers
4. National training sessions
5. Other local companies
6. Other independent contractors

JMT is positioned to be the strongest competitor, due to its current client base, and the personality and sales skills of its owner, Janice Tuffrey, and its potential to associate with national franchise training operations. However, JMT's current training staff and materials are of inconsistent quality, and current clients have expressed dissatisfaction with the lack of quality control. Moreover, JMT lacks skilled management of its financial affairs, resulting in insufficient capital for marketing and updating equipment. No other local companies have either the financial or personnel resources to adequately respond to a well-organized, sufficiently funded competitor.

Ranks competitors and describes strengths and weaknesses.

Seth Rose has established a reputation as an effective trainer of spreadsheet programs and has a loyal client base. However, he has expressed a lack of interest in expanding his operation by hiring additional trainers, and he has reached full or near-full capacity. ComputerEase has begun negotiating a strategic partnership with Mr. Rose to sell additional training to his current customers. No other independent contractor has a substantial client base or adequate resources to respond to new competition.

National training companies market their services entirely through direct mail and have little or no ongoing contact with their customers. Their customer base is neither loyal nor particularly satisfied with the service.

Barriers to Entry

It is relatively difficult for new competitors to enter the field. Substantial start-up costs are involved with purchasing or leasing equipment, and high-

SAMPLE PLAN: The Competition (continued)

Considers potential future competition.

quality trainers are difficult to find. Moreover, software providers are becoming increasingly selective about which companies they will allow to serve as "Authorized Training Companies." These relationships are crucial in terms of receiving prerelease, below-cost copies of software, co-sponsoring product introduction events, and customer perception.

However, the long-term outlook for the industry points to nationally franchised local training companies. This represents the most substantial threat. Recognizing this evolution, ComputerEase plans to affiliate with the highest-quality national franchise or independent trainers association as soon as practical.

Strategic Opportunities

The market for computer training services is highly dissatisfied at present as shown by a survey of human resource directors of target companies. Their level of satisfaction with current training arrangements is shown below:

Highly satisfied	8%
Somewhat satisfied	18%
Somewhat unsatisfied	43%
Highly unsatisfied	31%

This unusually high dissatisfaction level with current providers represents a unique opportunity for ComputerEase in a rapidly expanding market.

Chapter 9

Marketing Plan & Sales Strategy

*Tell them what they get,
not what you do.*

Reaching Customers Is Key to Successful Marketing

If you can't reach customers, you can't stay in business: It's the most basic business truth. That's why an effective marketing plan to contact and motivate customers is vital for your business success. Because reaching customers costs money, and money is always limited, your marketing strategy must be carefully and thoughtfully designed.

Address Both Marketing and Sales

If you are developing a business plan to seek outside funding, remember that many investors read the marketing plan portion first or second. They want to know that you have a realistic and price-conscious plan to get your product or service into the hands of the customers.

In your marketing plan you define:

- How you make customers aware of your product or service.
- What message you are trying to convey to customers about your product, service, or company.
- Specific methods you use to deliver and reinforce that message.
- How you secure actual sales.

Note that marketing and sales, although closely related, are two different activities. Marketing is designed to increase customer awareness and deliver a message; sales is the direct action taken to solicit

"Some people think it's either win or lose. But every game is followed by another. An analogy in business is that every sales call will be followed by another. You're always preparing for the next one. So it's important to make each game as close as possible, do as well as you can on each call. Even in the process of losing, even if you don't make the sale, you're improving and refining your skills, and how well you perform when you lose is important in determining whether you will eventually win."

Bill Walsh
Former Coach and
President, S.F. 49ers

"Even in a small business, you've got to come up with a concept that's just a little bit different. Finding the concept is critical. We went for a European coffee bar atmosphere, with people standing at a bar for coffee and cappuccino; no one else was doing that at the time. We reinforced the concept by paying attention to details. Little things make a big difference. We have hooks under the bar for customers to hang hand-bags or hats; we have books as well as newspapers for customers to read. Using large European bowls, instead of cups, to serve our cafe lattes made us memorable, and now they are widely copied."

Martha Johnson
Owner, Suppers
Restaurant

and procure customer orders. Thus, marketing includes activities such as advertising, using brochures, and public relations; sales encompasses telemarketing, sales calls, and direct-mail solicitations.

In devising and implementing your marketing strategy, you may wish to use the services of specialists such as marketing consultants, advertising agencies, and public relations advisors. While these professionals can increase the focus and effectiveness of your efforts, you must never relinquish the marketing program entirely to outsiders — it is far too crucial to the definition and success of your business.

This chapter provides the basic tools you need when outlining a marketing strategy to be included in a business plan document. For more thorough internal planning purposes, consult the book *Power Marketing,* by Jody Horner published by The Oasis Press.

Your Company's Message

Anyone who's ever seen an ad for Calvin Klein jeans, with an attractive model seductively suggesting, "Nothing comes between me and my Calvins," quickly gets the message, and it has nothing to do with price or durability. This company is selling sex appeal by telling customers, "Wearing Calvin Klein jeans will make you more attractive."

Every business sends a message in its marketing. This message, based on the competitive position the company stakes out for itself, emphasizes particular attributes, such as "low-price leader" or "one-day service." Or perhaps the message exploits a market niche: "specialists in estate planning" or "software for architects." Maybe the message is less direct and aimed more at the customer's self-image: "the choice of a new generation" or "you deserve a break today."

The Four P's of Marketing

What messages do you give customers to motivate them to purchase your product or service? Traditional marketing experts emphasize the elements described below, known as "the Four P's," in influencing customers to buy.

1. **Product.** The tangible aspects of the product or service itself.
2. **Price.** The cost advantage.
3. **Place.** The location's convenience and decor.
4. **Promotion.** The amount and nature of the marketing activities.

These elements leave a lot out of the marketing picture, however. Especially as customers have become more discriminating over the years and look for products or services not just to fill an immediate need but to enhance their overall sense of well-being.

Most marketing strategists agree that people buy benefits, not features. In other words, customers are more concerned about how a purchase will affect their lives than about how the company achieves those results. So your marketing message must tell customers what they get, such as security or an enhanced self-image, rather than just the detailed specifics of what your product or service does.

What Customers Want: The Five F's

"The Five F's," shown below, are a convenient way to sum up what customers want.

1. **Functions.** How does the product or service meet their concrete needs?

2. **Finances.** How will the purchase affect their overall financial situation, not just the price of the product or service, but other savings and increased productivity?

3. **Freedom.** How convenient is it to purchase and use the product or service? How will they gain more time and less worry in other aspects of their lives?

4. **Feelings.** How does the product or service make customers feel about themselves, and how does it affect and relate to their self-image, and will they like and respect the salesperson and the company?

5. **Future.** How will they deal with the product or service and company over time, whether support and service will be available? How will the product or service affect their lives in the coming years, and will they have an increased sense of security about the future?

Customers, of course, want to receive benefits in all these areas, and you should be aware of how your product or service fulfills the entire range of their needs. However, your primary message must concentrate on one or two of these benefits that most effectively motivate your customers and that stake out a competitive position for your company. You communicate these benefits through every interaction you have with your customers, not just through advertising. Naturally, your company slogan and any words you use in advertisements deliver an overt statement to the potential customer. Perhaps the name of the business itself is a direct message, for example, "One-Hour Photo."

Power of the Indirect Message

Indirect messages can leave an even stronger impression with customers. If brochures are cleanly designed and sales representatives conservatively dressed, it says the company is professional and responsible. If the decor features trendy colors and rock music plays in the background, the implication is that the company is youthful and contemporary.

Sometimes, unfortunately, a company sends out mixed messages; for example, nicely dressed salespeople but poorly printed sales material. How will you convey an image to your customer that reinforces your direct message? How will you add value to your product or service through design, packaging, and presentation?

"We're always looking for ways to maintain a positive image. For instance, when we decided we wanted to make sure we were exposing our product to health conscious people, we supplied our lollipops to runners after a footrace. At a convention of physicians, we had a table promoting the idea of nutritional balance. Our product can be part of a healthy lifestyle, and we want to reinforce that idea."

Charles Huggins
President, See's Candies

"Everything supports the vision. That's the key in retailing. Everything must reinforce the central concept you are trying to convey to your target market, including your product lines, the customer service you offer, architectural design, the hours you're open, even the type of bags you use."

Nancy Glaser
President, Golden Gate Chips

The Five F's worksheet on the opposite page helps you organize your answers to these questions; the information then can be incorporated into the Marketing section of your business plan. This worksheet helps you summarize how you reinforce your company's image and what you are trying to tell customers about your product or service. Use the information for internal planning as well as in your business plan.

Marketing Vehicles

Once you have clarified what you want to tell customers about your company, you must describe how you disseminate that information.

How do you reach potential customers? Do you advertise? If so, where? Do you send direct mail? If so, to what mailing lists? Do you participate in trade shows? If so, which ones and how frequently?

Since every marketing vehicle costs money, carefully plan how you intend to spend your marketing dollars. In devising your overall marketing program, be sure you look for:

- **Fit.** Your marketing vehicles must reach your actual target customer and be appropriate to your image.
- **Mix.** Use more than one method so customers get exposure to you from a number of sources.
- **Repetition.** It takes many exposures before a customer becomes aware of a message.
- **Affordability.**

Use the upcoming Marketing Vehicles worksheet to document how you employ various marketing vehicles in your business.

Be Resourceful

Often the best marketing vehicles are not the most obvious or the most expensive. A large ad in a specialty publication may prove far more effective and less expensive than a small one in a general newspaper.

A well-stocked public library can be an excellent source of marketing information. In particular, you may want to consult the *Standard Rate and Data Service* to find names and prices of specialty and general publications.

To find information on trade shows, refer to books, such as the *Trade Shows and Professional Exhibits Directory*, published by Gale Research; *Trade Show & Exhibit Schedule*, published by Successful Meetings Data Bank; or *Trade Show Week Data Book*, published by Trade Show Week.

If you are marketing to businesses, identify potential customers for direct mail or telemarketing efforts through the *Thomas Register*, an invaluable source similar to a giant, national *Yellow Pages* directory.

The Five F's

Keeping the Five F's in mind, describe the message you are trying to convey to customers about your product or service.

Functions: _____

_____

Finances: _____

_____

Freedom: _____

_____

Feelings: _____

_____

Future: _____

_____

Which of these messages is the most important in motivating your target market to purchase? _____

_____

How will you express this message to your customer in the areas listed below?

Business Name: _____

Slogan: _____

Key Words in Marketing Material: _____

_____

Product Design: _____

Logo: _____

Other Graphic Images/Design: _____

_____

Packaging: _____

Decor: _____

Style of Clothing Worn by Employees: _____

Merchandising/Displays/Presentation Materials: _____

_____

Other: _____

_____

_____

Some of the marketing vehicles you may choose include:

- **Brochures.** Leaflets, flyers, or other descriptive circulars; these are particularly useful for service businesses.
- **Print Media.** Newspapers, magazines, and specialty publications.
- **Broadcast Media.** Radio can be targeted to specific markets; television can be expensive, especially on network stations.
- **Advertising Specialties.** Items imprinted with the company name given to customers, e.g., calendars, caps, desk sets, and gifts.
- **Direct Mail.** Flyers, catalogues, brochures, and coupons.
- **Public Relations.** Free feature and news articles in the media and other publicity, usually secured by public relations specialists.
- **Sampling.** Distribution of free product samples, or coupons entitling recipients to free or discounted samples of your product or service.
- **Informal Marketing/Networking.** Activities such as joining organizations, public speaking, or attending conferences.

Marketing Tactics

In addition to direct marketing methods, you can employ a number of creative strategies to promote your company. These tactics often involve little or no extra cost and can be the source of substantial increased revenues. Complete the upcoming Marketing Tactics worksheet to indicate marketing tactics you utilize to increase sales.

Various industries have particular marketing tactics, and enterprising entrepreneurs devise unique methods to reach customers. A few important strategies to consider in your marketing approach are described below.

Media Advertising

Advertising works. Customers expect to learn about products and services from ads in newspapers and magazines and on the radio or television. Advertising gets your company's name and message to a large number of people with relatively little work on your part. But it costs money. Don't buy ads based merely on the number of people reached; make sure the ad is reaching the right people: your target market. A badly designed and written ad may be worse than no ad at all, so spend the time and money to develop a good one. Run ads repetitively; professionals estimate it takes nine exposures to an ad before someone even notices it.

Customer-Based Marketing

Often neglected, this is one of the most fruitful types of marketing. Two particularly effective approaches are to emphasize repeat sales

"Our marketing strategy included a large opening party for neighbors, bankers and insurance providers; limited advertising targeted only to neighborhood publications; menu distribution to all major institutions and employers in the area; and word-of-mouth to friends and local businesses."

Martha Johnson
Owner, Suppers
Restaurant

Marketing Vehicles $ ▶ $$ ▶ $$$

Use this worksheet to outline your marketing schedule, listing each type of marketing vehicle, the frequency with which you use it, and what it costs you annually. This is the basis of your marketing budget and will be used in the Financials section of your business plan.

Vehicle	Specifics	Frequency	Cost per Year
Professional Assistance			
Marketing/PR Consultants			
Advertising Agencies			
Direct Mail Specialists			
Graphic Design			
Brochures/Leaflets/Flyers			
Merchandising Displays			
Sampling/Premiums			
Print Media			
General Newspapers			
Magazines			
Specialty Publications			
Broadcast Media			
Television			
Radio			
Phone Directories			
Advertising Specialties			
Prospective Customers			
Current Customers			
Direct Mail			
Trade Shows			
Signs/Billboards			
Public Relations/Publicity			
Informal Marketing/Networking			
Other			
Total			$

by positioning your product or service to be consumed or replaced, and add-on sales, whereby you increase the total revenues per customer through the sale of extra products or services.

Another approach is point-of-purchase promotion: merchandising displays or other offers presented to customers at time of sale to encourage impulse purchases.

Strategic Partnerships

Identify a related company with which to associate for promotion, sales, or distribution. Ways in which you might use such a partnership include:

- **Cooperative Advertising.** This type of advertising occurs when two companies are mentioned in an advertisement and each company pays part of the costs. This is a frequent practice in many industries.
- **Licensing.** One company may grant permission to another to use its product, name, or trademark. For instance, instead of selling your computer software program directly, you might license it to another software publisher to incorporate in its program.
- **Distribution Agreement.** An agreement whereby one company carries another's product line and distributes another company's products or services.

Marketing Tactics $ ▸ $$ ▸ $$$

Customer-Based Marketing: How do you increase sales to current customers? _____

_____

Strategic Partnerships: What relationships do you have with other companies to help promote, sell, or distribute your product or service? _____

_____

_____

Special Offers/Promotions: What reduced-priced values do you offer to encourage sales? _____

_____

_____

Premiums: What gifts or prizes do you offer to build goodwill and sales? _____

_____

_____

Other Tactics: _____

_____

- **Bundling.** This is a relationship between two companies where one company includes another company's product or services as part of a total package.

Special Offers/Promotions

Special offers and promotions enable you to increase sales revenue and build market share by offering customers special values. The tendency is to consider this primarily a retail tactic, but service companies and business-to-business marketing can also incorporate the practice.

Strategies include leader pricing — products or services on which you make little or no profit — to entice first-time customers and increase patronage, and introductory or limited time offers to build cash flow at critical points.

Premiums

The use of premiums in marketing includes encouraging sales and creating good-will through gifts, sweepstakes, discounts, and other perceived added values. These "extras" can be packaged with products or services, such as free wine glasses with a two-bottle box of wine, given as gifts with a purchase, or offered as discounts, often in conjunction with other companies (such as travel discounts), for established customers.

Your Sales Structure

Directly related to your marketing strategy is your sales structure — how you achieve actual customer orders. In this section of your plan, describe the two main components of your sales system: the sales force and the sales process.

If your business plan document is being used for external funding requests, you don't need to go into great detail; it is enough to provide a general outline, giving a sense of your understanding of what is necessary to produce sales. For internal planning, however, you should flesh out these concepts more thoroughly.

The Heartbeat of Your Sales Force

At the center of your company's income-producing activities are those members of your staff with specific sales responsibilities. These are the people who come in direct contact with your potential customers and who most immediately determine whether your product or service is actually purchased. These key staff members are your sales team, and you must carefully plan how you make the best use of their skills and time.

What responsibilities do you give your sales team? What commissions and incentives do you provide? How do you train and supervise the people responsible for bringing in your revenues?

"We want our salespeople emotionally involved with the product. We let them know about new products and encourage employees to sample the product. We also provide periodic seminars and training programs. We offer opportunities for advancement, and we have bonus incentives based on the overall performance of all shops in a manager's area for all employees in that area."

Charles Huggins
President, See's Candies

"With public relations, you need to keep your best foot forward at all times. You should be scrupulously honest, as direct as possible; at the same time, you want to protect your long-term goals and the reputation and dignity of any individuals involved. It's important to maintain a certain public perception of your organization, so you can't go into all the details of each decision. The public has a hard time handling negatives. You must have standard, acceptable methods and forms of response to critical questions and inquiries."

Bill Walsh
Former Coach and
President, S.F. 49ers

Of course, every employee actually has a part in attracting and retaining customers: If the janitor does a poor job, and the store looks dirty, customers may not want to buy from you. Thus, some companies incorporate some form of sales-related training for all personnel. But certain staff members (and nonemployees, as well) have particular responsibilities for securing sales, and these individuals are the center of your sales team.

Sales Activities

Sales activities can be conducted either on your business' premises or by calling on customers at their homes or places of business. And your sales force can consist of either inside or outside salespeople.

- **Inside Sales Personnel.** Employees who remain on the company's premises to secure sales; includes floor salespeople in retail stores, personnel who take phone orders, and telemarketing.
- **Outside Sales Personnel.** Salespeople who go to customers' locations to solicit orders; these can be company employees working on salary alone, salary plus commission, or straight commission; or they can be independent contractors — sales representatives and manufacturer's agents, either representing many product lines or handling one company's products exclusively, usually on a commission-only basis.

You can also hire independent telemarketing services to conduct your telephone sales from their place of business, using their employees.

Once you determine the nature of your sales team, delineate how you divide responsibilities among personnel, for example, assign sales representatives by territories, product lines, or customer types.

Employee Compensation and Training

How do you pay your sales force? Some form of commission is usual in most selling situations. What commission percentage do you provide? Do you give bonuses for reaching certain goals?

Do you use other incentives, such as awards, gifts, or vacations? Do district managers or other supervisors receive commissions on their staffs' sales?

You also need to consider how you continue to train, motivate, and supervise your sales force. Selling is a difficult, often dispiriting, task, and salespeople need frequent encouragement and support. Who will be responsible for this? The upcoming Sales Force worksheet helps you outline the structure of your sales team.

Sales Process

Finally, you need to identify the procedures you use in making sales calls and presentations, and the level of results you expect from your sales force. Although this information is not necessary to include in a business plan prepared for external financing purposes, the data on sales productivity is important in developing realistic sales forecasts.

Some of the aspects you should consider in evaluating your sales process include:

- **Cold-Calling.** Contacting targeted customers before they have indicated any interest in purchasing your product or service; this can be done in person or on the phone.
- **Leads.** Developing or purchasing names of potential customers who have expressed at least some level of interest in your product or service.
- **Productivity.** The amount of time it takes to secure sales, and the level of sales realistically expected from each salesperson.
- **Order-Fulfillment.** Ensuring that orders are completed promptly and accurately, an essential completion of the sales process.
- **Goals.** Establishing specific, measurable objectives for each salesperson and the total sales force; realistically assessing the number of sales possible for each sales representative given the nature of his or her assigned territory/product line/customer base; setting sales quotas base; setting sales quotes based on these assessments.
- **Follow-up Efforts.** Ensuring that the sales representative maintains ongoing contact with the customer after the sale and seeks out repeat sales opportunities.

Use the upcoming Sales Process and Productivity worksheet to outline the procedures and productivity levels you expect in your sales efforts.

Preparing the Marketing Section of Your Plan

You need to distill the highlights of your marketing and sales planning into a concise and compelling statement of how you reach customers and convince them to purchase from your company. The Marketing section of your business plan should include:

- The message you attempt to send customers; how you position your company in the market.
- The marketing methods and vehicles you use.
- The sales force and sales procedures you use.

The Monthly Marketing Budget and Monthly Sales Projections worksheets and Plan Preparation Form on the next several pages help you organize information for completion of your business plan's Marketing section.

Refer to the previous worksheets in this chapter when completing your marketing budget estimates for the Monthly Marketing Budget worksheet. Some of this information will also be used in the Financials section

"We book travel packages together (air transportation, hotel, etc.) with our strategic partners. We work in tandem with their salespeople. They may be making a heavy volume of sales calls, and they sell our hotel along with their product."

Andre Tatibouet
President, Aston Hotels

Sales Force

List below the type of sales force you use, and how many salespeople you have in each category.

Inside Sales Force: _____

Outside Sales Force (company–employee): _____

Outside Sales Representatives, Agents (nonemployee): _____

Telemarketing Services: _____

Other: _____

_____

How do you divide responsibilities, e.g., by product line, territory, customer type, etc.? _____

_____

_____

Do sales personnel have additional responsibilities as well as sales? _____

What commissions do you pay sales personnel? _____

Do commissions vary by product line or goals achieved? _____

_____

What other incentives or bonuses do you provide? _____

_____

For which expenses do you reimburse sales personnel, e.g., travel, entertainment? _____

_____

What expenses must sales personnel pay for themselves? _____

_____

Who supervises sales personnel? _____

Do they receive any commissions or bonuses based on performances of people they supervise? ☐ Yes ☐ No

Who trains sales personnel? _____

How often is training provided? _____

What kind of training is provided? _____

Which other employees are involved in generating sales? _____

Sales Process and Productivity

On this worksheet outline the procedures and productivity levels you expect in your sales efforts.

Customer Identification

How do you identify potential customers? _____

Do you use "cold-calling"? _____

What prospect lists, if any, do you purchase? _____

What other methods do you use to determine customer interest? _____

Customer Contact

Who contacts potential customers? _____

How many times is a potential customer contacted before he or she is discarded from the list? _____

When are potential customers contacted? _____

How long does each contact take? _____

How frequently are current customers contacted for additional follow-on sales? _____

Who contacts current customers? _____

Sales Productivity

What are your sales goals? Delineate volume and revenues expected within a certain time frame. _____

_____

How many times, on average, must a potential customer be contacted before securing:

An appointment? _____   A sale? _____

What percentage of potential customers agree to an appointment or demonstration? _____

What percentage of those agreeing to an appointment or demonstration subsequently purchase? _____

How many calls will each salesperson be expected to make, and in what time period? _____

Who takes phone orders? _____

Who ensures orders are filled promptly and properly? _____

Does this information get reported to the salesperson?   ☐ Yes ☐ No

How? _____

Who checks credit? _____

Other Sales Procedures: _____

_____

_____

of your business plan. To complete the Monthly Sales Projections worksheet, estimate income by each product line, then total the income from all product lines and transfer this information to the appropriate financial forms in Chapter 13.

Chapter Summary

Your marketing plan and sales strategy are at the heart of your company's business. To stay in business you have to reach customers and secure sales. That is why this section of your plan is likely to be the first or second section reviewed by prospective investors. When studying your marketing plan, these investors want to see that you have a realistic, cost-effective approach to positioning your products or services in the market and to motivating customers to purchase.

In your sales strategy section, potential funders want to see that your sales methods are appropriate for your business and that your sales force is both large enough and trained well-enough to be able to secure the sales levels necessary to sustain your business.

"When I buy mailing lists from magazines, I request only those four-line addresses, rather than those with three-lines. These are more likely to be businesses instead of individuals."

Charles Orr
President, Productivity
Point International

Marketing and Sales Strategy Plan Preparation Form

Use the information recorded on this form to summarize the points you will cover in the marketing portion of your business plan.

Describe the message you are attempting to send customers: _____

_____

_____

_____

_____

_____

_____

Describe how you are positioning your company in the market: _____

_____

_____

_____

_____

_____

_____

_____

Describe the marketing methods and vehicles you use: _____

_____

_____

_____

_____

_____

_____

_____

Describe your sales force and procedures: _____

_____

_____

_____

_____

_____

_____

Use this information as the basis of your plan's Marketing section.

Monthly Marketing Budget	January	February	March	April	May
Professional Assistance					
Marketing/PR Consultants					
Advertising Agencies					
Direct Mail Specialists					
Graphic Design					
Brochures/Leaflets/Flyers					
Merchandising Displays					
Sampling/Premiums					
Media Advertising					
Newspapers					
Magazines					
Other Publications					
Television and Radio					
Phone Directories					
Advertising Specialties					
Direct Mail					
Printing					
List Purchases					
Postage					
Mailing House					
Trade Shows					
Fees and Setup					
Travel/Shipping					
Exhibits/Signs					
Public Relations Activities					
Informal Marketing/Networking					
Memberships					
Entertainment					
Other:					
TOTAL					

June	July	August	September	October	November	December	TOTAL
							$ ▶ $$ ▶ $$$

Monthly Sales Projections

	January	February	March	April	May
Product Line #1					
Unit Volume					
Unit Price					
Commissions					
Returns and Allowances					
Gross Revenue					
Net Revenue					
Product Line #2					
Unit Volume					
Unit Price					
Commissions					
Returns and Allowances					
Gross Revenue					
Net Revenue					
Product Line #3					
Unit Volume					
Unit Price					
Commissions					
Returns and Allowances					
Gross Revenue					
Net Revenue					
Product Line #4					
Unit Volume					
Unit Price					
Commissions					
Returns and Allowances					
Gross Revenue					
Net Revenue					
Totals for All Product Lines					
Unit Volume					
Commissions					
Returns and Allowances					
Gross Revenue					
TOTAL NET REVENUE					

							$ ▶ $$ ▶ $$$
June	July	August	September	October	November	December	TOTAL

SAMPLE PLAN: Marketing Plan

Marketing Plan

ComputerEase distinguishes itself from its competitors by better understanding the needs of its customers. Other computer software training companies in the Vespucci area market their services as if their customer were the individual student taking the class. ComputerEase, on the other hand, knows that the customer is actually the student's employer, the business that has contracted with ComputerEase.

ComputerEase Meets Customers' Needs

Employers have slightly different motivations than the students themselves. Although the companies, as well as the students, want high-quality, easy-to-understand training, the businesses also want:

- Increased overall productivity.

- One company to deal with for all computer training needs.

- Ongoing support for their employees.

- The convenience of not having to disrupt the workplace for computer training sessions.

These business customers want to deal with a training company with which they can have an ongoing relationship.

Describes the company's message.

ComputerEase incorporates reassurance and relationship in all its marketing efforts. The slogan "We speak your language" is designed to imply not only that the training will be comprehensible, but that ComputerEase is able to maintain ongoing communication with the business customer. Also, as a play on the word "computerese," the name is designed to be memorable, with the implication that the company makes dealing with computers easy.

ComputerEase Emphasizes Training

ComputerEase emphasizes high-productivity training. This is accomplished by selling training not only at the introductory, basic user-level, but additional, advanced training to substantially increase the benefits to the corporate client. This additional training expands the number of services ComputerEase can sell each customer, and increases the revenues produced from each sale.

Tells sales mechanism.

Since the average training contract is projected at approximately $5,000 per training session, and the goal is to target companies for regularly repeated sessions, most of the marketing will be done by face-to-face solicitation. An outside sales force, currently consisting of the company president and vice-president for marketing — both of whom have experience selling to the target market — will call on human resource directors to introduce the company and make sales presentations. Appointments are generally made by the vice- president for marketing, except in those cases where the president has existing relationships with potential customers.

Organization of Sales Team

All company personnel are considered members of the sales team. The registrar, who takes phone registrations, is trained in phone manners and order solicitation, and she is given incentive gifts for registering targeted numbers of students for "add-on" classes. Even the software trainers themselves participate in monthly sales training meetings. All employees receive financial bonuses if the company reaches overall sales goals.

Quality printed sales material has been prepared (see the Appendix) to support personal sales calls and for mailing in responses to phone requests (The Registrar is trained to attempt to set up personal sales presentations for larger businesses phoning in.) In year two, funds are budgeted to produce a computerized video presentation, to augment the printed material and enhance the sense of professionalism and computer expertise.

Direct Mail Program Key

Direct mail is key in the company's marketing. A schedule of ComputerEase's classes is sent out every two months to the target audience. (Currently 3,500 pieces are sent; the company purchases lists of human resource directors and subscribers to a leading computer magazine, both limited to names in the greater Vespucci area.) Once a year, a four-color brochure explaining ComputerEase's services is inserted in the schedule.

The company's advertising is aimed at supporting its other marketing and sales efforts rather than securing actual sales. Two main vehicles are used: a small ad in the *Yellow Pages*, and a half-page ad in each quarterly issue of the newsletter of the Vespucci Association of Human Resource Directors.

Cooperative Marketing Plans

A number of cooperative marketing activities are planned with software publishers. These include cooperative advertisements and sponsoring events to introduce business customers to new software. The goal of such efforts is to give ComputerEase added exposure to potential customers and increased stature through being associated with leading software publishers.

Two local computer hardware stores, and four computer hardware consultants, now refer customers to ComputerEase for training, and the company will continue to seek referral programs with other hardware suppliers.

The company is currently negotiating with Seth Rose, a well-regarded independent trainer, to conduct joint marketing activities, so that the company may benefit from his established client base.

Indicates sales training for staff.

Gives specifics of marketing plan.

SAMPLE PLAN: Marketing Plan (continued)

ComputerEase is also a member of the Vespucci Area Chamber of Commerce and will participate in the Chamber's annual trade show, which features providers of business services and products.

The company receives additional revenue from its Saturday training classes, which are aimed at individual students and businesses smaller than 50 employees. These classes are conducted primarily as a way to use the training center's excess capacity. These Saturday classes realize a lower profit margin than corporate training, and far less emphasis is placed on promoting these classes.

The marketing plan for these Saturday classes consists of printing additional copies of the ComputerEase schedule (presently 6,500 extra) and distributing them at local computer hardware and software retail stores, office supply stores, and college campuses. No paid advertising is done for these classes.

Chapter 10

Operations

Ninety percent of success comes from
properly executing the fundamentals.

Describing How You Run Your Business

How are you actually going to run your business? The Operations section of your business plan is where you begin to explain the day-to-day functions of your company. This is where you translate your theories into practice.

Much of the information in this chapter appears mundane, for instance, how you keep track of inventory, or what equipment you need and when it must be replaced. These seem like the kind of details that take care of themselves. But there's a far greater chance that a business will fail because fundamentals aren't handled properly than because the basic business concept is faulty.

Examining your basic operation is particularly important for internal planning. A capable manager does not take any activity in the business process for granted. Each step is worthy of evaluation and improvement. A little bit of extra planning in operational areas can mean marked improvements in profit margin. Assessing and developing the underlying mechanisms of your business will certainly pay off.

To do a thorough job planning your internal operations, you may want to develop a separate operations or procedures manual. Such a manual should describe the specific details of the processes by which you produce, distribute, or maintain your products and services.

For the purpose of preparing a business plan, however, your Operations section does not need to be thoroughly detailed. Be brief. Describing your operations too specifically in a business plan is not only unnecessary, it may be counterproductive, especially if you are seeking outside funding. Focusing on very small details may make it appear that you are not seeing the big picture in your business.

What Your Operations Section Should Cover

This chapter describes most of the subjects commonly included in an Operations section of a business plan. In your own plan, you do not necessarily need to address each of these topics. Rather, limit your Operations section to those issues that:

- Are essential to the nature and success of your company.
- Provide you with a distinct competitive edge.
- Overcome a frequent problem in businesses of your type.

Thus, if yours is a manufacturing business in which distribution is often a major difficulty, you may want to include one or two paragraphs clarifying your company's improved approach to distribution. However, if yours is a retail business, distribution may not be an issue at all, and you needn't discuss it.

Of course, if your business is an enterprise that develops or relies heavily on new technology, you need to explain those aspects fairly thoroughly. Likewise, if you are counting on a new manufacturing or merchandising method to significantly improve your competitive position, you must describe the mechanisms and importance of those techniques.

Many sources of information exist if you need to locate resources to prepare your Operations section. Commercial real estate agents can easily describe the advantages, disadvantages, and resources available in your location. Trade associations can assist in helping you find consultants for plant and manufacturing design and direct you to sources of equipment. The *Thomas Register*, available in most large libraries, is an invaluable source of suppliers, distributors, and equipment manufacturers. Information about office equipment is also available in libraries, from sources such as *Buyers Laboratories Reports* or *Datapro Office Automation Reports*.

Operations, naturally, have many financial implications. You should note these in the Flow-Through Financial worksheets in this chapter and transfer the numbers to your financial statements in Chapter 13. If yours is a new business, you should include the Start-Up Costs worksheet in your business plan. For both new and existing businesses, the Equipment Schedule worksheet, which you need for internal financial projections, can also be included in the Appendix of your business plan.

Facilities

In real estate the old saying is that the three most important factors are location, location, location. In business, as well, location can prove the critical factor for success. For example, with retail operations, a bad location can mean you just don't attract enough customers to your store. Likewise, in manufacturing and distribution companies, a location lacking adequate access to transportation or suppliers may prevent you from manufacturing or distributing your product in a timely or cost-effective manner.

The physical aspects of the facilities themselves can be extremely important for a company's continued growth. Are your facilities large enough to accommodate expansion in the coming years? Are the necessary utilities available and energy efficient? Are you near an airport or rail terminal? Or, are you locked into an inadequate facility that reduces your overall production and distribution capacity?

Occasionally, the length and terms of a lease may be a particularly attractive (or problematic) aspect of a business. Having a long-term, low-rent lease in a desirable area may be, in and of itself, a significant business asset. A lease that needs to be renegotiated in the near future may spell trouble for your company, as you may be facing substantially increased rents. In a new lease, look to negotiate certain concessions, such as leasehold improvements or a few months' free rent (particularly while construction is occurring).

When evaluating your facilities, examine those aspects most important for your particular business. Do you need a prestigious address in a downtown office building for your law firm? Do you need to be close to key suppliers for your manufacturing plant? Do you need access to environmentally approved disposal sites for your chemical company?

In the upcoming Facilities worksheet, describe all the facilities in which your company operates, emphasizing any competitive and cost-saving advantages they may have. Specific points to mention are listed below.

Location

Include company headquarters, retail store(s), branch offices, additional plants, distribution centers, etc. Describe any mobile facilities. List square footage, and how the square footage is allocated (office space, retail, production, shipping, etc.). Describe access to parking and transportation; air, rail and surface shipping access, and loading docks, warehouse, and other necessary facilities.

Lease

What are the terms and length of the lease? Do you pay straight rent or rent plus a percentage of gross or net profits? Can you sublet? Did you receive concessions in the lease? What restrictions are in the lease (for

"People have no idea you're there if they can't see you. Get a good location; it's money well-spent. As a start-up, it's hard to advertise; so, instead of a big advertising budget, spend the money on a better location. Find a good real estate broker with retail experience. Have them identify successful businesses serving your target customer and then locate near them. Capture their customers."

Nancy Glaser
President, Golden
Gate Chips

instance, hours of operation or promotional activities that are often mandated in mall leases)?

Improvements

What additions, such as walls, signage, or utility hook-ups, have been made to the property, or remain to be made? Who pays for such improvements — you or your landlord?

Utilities/Maintenance

Include the costs of gas, water, and electricity. Note seasonal or production level variation. List the cost of janitorial, trash-removal, and other ongoing facility maintenance expenses. Emphasize energy- efficient measures.

Key Factors

What aspects of your facilities are most likely to affect your company's success? Are you near your target market? Are you in a prestigious or convenient location? Does your lease have particularly favorable terms? Will you be able to grow in these facilities without moving?

Production

Every manufacturing business has a production process — the way it goes about fabricating a raw or component material and creating an item with greater usefulness or desirability. But even if yours is a service or retail business, you have a method of "producing" something of value for your customers, although you may not have given this process much thought.

Take time to evaluate and assess your production plan to see if you can enhance efficiencies, improve the quality of the finished "product," and, in the long run, increase your profit margin. Look at the various stages involved in creating your product or service: Can these stages be shortened? If so, you will be able to produce and sell more in less time.

Examine how you organize and deploy your work force. Do you use a team approach — with one group of workers responsible for a job from start to finish? Or, do you use a production-line approach, with a worker doing the same portion of each job and then passing it along to someone else? Do you have clear-cut lines of authority, or do workers often not know who is responsible for making decisions?

Increasingly, companies are utilizing variable labor in addition to permanent employees, as an integral part of their workforce. Variable labor — employees hired to perform a specific task for a specific period of time — is particularly useful for seasonal work or unusually

Facilities $ ▶ $$ ▶ $$$

Describe the attributes of your facilities.

Principal Location(s)

Location: _____

Square Footage: _____

Description of Use: _____

Parking/Transportation: _____

Shipping Access/Facilities: _____

Warehouse Facilities: _____

Other: _____

Branch Offices/Additional Plants/Distribution Centers/Other Facilities

Number: _____

Locations: _____

Square Footage: _____

Description of Use: _____

Other Aspects: _____

Lease(s)

Length of Lease: _____

Rent/Terms of Rent: _____ Other Terms: _____

Restrictions: _____

Concessions: _____

Improvements

Existing: _____

To be made: _____

Paid by landlord: _____ Paid by company: _____

Utilities/Maintenance

Average monthly utility costs? _____ How do costs vary seasonally? _____

How do costs vary due to production levels? _____ Are there energy-efficient methods in use? _____

Average maintenance costs? _____ Do any maintenace costs vary? _____

Other: _____

> *"We wanted to have neighborhood pricing and high quality. That meant we had to keep our food costs under control. To do so, we spent about six months testing different recipes, so we would know the exact cost of each item."*
>
> **Martha Johnson**
> **Owner, Suppers**
> **Restaurant**

large or special orders. Many companies even use variable labor, in the form of consultants, for professional positions. Utilizing variable labor gives you more control over ongoing expenses, since you can add these employees in good times but don't have them on the payroll when business is slow. Maintaining high quality in a variable labor force is frequently difficult, however, and employee motivation is often low.

Another way to increase flexibility in fixed costs is to subcontract various aspects of production to other companies. These companies then have the responsibility for maintaining the workforce, facilities, and equipment necessary to produce their component piece. While the per piece cost to you includes a profit to these companies, and thus, your per piece cost is probably greater than if you had all the necessary means of production in-house, the advantages of not having your money tied up in overhead may be well worth the additional cost. Even service businesses should consider the various ways to subcontract portions of their contracts.

How You Utilize New Technology

In your production analysis, examine the use you make of new technologies. Virtually every industry has experienced rapid advances in production, information processing, and inventory control as a result of technological developments. How can you utilize computers, robotics, optical scanners, or other new devices to reduce costs and increase productivity in your production process? Through the use of new technologies, you can often significantly improve productivity and profitability and gain a competitive edge. If you have incorporated such advances into your production process, you should feature that information in your business plan.

Of course, some companies are specifically in the business of developing or exploiting new technology. In these companies, the technology is central to the very heart of the business, and potential investors will want more detailed information about the state of your technology and how you develop and use it. Thus, for a technology-based business, you might include an additional section in your business plan.

This additional section should be entitled, "The Technology" and describe the basic concept and features of your technology, science, or engineering. The level of detail should be geared to your potential reader. If you are sending your business plan to a venture capital firm with a specialty in your area, expect that they will have an expert on the staff who will want to scrutinize your technology in fairly great detail. In this case, you need to be careful to provide the data necessary to show the viability of your concept without revealing your company's secrets. Extremely sensitive data should not be put in a business plan.

If, on the other hand, you are seeking conventional financing (e.g., bank loans) or investment from less knowledgeable sources, then your technology description should be fairly general. If your plan is for internal use only, your technology section may be very detailed and include sensitive information about product development. In this case, be extremely cautious as to how the plan is distributed; you don't want it to fall in a competitor's hands.

Assessing Your Production Plan

Two worksheets on the next few pages help you evaluate your production process. The Production worksheet covers the major aspects other than equipment, which is handled on a separate form, the Equipment Schedule worksheet. You may wish to include the Equipment Schedule in the Appendix of your business plan. If yours is a manufacturing business, you might also wish to include a flow chart of your production process in the Appendix.

The aspects covered in the Production worksheet are:

- **Labor/Variable Labor.** What kinds of and how many employees do you require to produce your product or service? How do you utilize them? How are decisions reached in the workforce? What is the chain of command? Do you use variable labor — employees hired only when you have certain orders in hand?

- **Productivity.** Productivity measures how long and how many people it requires to produce your product or service. This can have a major impact on your profit margin.

  If you can produce more goods in less time, you increase the amount of profit earned from every dollar spent on salaries, equipment, and rent. What methods can you use to increase productivity without reducing quality?

- **Capacity.** Capacity is the measure of how much work your current facilities, labor force, and equipment can handle. If you have excess capacity, you have the ability to produce more than you are currently selling using your current work force, equipment, and plant.

  Excess capacity represents a waste of already paid-for earning potential. Can you find ways to use or reduce excess capacity? If you are operating at close to full capacity, what plans do you have for expansion, to handle growth?

- **Quality Control.** All the various measures you take to ensure that you maintain the same standards with each product or service come under the category of Quality Control.

  Such activities include regular inspection throughout the production process, occasional testing or sampling of randomly-selected goods, employee-involvement training and reward programs for quality assurance, and solicitation of customer comments.

"To plan for change, you must build flexibility not only into the process, but into the workforce as well, because team members will be called on to do many jobs."

Michael Damer
New United Motor
Manufacturing Inc.

Production

Describe the key factors (other than equipment) involved in producing your product or service.

Processes

What are the stages of production? _____

_____

How does the product/work get transferred from one stage to another? _____

_____

How does the process utilize new technologies? _____

_____

What are the advantages of your production process? _____

_____

What are the drawbacks of your production process? _____

_____

What components are contracted for others to produce? _____

_____

What are the costs of these outside services/components? _____

_____

Briefly describe the subcontracting company(s): _____

_____

What other costs are directly associated with the production process? _____

_____

Labor

Total number of employees: ___ permanent: full-time: ___ part-time: ___ variable: full-time: ___ part-time: ___

When do you use variable labor? _____

How many shifts do you operate? ____How long are the shifts? ____ What are the hours of operation? ____

What are the basic qualifications required of employees? _____

_____

How are employees organized: ☐ team approach?   ☐ production line?   ☐ other? _____

Who supervises employees? _____

_____

Other labor issues: _____

Other labor costs: _____

Productivity

For each product or service, list how many minutes, hours, days, weeks, and workers it takes to produce one unit.

_____

_____

_____

_____

How many units can each worker produce in a minute, hour, day, week? _____

What methods could reduce the amount of production time required without reducing quality? _____

What other methods can you use to increase productivity? _____

Capacity

How many units of goods or services can be produced in your current facility in a day___week___month___?

How many units of goods or services can your workforce handle in a day, week, month? _____

At what percentage of capacity are you now operating in terms of workforce____ equipment____ facilities____?

How is excess capacity currently utilized? _____

What are other ways to use excess capacity? _____

How can you provide for increased capacity, if needed for growth? _____

Quality Control

Who is responsible for overall quality control issues? _____

What steps are taken to inspect finished goods or services? _____

What intermediate steps are taken to ensure quality in the process? _____

Are products and services tested for quality? _____

How are employees motivated to ensure quality? _____

How do you solicit customer comments? _____

What other steps are taken for quality control? _____

Equipment Schedule

$ ▶ $$ ▶ $$$

List your company's existing and anticipated equipment.

Currently Owned Equipment

Description (Name/Model #)	Status	Date Purchased	Cost	Payments

Equipment to Be Purchased

Description	Purchase Date	Cost	Terms	Payments

- **Equipment and Furniture.** (List separately on the Equipment Schedule worksheet). Include manufacturing equipment, transportation vehicles, store fixtures and office equipment, computers, and furniture. List any payment obligations or leases. Under "Status" describe the state of the equipment in terms of future use potential, technological development, and substantial maintenance required. Also indicate date to be replaced, if known.

Inventory Control

Many businesses overlook the vital contribution that careful inventory management makes to the profitability of a company. How much money you have tied up in supplies or finished product sitting in your warehouse makes a direct impact on your bottom line. Every box of raw material is not just taking up space; it's money sitting around, losing value.

Of course, if you don't have sufficient inventory, you occasionally can't make sales. Every business dreads the possibility of receiving lucrative orders it can't fill due to inadequate supplies. And sometimes you don't just lose sales; you lose a customer. This is the risk in maintaining too low an inventory.

The answer is to develop inventory management systems that substantially increase the flow of information from the sales point to the production and purchasing teams. Information can reduce the amount of guesswork that goes into maintaining inventory. Know how sales are going, even on a daily basis.

Suppliers can help. Work with them to see how to reduce the amount of time necessary to receive goods and to explore the potential of lowering the amount of minimum orders. Large businesses often have significant clout with suppliers, but even smaller companies should look for suppliers who are willing to increase flexibility in their orders and deliveries.

Methods of Inventory Management

One of the approaches to inventory management is "just-in-time" inventory control. This concept emphasizes keeping inventory stocked only to the levels needed to produce goods just in time for delivery, usually in response to orders in-hand. Such a system is highly dependent on adequate communication systems and good supplier relationships.

In devising your inventory control and communication procedures, you will want to devise a Management Information System (MIS). Usually such a system centers around the computerized maintenance and communication of information, such as order and stock levels, reorder dates, historical tracking of sales, and so forth. Computer professionals can help you select and adapt an MIS for your company.

> *"We take inventory in each store daily. This information is sent to the main computer through the telephone, and this determines what will be manufactured. Very perishable items are made to order the day before delivery. We have two manufacturing plants, and stores receive two deliveries a week. So product is delivered to stores, even those in Hong Kong and Hawaii, no more than the third morning after production. It's fresh."*
>
> **Charles Huggins**
> **President, See's Candies**

Inventory Control

This worksheet helps you get a clear picture of your inventory control procedures.

Who is responsible for inventory control? _____

What is the minimum level of inventory necessary to be maintained at all time? _____

_____

What is the minimum amount of time necessary to get materials from suppliers? _____

_____

What is the minimum amount of time necessary to produce goods to order? _____

_____

_____

What is the minimum amount of time necessary to ship goods? _____

_____

_____

How is information about sales translated to the production and purchasing departments? _____

_____

_____

What Management Information Systems does your company use? _____

_____

_____

_____

What steps do you take to reduce theft of inventory? _____

_____

_____

_____

What other inventory control steps does you company take? _____

_____

_____

You will also need to discuss how you want to value and record your inventory. Two commonly used methods are LIFO — last in, first out, or FIFO — first in, first out. These are basic methods of valuing your remaining stock, and they can have significantly disparate tax implications, so this decision should be reached in consultation with your accountant. Complete the worksheet on the opposite page to assess your inventory control procedures.

Supply and Distribution

Almost every business has goods or materials coming in to the company and finished products or services going out. The companies you rely on to provide you with incoming goods, and the methods you use to sell and distribute your product are essential to the continuing well-being of your business.

Most businesses will experience difficulties with their suppliers or distributors at some point. So it can serve you well to explore the abilities, flexibility, and alternatives of your current suppliers and distributors.

Try not to be dependent on just one supplier or distributor; your financial future will be too vulnerable if they fail you. Work to develop excellent relationships with your suppliers and distributors; you want them to feel that you are in a partnership together so that they will try to do everything possible to meet your needs. Be responsive to their needs as well; work out payment plans and communication methods to reduce pressures on them.

Select Suppliers that Understand Your Needs

Usually, competitive supply sources exist, giving you a number of choices and enabling you to negotiate better prices. But don't make your decisions based on price alone, for you may find the price right but the delivery time and quality problematic. Select suppliers with whom you can communicate well; make certain they understand your specifications and can consistently meet your standards.

Reliable Distribution Is a Must

Reliable distribution often presents a far more difficult problem. If your product is distributed through a wholesaler or "middle-man", you need to carefully examine your choice of such distributor(s). Your selection of distributor(s) may be one of the single most important decisions you make, especially if they are responsible for most of your sales.

Once again, try not to put all your eggs in one basket. If you can ethically use more than one distributor, do so. Ask retailers or consumers about the reputation of distributors who sell to them so that you can be certain you are dealing with a reliable company and one that is well-regarded.

"To finance our growth rate, we opted to lease everything. The only thing we purchased was the equipment necessary for our patents. From an ultimate financial strategy, leasing was the only way we could grow the way we did. For us growth was the objective rather than net profit."

Larry Leigon
President, Ariel Vineyards

Supply and Distribution

$ ▶ $$ ▶ $$$

These questions help you evaluate your current supply and distribution needs.

Suppliers

Who is responsible for your purchasing decisions? _____

What are the key goods or materials necessary? _____

What are the average costs of these goods? _____

List your sources of key goods or materials: _____

List any alternative sources of these supplies: _____

Are any goods available from only one or two suppliers? ☐ Yes ☐ No

If so, how reliable or secure are these suppliers? _____

Can your suppliers provide you with "on demand" or short-notice goods? ☐ Yes ☐ No

If so, what additional costs do you incur? _____

Will your suppliers negotiate no- or low-minimum order contracts? ☐ Yes ☐ No

What kind of credit terms will your suppliers offer? _____

What are your average credit costs? _____

Which key factors determined your choice of suppliers? _____

Other supplier issues: _____

Distribution

How is your product or service distributed to the consumer? _____

_____

Is there a wholesaler or distributor between you and the consumer? ☐ Yes ☐ No

If so, how many such companies do you use? _____

What are the key qualifications and advantages of such companies? _____

_____

What are the drawbacks of such companies? _____

If you use only one or two distributors, how secure are these companies? _____

What is their reputation among consumers? _____

What kinds of payments or commissions do these distributors receive? _____

Describe any alternative distribution methods available: _____

_____

Complete the Supply and Distribution worksheet on the opposite page to assess your sources of supply and distribution.

Order Fulfillment and Customer Service

Remember, your work is not finished when you produce a product or secure an order from a customer. You still need to make sure your customer receives the product he or she wanted, in good condition, and in a timely fashion. You need to know that you have satisfied your customer.

Surprisingly, many companies pay relatively little attention to order fulfillment and customer service since they do not seem like pressing concerns or sources of increased profit margin. However, order fulfillment is part of any current sale, and customer service is part of any future sale.

Customers are constantly demanding better and better service. They expect to get what they want, when they want it, and to be treated graciously and fairly in the process. Many companies are renowned for their customer service and have built entire marketing strategies around it.

Some companies assume they are doing just fine in the way of customer service because they don't receive many complaints. But you can't judge how well you are serving your customers just by the number of complaints you receive; the unhappy customer who doesn't complain is almost certainly a lost customer. At least a customer who tells you the problem gives you a chance to make it right.

So, it is your job to make certain customers have little reason for complaints. Training all employees — from the shipping clerk to the sales representative — in customer service can pay off for you in customer retention and referrals. Build sufficient flexibility into your policies so that you can easily handle unusual or difficult requests. Empower employees to make certain decisions on the spot (such as accepting returns) instead of requiring each customer request to be approved by a manager. Make it easy for your customers to let you know what they want by soliciting customer suggestions and feedback.

Evaluate Your Order Fulfillment Processes

Examine your order fulfillment processes. Often, orders are not communicated clearly or quickly to the processing department, and valuable time is lost due to inadequate internal communication. Assess the methods by which you prepare goods for shipping and deliver goods to customers. If you hire outside companies to ship or deliver your product directly to the customer, make certain they can deliver on emergency or rush time schedules, or line up other shippers for such deliveries.

> *"One method of insuring quality-control is to put guest comment sheets in each room. The comment sheets are read, assessed, and charted. Every month, we do detailed assessments of cleanliness, friendliness, ground maintenance, telephone service, and so forth, for each managed property."*
>
> **Andre Tatibouet**
> **President, Aston Hotels**

Order Fulfillment and Customer Service $ ▶ $$ ▶ $$$

Describe your company's order fulfillment and customer service practices.

Who processes orders? _____

How are orders communicated from the salesperson to the order fulfillment department? _____

_____

How are orders checked to be certain they are filled promptly and accurately? _____

_____

What percentage of orders are prepared incorrectly? _____

How are goods prepared for shipping? _____

_____

How do you ship products? _____

_____

What is the shipping cost of your average order? _____

Are your shippers able to ship on short or emergency notice?   ☐ Yes   ☐ No

If so, are extra expenses incurred?   ☐ Yes   ☐ No

Who pays these: ☐ you or   ☐ the customer?

What alternative methods exist to ship products? _____

_____

What service programs do you offer? _____

What maintenance or repair programs do you offer? _____

_____

What percentage of your orders require repairs? _____

What is the average cost of the repair to your company? _____

What is your return policy? _____

What is your average rate of returns? _____

What is the cost of the average return? _____

Do you have a complaint or customer service department?   ☐ Yes   ☐ No

How do you solicit the opinions of customers? _____

_____

_____

Look at the kinds of services you provide customers after sale. Good customer service emphasizes developing an on-going relationship with your customers, so you need repair, service, warranty, and return policies that reassure customers that you continue to be interested in them even after you have their money.

Complete the worksheet on the opposite page to evaluate your order fulfillment and customer service practices.

Research and Development

A business that stands still is one that is almost certainly going to fail. You must keep on top of new developments that are going to affect your business. Your target market is always changing: growing older, developing new tastes, using new products. Your competitors understand this, so you need to stay aware of what they are doing if you wish to increase your ability to compete effectively.

All Companies Need Ongoing Product Development

Some companies need relatively large research and development components because they deal with constantly evolving technology or rapidly changing consumer preferences. But even companies that sell old-fashioned products (chocolate chip cookies, for instance) need to be developing new products based on changing customer values and concerns (such as low-fat cookies).

Your research and development activities may range from running a complete department staffed with researchers experimenting with new products and new equipment, to merely subscribing to certain publications and attending conferences. Regardless of the extent of such activities, research and development must be a priority in any business.

Examine the ways you plan to stay aware of developments likely to change your company's products, services, and practices. Make certain that key employees are likewise involved in research and development activities.

Complete the Research and Development worksheet on the next page to evaluate research and development in your company.

Financial Control

Amazingly, some businesses give relatively little attention to how they handle money. Businesses may have serious cash-flow problems just because they don't send out invoices in a timely manner. Or, they may incur substantial credit charges because they don't process their bills when due. Even very large companies are often guilty of inadequate financial control systems.

"Stay on top of your billings. You can't have money coming in if you don't have bills going out. Every month I do a 'Cash In, Cash Out' analysis. From the cash in, I subtract returns, loans. From cash out, I subtract major or unusual expenses. This gives me a quick picture of our operational profitability."

Charles Orr
President, Productivity Point International

Research and Development $ ▶ $$ ▶ $$$

This worksheet helps you assess your ongoing research and development efforts and costs.

Describe any new products currently in development: _____

_____

_____

_____

Describe any new services currently in development: _____

_____

_____

_____

Which staff members have research and development responsibilities? _____

_____

How are staff members used for research and development? _____

_____

What percentage of your staff's time is devoted to research and development? _____

Costs: _____

What equipment is needed for research and development? _____

Costs: _____

What supplies are needed for research and development? _____

Costs: _____

What publications are needed? _____

Costs: _____

What conferences will your employees attend for research and development purposes? _____

_____

Costs: _____

List any other research and development activities your company is involved in: _____

_____

_____

Costs: _____

Set up procedures to ensure that your financial information is handled promptly and accurately. Invoices should be sent out quickly, and a system of regular followups should be established for delinquent accounts. Accounts payable records should be thorough and easily retrieved, and sent regularly to appropriate decision-makers within the company. Make certain your accounting practices and data retrieval systems are such that you can receive ongoing information on sales and expenses. Don't depend on monthly reports.

One particularly difficult problem is how to make certain that employees do not have the opportunity to embezzle or pilfer. Work with your accountant to set up practices that ensure there are adequate safeguards against theft in your financial procedures. Bring in a computer consultant to design safeguards in your data processing programs as well.

Design your financial systems to be a source of regular information and constant feedback. Avoid cumbersome systems that bury your employees in paperwork; this increases your costs and reduces efficiency. Streamline the process as much as possible.

Complete the Financial Control worksheet on the next page to examine your financial control systems.

Other Operational Issues

A variety of other operational concerns will face your company, depending on the size and nature of your business. Some of these topics might include protecting the safety of your workers, protecting the environment, dealing with governmental regulations, arranging for adequate insurance protection, or exporting goods.

For in-depth information on many of these subjects, contact The Oasis Press at 1-800-228-2275. Among the publications you might find particularly helpful, depending on your needs, are *Export Now, The Business Environmental Handbook, California Safety Law Compliance Manual,* and *A Company Policy and Personnel Workbook.*

To briefly look at some of these concerns, complete the upcoming Other Operational Issues worksheet.

Financial Control

This worksheet helps you evaluate your company's financial control methods.

Who is primarily responsible for designing financial control procedures in your company? _____

_____

Which other employees are involved in financial control processes? _____

_____

_____

Who is responsible for invoicing? _____

What is the average amount of time that elapses before an invoice is sent after an order? _____

How are delinquent accounts handled? _____

_____

Who is responsible for handling your accounts payable? _____

What is your company's policy on paying outstanding bills? _____

☐ Pay when due

☐ Pay when received

☐ Pay on 30 days

☐ Other _____

Who makes decisions on variations in payment or billing procedures? _____

What protections have been designed to reduce theft? _____

_____

_____

What systems have been designed to produce ongoing reports of financial status? _____

_____

_____

_____

What other financial control systems have been devised? _____

_____

_____

_____

_____

Other Operational Issues   *$ ▶ $$ ▶ $$$*

The questions below elicit your company's concerns and plans involving other operational issues.

Safety and Health

What procedures do you take to protect the safety and health of your workforce? _____

_____

What safety programs do you have in place to encourage your workers to maintain safety precautions? _____

_____

Other safety issues: _____

_____

Insurance and Legal

What types of insurance do you need for your business? (include fire, accident/liability, malpractice, auto, etc.)

_____

_____

What amounts of coverage do you require to be adequately protected? _____

_____

What kinds of legal problems do you face in your business? _____

_____

Does your company need on-going legal advice and assistance? _____

Other insurance and legal issues: _____

_____

Regulations and Environmental

What licenses or permits are you required to have by law? _____

_____

What kinds of regulations cover your type of business? _____

_____

What kinds of environmental regulations affect your business? _____

_____

What precautions can your company take voluntarily to protect the environment? _____

_____

How can your company use products or processes that don't cause harm to animals? _____

_____

Other regulatory or environmental issues: _____

_____

Other operational issues: _____

Preparing the Operations Section of Your Business Plan

In preparing the Operations section of your business plan, emphasize these aspects of your operations:

- Key characteristics
- Competitive advantages
- Cost and time efficiencies
- Problems addressed and overcome

The aim of this section is to show that you have a firm grasp on the operational necessities of carrying out your business, that you understand how those operations relate to your overall business success, and that you have taken steps to achieve maximum efficiency at the least cost. You do not want to give a step-by-step explanation of how your company functions or go into the specific details of your activities. Save that information for your internal procedures manual.

The adjacent Plan Preparation Form lays out the basic areas you should cover in your written document. The Start-Up Costs worksheet that follows can be used by new businesses to explain the initial investment necessary to begin their operations.

Chapter Summary

While the Operations section of your written business plan should not be overly detailed, careful planning in this area brings you meaningful rewards. Analysing the day-to-day operations of your business will pay off in the form of increased profits as you find ways to reduce costs and improve productivity. You can find ways to make your money work harder and go farther, at the same time improving the quality of the product or service you produce and enhancing the work environment for your employees.

Operations Plan Preparation Form

On this form record specific information relating to your company's operational processes.

Key Aspects of Operations (possibilities include facilities, production process, equipment, labor force utilization):

_____

_____

_____

_____

_____

Cost and Time Efficiencies: _____

_____

_____

_____

_____

_____

_____

_____

Competitive Advantages: _____

_____

_____

_____

_____

Problems Addressed and Overcome: _____

_____

_____

_____

_____

_____

Use this information as the basis of your plan's Operations section.

Start-Up Costs

List the specific details of your initial cash requirements in the areas listed below and submit this information with your business plan.

		January	February	March	April
Facilities	Initial Rent/Purchase				
	Deposits (Security/Utility/Water/Other Hook-Ups)				
	Improvements/Remodeling/Fixtures/Signs				
	Other				
Equipment	Furniture				
	Production Machines/Equipment				
	Computers/Software				
	Cash Registers				
	Telephones				
	Vehicles				
	Other				
Materials/	Starting Inventory				
Supplies	Production Materials/Components				
	Stationery/Office and Packing Supplies				
	Brochures/Pamphlets, Other Descriptive Material				
	Other				
Fees and	Licenses/Permits				
Other Costs	Trade or Professional Memberships				
	Accounting				
	Legal				
	Insurance				
	Marketing/Management Consultants				
	Design Consultants				
	Advertising/Promotional Activities				
	Other				
Cash	For Salaries				
Reserves	For Operating Expenses				
	For Unanticipated Costs				
	Other				
TOTAL					

| | | | | | | | | $ ▶ $$ ▶ $$$ |
May	June	July	August	September	October	November	December	TOTAL

SAMPLE PLAN: Operations

Operations

At the core of ComputerEase's strategic concept is the corporate training center. These centers — classrooms equipped with computer stations — will be the location for conducting the largest percentage of the company's software training programs.

Operating these centers is vital, because most of ComputerEase's potential customers have limited, if any, extra computer facilities on their premises. Thus, ComputerEase can grow to an adequate level of income only if it has training facilities of its own to offer.

Corporate Training Centers

On August 1, 1993, ComputerEase opened its first corporate training center, at 987 South Main Street in Vespucci, along with its company's headquarters. This training center is equipped with 10 personal computer stations. Prior to the opening of the training center, ComputerEase was limited to conducting training programs at the client's place of business (referred to as on-site programs).

Cost and Time Effective Programs

These on-site programs produce lower profit margins than training center classes. Generally, fewer students attend each on-site training session; instructors spend additional time for travel and setup, and costs arise from transporting training materials. While ComputerEase charges higher fees per student in these on-site classes, the market will not bear prices that truly absorb the increased costs.

Moreover, the potential customer base for training center classes is substantially larger than that for on-site programs. Research shows a much larger number of businesses can afford to send a few employees to a class at the center, or even have a class developed for them at the center, than to incur the costs of an on-site program.

Thus, ComputerEase's strategic plan called for the opening of at least one classroom as quickly as possible.

ComputerEase will open a second training center in January 1994, dependent upon receiving the capital investment currently being sought. This addition will be either a second classroom at the present location, or a satellite classroom in the city of Abergel Peak (where many of ComputerEase's target corporate customers are located).

Competitive Advantages

The training center also offers Saturday training classes primarily for individuals or operators of very small businesses. The fee per student for Saturday classes is less than half the average fee of the corporate classes. However, ComputerEase reduces costs for these classes by utilizing more concise training materials and by requiring students to pay fees in full at the time of registration. (Corporate clients, on the other hand, pay 50% at time of class, and 50% within 30 days; contract clients are billed monthly.) Thus, these Saturday classes provide a quick source of cash while using the excess capacity of the training center.

Management decided early on to lease rather than purchase the computer equipment necessary for the current training center. This not only significantly reduced the amount of initial capital outlay, which would have exceeded $50,000, but it also ensures that ComputerEase will always be able to provide its students with the latest computers.

Problems Addressed

With the type of corporate training offered by ComputerEase — high quality, premium price — a major cost arises from the printed training materials provided to each student. Not only are substantial costs incurred in developing and writing the training manuals for each software program (revised for each new edition; the average life span is only six months), but the actual production costs can be staggering (average cost is $45 per student, per class). ComputerEase has reduced the amount of waste (to virtually none) by printing manuals just one day before each class begins (enabled by the purchase and lease of high-speed copying, collating, and binding equipment).

Nevertheless, ComputerEase must work to substantially reduce materials costs in the future. To share the costs of developing and producing such materials, national associations of software training companies are now forming. ComputerEase will join such an association, (or participate in creating one) as soon as practical (projected by July 1994).

ComputerEase emphasizes high-quality, productivity-oriented training. To help ensure quality, the company conducts interviews with each corporate client approximately one week after the training session to ascertain that the customer is satisfied. In the case of problems, the company offers free remedial training, preferably at the training center. To date, only two students have required remedial training.

In the future, ComputerEase, in conjunction with appropriate industry associations, intends to develop interactive computerized multi-media training programs. Such programs should substantially reduce materials costs.

Indicates how excess capacity is utilized profitability.

Details way to minimize inventory and cost of goods.

SAMPLE PLAN: Operations (continued)

Explains choice of location.

The choice of location for the training center was key. It had to be within walking distance of a large number of Vespucci target customers (located in a five-block radius in the central downtown business district). It needed to be close to transportation and parking facilities and had to present a professional image. And, of course, rents had to be affordable. For this reason, South Main Street stood out as the best choice. It is downtown, immediately available to the prime office locations, but it offers significantly lower rents than offices on the north side of Main.

Chapter 11

Management & Organization

No matter what you sell,
you're selling your people.

Your People Determine Your Success

People are the heart of every business. Overwhelmingly, the quality of the people determines the success of the business. Many investors base their investment choices almost entirely on the strength of the people involved in the enterprise. They know that the experience, skills, and personalities of the management team have a greater impact on the long-term fortunes of a company than the product or service provided.

For this reason, investors and lenders are likely to review the management portion of a business plan before they read many other sections. They read this section thoroughly, carefully scrutinizing the qualifications of the people behind a business. They look not only to see if the management team has the expertise necessary to run the business, but also if the internal structure makes maximum use of the talents of team members.

So, if you are preparing your business plan for financing purposes, you need to take particular care in crafting your Management section. Even if you are developing your business plan solely for internal use, an honest evaluation of your key employees' strengths and weaknesses will help you make the best use of your management team.

Most entrepreneurs give serious thought to choosing people for key positions. They may undertake extensive recruitment efforts, often

"Part of planning is 'people planning.' We want our managers to tell us about their people resources. People issues make up one of the largest sections of our business plan. We want to know how people will be used, and how managers are training their people and preparing for succession."

Georges James
Sr. V.P. & CFO
Levi Strauss & Co.

using professional executive search firms, to find just the right person. But what do they do with that man or woman once on board?

All too often, no one gives careful consideration to creating clear lines of organizational responsibility and developing a management style that motivates employees. Even the very best people will only do their best work in a system that encourages, recognizes, and rewards achievement. If you can create such an atmosphere, you can give yourself a true competitive edge.

Thus, in developing your Management plan, focus on two main areas: 1) the people who run your business; and 2) your management structure and style. Together, these two thrusts represent the core of your management system.

Your Management Team

Who are the people most important to your company's future? Who are the people determining the strategies you will pursue? Who makes final decisions? Which members of your management decide on the products or services you will sell and the prices you will charge? Who is in charge of your sales efforts?

In all but the smallest businesses, these tasks are assigned to or shared by many people. So when you evaluate your management team, include:

- Key Employees/Principals
- Board of Directors
- Advisory Committee
- Consultants and Other Specialists
- Key Management Personnel to Be Added

Key Employees/Principals

Usually, the most important person in a business is the founder or founders, especially if the company is a startup. In startups, the founders usually serve as the top managers and exercise day-to-day control over affairs. For this reason, the first person to evaluate in your management assessment is the founder, even if it is yourself.

Occasionally, either the founders themselves or major investors will bring in others to serve in top positions, such as president and chief executive officer. But if the founders remain active in the business in any way, either by serving on the Board of Directors, remaining as a company consultant, or taking a secondary management position, their skills and qualifications must be described in your plan.

Other managers to evaluate in your business plan include:

- Top decision makers: president, chief executive officer, division presidents.
- Key production personnel: chief operating officer, plant manager, technical director.
- Principal marketing staff: director of marketing, director of sales.
- Primary human resources staff: personnel director, training director.
- Head of research and development.

In looking at these key players, ask yourself:

- Do they possess the skills necessary for their specific jobs?
- Do they have a record of success?
- Have their business setbacks given them insights that will help them in their current roles?
- Do their personalities make them effective members of the team?
- If they have supervisory responsibility, are they able to direct and motivate employees effectively?
- Taken as a whole, does your team incorporate the full range of expertise and management skills you require?

If you are preparing your business plan solely to seek outside financing, you should limit the number of key employees discussed in this section to no more than five or six. Focus only on those who are most responsible for the company's long-term success.

Some companies are fortunate enough to have enlisted the services of "stars," individuals with particularly outstanding track records. If you have such a star associated with your company, be certain to highlight the role that he or she plays in your enterprise.

If you choose, you can include the resumes of key personnel in your plan's Appendix.

Complete the Key Employees Evaluation worksheet on the next two pages to outline the attributes of your top managers. Assess their:

- **Experience.** State the specific positions held and job responsibilities that directly relate to the current position. This is not a resume, so do not list every previous job, only those that indicate a skill or talent transferable to the job at hand.
- **Successes.** Describe noteworthy successes, particularly those that can be quantified. Include accomplishments that indicate the ability to plan, manage, overcome obstacles, and reach a goal.
- **Education.** Include education in the written plan only if the person is new to business or the education is directly related to or necessary for the task at hand.

Key Employee Evaluation

Describe the attributes of your top managers.

President/CEO: _____

Experience: _____

_____

Successes: _____

Education: _____

Strengths: _____

Areas Lacking Strength: _____

Chief Operating Officer: _____

Experience: _____

_____

Successes: _____

Education: _____

Strengths: _____

Areas Lacking Strength: _____

Chief Financial Officer: _____

Experience: _____

_____

Successes: _____

Education: _____

Strengths: _____

Areas Lacking Strength: _____

Marketing/Sales Director: _____

Experience: _____

Successes: _____

Education: _____

Strengths: _____

Areas Lacking Strength: _____

Production Manager: _____

Experience: _____

Successes: _____

Education: _____

Strengths: _____

Areas Lacking Strength: _____

Human Resources Director: _____

Experience: _____

Successes: _____

Education: _____

Strengths: _____

Areas Lacking Strength: _____

Research Director/Technical Director: _____

Experience: _____

Successes: _____

Education: _____

Strengths: _____

Areas Lacking Strength: _____

Other Key Personnel: _____

Experience: _____

Successes: _____

Education: _____

Strengths: _____

Areas Lacking Strength: _____

Other Key Personnel: _____

Experience: _____

Successes: _____

Education: _____

Strengths: _____

Areas Lacking Strength: _____

- **Strengths.** Describe the individual's best attributes in a business setting, including traits such as the ability to motivate others, industry knowledge, and financial capabilities.
- **Areas Lacking Strength.** Describe the attributes the individual must enhance to become a more effective manager; such traits might include specific skills or knowledge, better communication techniques, or ability to handle additional tasks.

Management Compensation and Incentives

Next, you need to discuss the compensation and incentives you offer your key employees as a way of retaining and motivating them to succeed. Most incentives have monetary implications, and investors often want to know the financial stake top management has in the company.

Some of the incentives you can offer include:

- **Salary.** Amount of money paid annually to the manager, regardless of company or personal performance.
- **Bonuses**. Additional cash given, usually at the end of the year, based on company or personal performance.
- **Commissions.** Cash given based on a percentage of sales made; rarely given to top management.
- **Profit Sharing.** Cash distributed to all eligible employees, based on the company's annual profit.
- **Equity**. Stock in the company, which gives the employee a direct financial stake in the overall performance of the business.
- **Stock Options.** Ability to buy stock at a future date at a currently set price; if the worth of the company goes up, these options can be exercised, giving the employee a financial gain.

In the Compensation and Incentives worksheet on the opposite page, list the financial incentives given key employees.

Board of Directors/Advisory Committee

Businesses that are incorporated must have boards of directors. In very small corporations, the directors are usually just the principals running the company. The board then serves little more than a legal function.

In larger companies, however, the board often includes members outside of management. Most frequently, these board members are people who have invested large sums in the company. Venture capitalists often require board seats as a condition of their investment.

Obviously, investors serve on boards to protect their money; they want to exercise some control over the management and direction of the company. But management should not view these investor–directors only as "Big Brothers," watching their every move. They often bring

Compensation and Incentives $ ▶ $$ ▶ $$$

Describe the compensation package for each of your key employees.

President/CEO

Salary: _____ Bonuses: _____

Other Incentives: _____ _____

Chief Operating Officer

Salary: _____ Bonuses: _____

Other Incentives: _____ _____

Chief Financial Officer

Salary: _____ Bonuses: _____

Other Incentives: _____ _____

Marketing/Sales Director

Salary: _____ Bonuses: _____

Other Incentives: _____ _____

Production Manager

Salary: _____ Bonuses: _____

Other Incentives: _____ _____

Human Resources Director

Salary: _____ Bonuses: _____

Other Incentives: _____ _____

Research Director/Technical Director

Salary: _____ Bonuses: _____

Other Incentives: _____ _____

Other Key Personnel

Salary: _____ Bonuses: _____

Other Incentives: _____ _____

Other Key Personnel

Salary: _____ Bonuses: _____

Other Incentives: _____ _____

valuable insight and judgment to the company and contribute to its overall viability and success.

In forming your board of directors, you might also want to include members who bring you specific business expertise, such as financial acumen or industry knowledge. Such directors typically receive compensation for their service on the board.

Remember, however, that the board of directors has legal responsibility and authority for the corporation. Thus, outsiders should be chosen very carefully.

You may identify a number of individuals whose ongoing judgment and advice you want for your company, but whom, for legal considerations, you don't want on your board of directors.

One way of using their services, other than hiring them, is to institute an informal advisory committee. Such a committee would have little or no legal responsibility but could still render great assistance in your company's development.

An advisory committee can also be helpful to a propietorship or partnership that does not have a board of directors.

Complete the Board of Directors/Advisory Committee worksheet on the opposite page to describe the members of your board of directors and advisory committee, if applicable.

Consultants and Other Specialists

Smaller businesses often think that consultants and specialists are only for large corporations. But hiring consultants can bring you the specific expertise of highly qualified individuals without the expense of a full-time employee. Both large and small businesses benefit from the services of outside consultants and specialists.

The use of consultants can also enhance the image you present in your business plan. Being represented by one of the leading law firms in town, or having your accounts prepared by one of the major accounting firms, adds credibility to your company.

Consultants with particular skills can help fill in the gaps in your management team. For instance, you might not yet be able to hire a full-time marketing director, but you could use the assistance of a marketing consultant.

Every business, no matter how small, should use an attorney and accountant, at least to set up the initial books and review contracts and leases. If you can't afford their services, you can't afford to go into business. It is a foolish economy to forego their advice for the sake of a few hundred dollars.

Board of Directors/Advisory Committee

List the members of your Board of Directors, their financial stake in the company, and their professional expertise:

_____

_____

_____

_____

_____

_____

_____

_____

Describe how often the Board of Directors meets and its responsibilities: _____

_____

_____

_____

If you have an Advisory Committee, state its functions and responsibilities and how often it meets: _____

_____

_____

_____

List the members of your Advisory Committee, their professional expertise, and their compensation, if any:

_____

_____

_____

_____

_____

_____

_____

_____

_____

Consultants and specialists you might use, other than attorneys and accountants, include:

- **Management Consultants.** To help you plan your business, develop strategies, solve particular problems, and improve management techniques.
- **Marketing Consultants.** To design ways to position your company in the market, oversee the creation of advertising and promotional materials, and structure your sales strategy.
- **Designers.** To add perceived value and improve your company's image through the talents of graphic design, product design, packaging design, or interior design.
- **Industry Specialists.** Every industry has areas requiring special knowledge or specific technical skills, and "experts" offer consultation in these areas; examples might be kitchen design for restaurants, production line design for manufacturing companies, or merchandising specialists for retail stores.

Complete the Consultants and Other Specialists worksheet on the opposite page to describe the consultants and specialists utilized by your company.

Key Management Personnel to Be Added

Don't worry if your management team is not fully complete, especially if your company is a startup. Investors and bankers are accustomed to seeing plans for companies that have key positions vacant.

You must, however, indicate the positions you intend to add in the future and the qualifications of the individuals you will seek to fill the positions. This gives a more complete picture of your overall management team and indicates that you understand the gaps in your organization.

When thinking about what you are lacking, consider not only the specific functional responsibilities that have yet to be covered, but also how you can create a sense of "balance" in your total team.

If most of your current management has strong technical experience in your industry, but less in business management, business experience should be a primary requirement of your new managers.

Sometimes your top manager is a good "inside" person, able to run production, supervise employees, and manage accounts, yet you still need a strong "outside" person, able to secure sales, entertain clients, and conduct promotional activities.

Complete the upcoming Key Management Personnel to Be Added worksheet to describe the key employees you intend to add to management.

"Building a sense of the 'team' must be planned and orchestrated. You must continually note that the team is all-important. The only bottom line, the only true satisfaction, is when the team does well. Team-building is an on-going process. In your training, use every conceivable example from other fields to bring home the importance of the concept of the team. Look to develop an atmosphere where players expect and demand a lot of each other, where they feel that individually they are an extension of their team-mates. This doesn't just happen, it must be planned."

Bill Walsh
Former Coach and
President, S.F. 49ers

Consultants and Other Specialists

Profile your key consultants below.

Attorney

Firm Name: _____

Lawyer's Name: _____

Specialty Area, if any: _____

Other similar or successful companies represented by firm: _____

Ways used by the company: _____

Accountant

Firm Name: _____

Accountant's Name: _____

Other similar or successful companies handled by firm: _____

Ways used by the company: _____

Management/Marketing Consultants

Firm Name: _____

Consultant's Name: _____

Specialty Area: _____

Qualifications: _____

Ways used by the company: _____

Industry Specialists

Firm Name: _____

Specialist's Name: _____

Specialty Area: _____

Qualifications: _____

Ways used by the company: _____

Others

Firm Name: _____

Specialist's Name: _____

Specialty Area: _____

Ways used by the company: _____

Key Management Personnel to Be Added   *$ ▶ $$ ▶ $$$*

Describe the factors concerning management personnel you intend to add to your staff.

Position: _____

Qualifications Sought: _____

_____

_____

Approximate Date to be Added: _____

Approximate Level of Compensation: _____

Other Incentives to be Offered: _____

Position: _____

Qualifications Sought: _____

_____

_____

Approximate Date to be Added: _____

Approximate Level of Compensation: _____

Other Incentives to be Offered: _____

Position: _____

Qualifications Sought: _____

_____

Approximate Date to be Added: _____

Approximate Level of Compensation: _____

Other Incentives to be Offered: _____

Position: _____

Qualifications Sought: _____

_____

_____

Approximate Date to be Added: _____

Approximate Level of Compensation: _____

Other Incentives to be Offered: _____

Management Structure and Style

How will you actually run your company? How will decisions be made? What are the lines of authority? How do you want employees to feel about the company? What voice do employees have when company policies and goals are set?

A company's organization and management style act as powerful invisible forces shaping both the daily working atmosphere and the future of the company. But all too often managers, especially new managers, pay only cursory attention to the development of their structure and style. In looking at your company's structure, examine both the formal lines of authority that exist and the informal ways in which decisions are made and employees are treated.

Lines of Authority

When examining their organization, managers usually begin with the formal structure — the official lines of authority. They decide how employees will be supervised and how job functions will be allocated. While clear lines of authority are vital in large organizations, they are equally important in small companies. A frequent source of tension in partnerships is the failure to plainly delineate areas of responsibility and decision making.

Some questions to ask when examining your company's structure are:

- Should responsibilities be allocated by functional area, product line, or geographic divisions? For example, should all your marketing efforts be assigned to a marketing department, or should each division handle all aspects of a product or service, including marketing?

- Which employees will each manager supervise, and over what functions will each manager have responsibility?

- Will you use a production line or team approach in producing your product or service? Thus, will each worker be responsible for one particular task, or will a group be responsible for many tasks?

Perhaps the quickest and clearest way to communicate your management structure is through a graphic organizational flow chart. You can use two kinds of charts: one describing areas of responsibility, and the other outlining reporting or supervisory relationships. Examples of each are shown on the next page. You should also provide a short narrative description explaining the relationships shown on the charts. If you do not wish to use a chart in your business plan, you need not do so. Just expand the verbal narrative to encompass the same material.

Informal Relationships

Flow charts describe your formal organizational structure, but every business also has an informal structure which can have at least as much

"Our management structure assumes people care about their jobs and want to belong to an organization that takes pride in what it makes. We demand more from our work force, but the trade-off for the worker is excellent pay and job security. We believe in developing employee potential through: mutual trust and respect; recognizing worth and dignity; developing individual performance; developing team performance; and improving the work environment."

Michael Damer
New United Motor
Manufacturing Inc.

Examples of Flow Charts

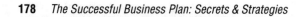

Examples of Flow Charts

Areas of Responsibility

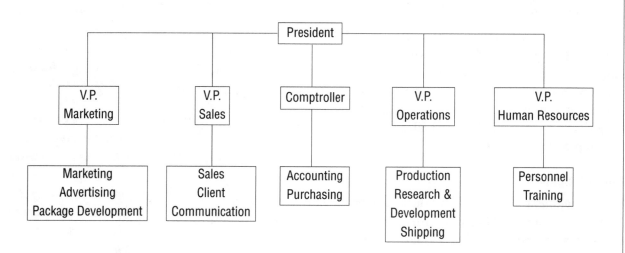

Reporting Relationships

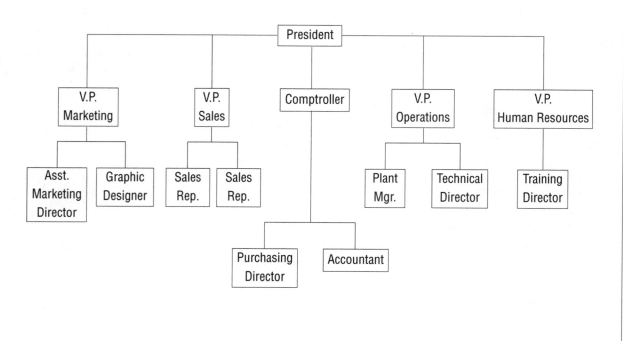

impact on the company. Although you should not discuss these informal relationships in a business plan prepared for outside funding, you should look at less formal relationships within your company when undertaking internal planning.

Questions to ask when evaluating your informal organization include:

- Which managers have the most impact on decisions?
- Which managers have ready access to the president or members of the Board of Directors?
- Do decisions at the top get effectively translated into action by others?
- Which subordinates have substantial influence on their superiors?
- Which divisions or groups of employees have the greatest morale problems? Who do they report to?

Generally, you want to evaluate how authority is distributed and how decisions are made in reality, not just on paper.

Management Style

All managers have management styles, even if they've never thought about their approach to management. Most managers define their jobs in terms of the tasks to be done rather than the methods to be used. They see their role as making widgets, rather than motivating and aiding the widget makers. Thus, their management styles are usually just extensions of their personal styles.

Managing people is far too important to be left to chance. Your employees are one of your most valuable resources. Just as you need to take care of other resources in your company, such as equipment and materials, you must make certain you are not wasting your human resources.

Moreover, you want to develop a management style that is independent of the personalities of your key managers and that instead fits your corporate culture. As discussed in Chapter 1, your corporate culture should permeate every aspect of your business and should reflect how you want your employees and customers to see you.

Your management style should reinforce your corporate culture and company message. If you are selling computers, for instance, and your corporate culture emphasizes creating an efficient tool for business, you might utilize a hierarchical management style with clearly defined tasks for each employee. On the other hand, if your computer company has a corporate culture centering on being an "alternative" to stuffy business computers, a more open management style accentuating the personal creativity of staff members may be more appropriate.

For most companies, especially smaller companies, building a sense of teamwork is essential. Help your employees feel they are an important

"We rotate jobs among members every two to three hours for safety, fairness, avoiding strains, and reducing boredom. Members are encouraged to make decisions on their own. Team members design the way the jobs will be done. The theory is the people closest to the function can best design how to perform the task."

Michael Damer
New United Motor
Manufacturing Inc.

"The best management is management by walking around. Employees know the boss is accessible and a real person they can identify with, not an anonymous entity. It gives management a personal quality. I shake hands with every employee; everybody calls me by my first name, from the mail room clerk on up. I'm listed in the telephone book; any employee or any guest can call me. With 1,500 employees and over one million guests, this could be a problem if we didn't have an effective operation.

Andre Tatibouet
President, Aston Hotels

"It's easy enough to acknowledge success. The tough part is finding the time and the right way to reinforce the person who made the effort but didn't quite succeed or the one who made sacrifices for the good of the team."

Bill Walsh
Former Coach and President, S.F. 49ers

part of the organization and that their contribution matters. Communication is a vital ingredient in team building; if employees know what's going on in the company, they feel a part of the whole picture.

Regardless of your management style, remember that everyone, whether mailroom clerk or company president, wants to feel important. Recognize achievement, both privately and publicly. Reward initiative with both monetary and nonmonetary awards. Acknowledge jobs well done. Solicit suggestions, and be responsive to concerns.

The five most important elements of your management style are:

1. Clear Policies

2. Communication

3. Employee Recognition

4. Employee's Ability to Affect Change

5. Fairness

Complete the Management Style worksheet on the opposite page to evaluate your company's management style.

Preparing Your Management Section

How you prepare the Management section of your business plan depends a great deal on whether it is being written for internal use only or whether it will be submitted to outside investors.

"What makes the difference in employee attitude is the relationship between the on-site manager and the employee, and the sensitivity and openness of management. You have to give your employees the opportunity to talk with management, the feeling that they're part of a winning team, and they have the opportunity to move ahead. They have to feel they are being treated fairly, and the golden rule is being applied. Treat people the way you want to be treated."

Robert Price
Chairman of the Board
The Price Club

If your plan is for internal use, emphasize the management aspects centering on structure, style, and gaps in personnel. However, if you are preparing the plan for financing purposes, you should focus primarily on the relevant backgrounds of your management team members. These summaries should be brief and written in an objective style. Even if your vice president for marketing truly is "highly motivated, results-oriented, and exceptionally creative," those types of judgments appear naive when read in a business plan.

The upcoming Management Plan Preparation Form enables you to outline the Management section of your business plan.

Chapter Summary

Management is the key to success for every business. It takes capable people, with appropriate experience and abilities, to develop both a management structure and style that make full use of the personnel and financial resources of the business and keeps the company focused on its mission. Thus, potential investors will thoroughly examine the backgrounds of the management team that will be running your company.

Management Style

Describe the nature and functions of your company's management.

How does your company's management style fit with your corporate culture? _____

_____

_____

_____

How do the personalities of your key employees complement or contrast with the company's management style?

_____

_____

How do you develop a sense of teamwork among your employees? _____

_____

_____

Do you have a clear set of company policies, covering items such as benefits, termination, and promotion? ____

_____

How do you ensure ongoing communication with your employees? Do you hold meetings, informal conferences, or print newsletters? _____

_____

_____

How do you recognize and acknowledge employees' achievements? What financial rewards do you give? What nonmonetary recognition do you provide? _____

_____

_____

How do you solicit and act on employee suggestions? How can employees affect the development of company products, services, or policies? _____

_____

_____

Are policies enforced evenly? Are rewards and acknowledgments given fairly? Does management play "favorites"?

_____

_____

Management Plan Preparation Form

List the key members of your management team, with a brief description of each person's relevant business background, responsibilities they have in your company, and the compensation they receive.

_____

_____

_____

_____

_____

_____

_____

_____

_____

_____

_____

_____

Key Decision-Makers and Advisors for the Company: _____

_____

_____

_____

_____

_____

_____

_____

_____

_____

_____

_____

Management Structure and Style: _____

_____

_____

_____

Use this information as the basis of your plan's Management section.

SAMPLE PLAN: Management & Organization

Management

Key Employees

<u>Scott E. Connors, President.</u> Prior to founding ComputerEase in January 1993, Scott E. Connors was the Regional Vice President for Chanoff's Computer Emporium, a franchised computer hardware retail chain, with 23 stores in the Midwest. Connors began his association with Chanoff's Computer Emporium as manager of the downtown Vespucci store in 1982. In his first year, he increased sales by over 42%, and in his second year by 39%. Because of these sales, he was named "Manager of the Year" in 1984 for the Chanoff's chain. In March 1985, Connors purchased a half-interest in the ownership of the Vespucci store. In October 1989, he sold this interest .

Gives examples of achievements.

Connors assumed the role of Regional Vice President of the Chanoff's chain in August 1987. In that position, he was responsible for the company's strategic development for Indiana, Ohio, and Illinois. His duties included approving franchise proposals, selecting locations, and providing direct assistance to store managers in marketing, operations, and administration. He remained in that position until October 1992, when he left to begin work on ComputerEase.

Shows relevant experience.

As Chanoff's Regional Vice President, Connors conducted an evaluation of the potential of adding software retailing and training components to augment the chain's computer hardware sales. This evaluation led Connors to believe that a substantial need for corporate software training existed but could not be met by a hardware retailer. Instead, a stand-alone operation should be formed. This was the concept behind ComputerEase.

Connors' association with Chanoff's Computer Emporium, coupled with the five years he spent as a sales representative for IBM, has given him extensive experience in selling technological equipment and services to large corporations.

Connors owns 60% of the stock in ComputerEase and serves as Chairman and Treasurer of the Board of Directors. He voluntarily reduced his salary for the years 1993 and 1994 to $30,000 and $40,000, respectively. In 1995 his salary will be $65,000.

Specifies ownership interest in company.

<u>Susan Alexander, Vice President, Marketing.</u> In March 1993, Susan Alexander joined ComputerEase with primary responsibility for the company's marketing and sales activities.

Prior to joining ComputerEase, Alexander served as Assistant Marketing Director for AlwaysHere Health Plan. Her responsibilities in this position included direct sales to human resource directors, developing marketing

SAMPLE PLAN: Management & Organization (continued)

Shows directly applicable experience.

materials and campaigns, and supervising sales personnel. She held that position from 1988 until coming to ComputerEase.

Alexander's experience marketing to the human resources community gives her the ideal background for ComputerEase, which sells its services primarily through human resources and training directors.

In previous relevant positions, Alexander was a sales representative for SpeakUp Dictation Equipment, where she sold technological equipment to corporations, and copy editor for Catchem Advertising Agency.

Alexander owns 10% of the stock in ComputerEase. In 1993 and 1994 she took reduced salaries in return for this equity ($24,000 in 1993; $32,000 in 1994). Her salary will rise in 1995 to $50,000. She also receives a 5% sales commission on all contracts she secures.

Lists management to be added at a later date.

Vice President, Training (To Be Selected). In January 1994, ComputerEase will add a third key management position, Vice President for Training. The individual selected will have substantial experience in conducting a training organization, teaching others to train, and supervising a training staff. The future vice president will possess outstanding training skills and have experience with computer software programs, either in teaching or developing such programs. Ideally, he or she will have experience in developing training manuals or other training material.

The Vice President for Training will be offered a 10% ownership in the company in return for a reduced salary. The salary budgeted for this position in 1994 is $30,000. In 1995 the salary is budgeted for $45,000.

Board of Directors
Scott Connors is the Chairman of the Board and Treasurer. The position of Vice Chairman has been reserved for an outside investor. The company's attorney, Cathy J.Dobbs, serves as Secretary.

Consultant
A.A. Arnold, Ph.D. Dr. A. A. Arnold, Professor of Instructional Media at Vespucci State University (VSU), serves the company as a consultant in the conception and development of training manuals. A specialist in the design of instructional materials, Dr. Arnold received his Ph.D. in Education with an emphasis on interactive computer-aided training. Currently, Dr. Arnold designs training programs for industry in addition to holding his position at VSU.

Advisory Committee

An informal Advisory Committee was formed in April 1993 to provide guidance to the officers and staff of ComputerEase. The committee meets quarterly, and members of the committee are available as resources to the company on an ongoing basis.

Members of the committee are:

Virginia Gross, Director of Human Resources, RockSolid Insurance Company

John Caruso, Director of Training, Vespucci National Bank

Mark Richards, Marketing Director, PSI Software

Dr. A. A. Arnold, Professor of Instructional Media, Vespucci State University

Additional members are expected to be added by the end of 1993.

Management Structure

President Scott Connors is involved in the day-to-day operations of all aspects of the company. He directs the administrative and financial aspects of the company and works closely with the vice presidents to help guide and support activities over which they have specific responsibility. However, each vice president is given a wide degree of decision-making authority in his or her assigned areas.

Management responsibilities in ComputerEase are divided as shown on the flow chart on the next page.

Advisory Board reflects business leaders and potential customers.

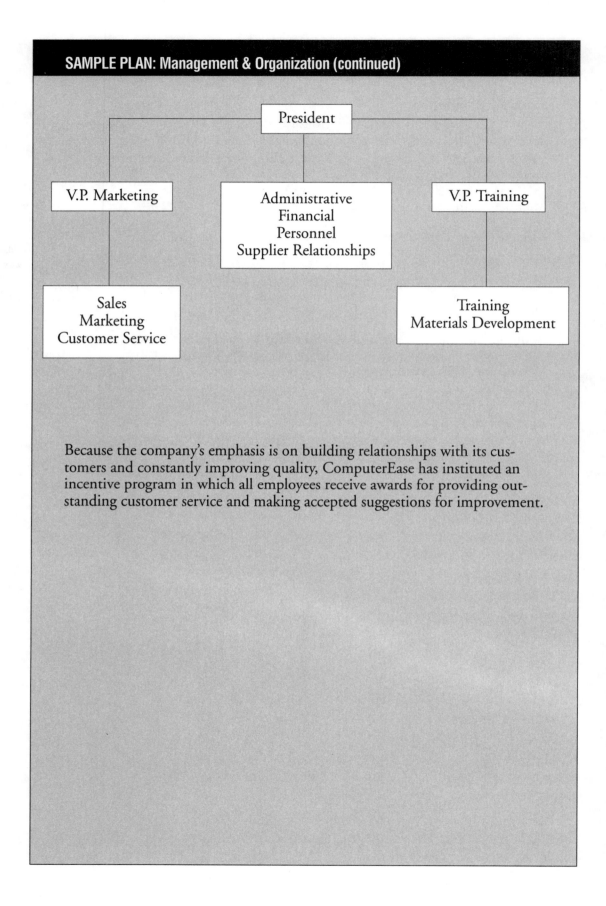

SAMPLE PLAN: Management & Organization (continued)

Because the company's emphasis is on building relationships with its customers and constantly improving quality, ComputerEase has instituted an incentive program in which all employees receive awards for providing outstanding customer service and making accepted suggestions for improvement.

Chapter 12

Long-Term Development & Exit Plan

You can't reach a goal
you haven't set.

Determine Your Business' Ultimate Destination

If a business plan serves as a road map for your company, then to use it properly you need a sense of your ultimate destination. What do you want your business to look like in three, five, or seven years? You can't hope to just stumble across success; you have to figure out how to get there. One of the most important aspects of the business planning process, therefore, is the examination of your long-term goals.

Moreover, in the course of your planning process you will find it useful to establish markers — milestones — to help keep you on track. By developing specific objectives, you have signposts to measure progress along your way.

Investors are greatly interested in this section of your business plan. When they invest capital in your company, they want to see what they are getting in return. They know how much money they can lose — the downside risk. But they also want to gauge what they might gain, how big the company might become — the upside reward. Lenders, on the other hand, are less interested in long-term growth than investors. They already know their upside potential; it's defined in the terms of the loan.

In this section you will spell out the specific ways whereby your company can be judged and the risks involved. You may find this prospect a bit unsettling, perhaps you even fear that it will scare off financing

"Every business grows in phases. I want to see one respectable phase in which they can succeed before they go on to the second and third phases. They can have other things in mind, but I want them to finish the first thing to show what they can do."

Eugene Kleiner
Venture Capitalist

sources. Don't be intimidated. Sophisticated investors and lenders give greater credence to entrepreneurs who acknowledge risk and are willing to be measured against clear-cut objectives. They understand that progress takes time and that risks are an inherent part of doing business.

In developing your company's long-term plans, you must evaluate your:

- Goals
- Milestones
- Risks
- Exit plan

Goals

What do you want in the future, both for yourself and for your company? In founder-led and small companies, the personal goals of the entrepreneur(s) and the goals for the business should reasonably relate to one another. Otherwise, the inherent tensions will undermine the success of the business. There's no use envisioning running a $50 million dollar company, when what you really want is to take long vacations and be home every afternoon by 3:00 p.m. That's just not a realistic fit.

You probably have a vision of what your company may be. The vision may not be well-formed, perhaps something like, "One day I'd like this company to be known for making the very best product of its type." Or the vision may be very specific, set by you or investors; it might be a goal such as "Sales of $10 million by 1996."

The vision that you and the other decision-makers hold for your company shapes the nature of your day-to-day activities and should determine the priorities for the expenditure of your resources. You want to emphasize those actions that support your eventual aims. Grow towards your vision.

In assessing your business concept, consider which of the following visions you have for your company and yourself:

- **Steady Provider.** Maintain a stable level of profit; earn a good, reliable income while owning your own business.
- **Innovator.** Produce new and different products or services; change the way the market views the product or service; act on your creativity.
- **Quality Leader.** Produce the product or service everyone would buy if price were no object; develop a reputation for excellence; take pride in creating the best.
- **Market or Industry Leader.** Dominate the market in terms of sales and products; have a well-known name and run a large operation.
- **Niche Leader.** Carve out a narrow place in the market that your company dominates; do only one thing, but do it extremely well.

- **Exploiter.** Take advantage of the trends of the moment or copy the successes of others; take risks for quick rewards.

These goals are not necessarily mutually exclusive, and you can choose more than one, if they aren't contradictory. Or, perhaps you have another vision for your company. Use the Company Vision worksheet on the next page to focus your thoughts about the future.

Although these concepts are relatively intangible, they have tangible consequences. If you see your company as an innovator, you may have to sacrifice short-term profits for the ability to experiment. If you want a company that is a market leader, you must position your company to grow to a substantial size.

To give substance to your vision, express your goals in concrete terms. This process will help you understand and articulate your goals; it is meant for internal planning rather than for inclusion in a written business plan, especially one prepared for outside funding.

Strategies

You now must consider what business strategy will take your company from its present situation towards your long-term goals. Developing an overall strategy gives you the basis for deciding on the priorities for specific actions and expenditures of funds.

Among the business strategies you might undertake are:

- **Market Penetration.** Gain a foothold in the market as you introduce either the company or a new product or service and attempt to develop sufficient sales to sustain your initial development.
- **Promotion and Support.** Intensify the marketing and development of your current product or service lines to increase sales and gain market share.
- **Expansion.** Add products or services in existing lines, additional locations, production capacity, or distribution systems in an effort to increase sales.
- **Increase Focus.** Narrow the scope of activities of your company by eliminating some products or services and marshaling your resources on your remaining line(s) to increase profit margin.
- **Diversify.** Add new product or service lines (or buy other companies), thus broadening the nature of the company, in an effort to expand the overall size and sales of the company and making you less dependent on your current products or services for survival.
- **Refocus.** Modify the essential nature of the company in terms of market, products, or services to respond to changing conditions or substantial business reverses.

Consider the above strategies when assessing the long-term development of your company.

"Our development strategy is aimed at keeping the company manageable for me. I wanted at least a year to learn the business, so I limited the number of stores and the geographic area served. Everyone was urging me to go fast, think big, but I needed to go at my own pace."

Deborah Mullis
Founder
D.A.M.E.'S Foods

Company Vision

Describe the vision you hold of your company for the next decade.

Overall Long-Term Development: _____
_____
_____
_____

Specific Goals	**One Year**	**Five Years**	**Ten Years**
Number of Employees	_____	_____	_____
Number of Locations	_____	_____	_____
Annual Sales	_____	_____	_____
Profits or Profit Margin	_____	_____	_____
Number of Products or Services	_____	_____	_____
Awards or Recognition Received	_____	_____	_____
	_____	_____	_____
	_____	_____	_____
Ownership Allocation	_____	_____	_____
	_____	_____	_____
Other:_____	_____	_____	_____
_____	_____	_____	_____
_____	_____	_____	_____

Business Strategies

One year: _____
_____
_____
_____

Five years: _____
_____
_____
_____

Ten years: _____
_____
_____
_____

Priorities

To implement those strategies you must undertake specific actions. For instance, if your strategy is to promote and support, you will want to use any additional resources, either of money or time, on your marketing efforts. If, on the other hand, your strategy is to diversify, you want to accumulate resources to expend on the introduction of new product lines or the purchase of new companies.

To clarify the significance of particular activities as they relate to the strategy for reaching your long-term goals, you must develop a set of priorities for the expenditure of your resources. A list of priorities is a critical tool for every business. Although this list does not need to be included in a business plan for outside financing sources, it would be wise to refer to it whenever making major business decisions.

On the upcoming Priorities worksheet, specify the relative importance of each activity when it comes to the expenditure of funds.

Milestones

How will you and your investors know that you are making sufficient progress towards your goals? If your long-term goal is to reach sales of $3 million in year five, how much do you need in sales by year two and year three?

In the daily press of business, it can often seem that you're making no progress at all. At any given time, you'll have a stack of bills to pay, troublesome customers, and problems with your staff. So you need a reminder that you have, in fact, been going forward.

A milestone list allows you and your financing sources to see just how much you've accomplished, and it sets out clearly delineated objectives. These objectives are part of your immediate business plan and are included with the written document.

A milestone list focuses on the specific objectives you intend to achieve and the dates by which you expect to accomplish them. These must be defined in concrete terms and a number assigned to any measurable activity. Thus, omit goals expressed in ways such as: "developing a substantial customer base." Instead, specify: "reaching annual sales level of 50,000 units by 1997."

When assigning dates to your milestones, remember that everything takes longer than planned; problems always arise. One of the frustrations of all entrepreneurs, but especially new entrepreneurs, is realizing how long everything takes to get done. Progress comes slowly. So allow yourself plenty of time when you are establishing chronological goals.

"Long-term planning must be a part of everything you do. You must continually work to stay contemporary. Be inquisitive and open-minded. Don't make comments like, 'We've always done it this way,' or 'We've tried it before.' Look for reasons to respond to new ideas and evaluate how they can improve your performance."

Bill Walsh
Former Coach and
President, S.F. 49ers

"Our strategy is to build sales in the stores we're in before expanding into more stores and a wider area. This gives us the opportunity to develop our product line, and to show retailers good sales figures when presenting our products."

Deborah Mullis
Founder
D.A.M.E.'S Foods

> *"A plan should tell us how, as funders, we will know you're making progress, that you're on the road to success. Spell out what challenges you face in getting to market, what specific accomplishments you must achieve to build your company. We want five or six milestones to measure as we go along. For us, these are 'risk-reduction points' — they let us know you're on the right track."*
>
> **Ann Winblad**
> **Venture Capitalist**

Complete the upcoming Milestones worksheet to outline your objectives. This list should be included with your business plan, whether used for internal planning or raising funds.

Risk Evaluation

Every enterprise involves risks. But you can take some of the hazards out of your business by anticipating potential problems and considering your response.

Investors make financing decisions based on an evaluation of the potential risks versus potential rewards. They will naturally consider what risks your company represents, whether or not you outline such risks in your plan. Showing that you have already assessed the potential risks in your business reassures investors that you are not just naively optimistic in your planning.

On the Risk Evaluation worksheet, which follows the Milestones worksheet, assess the nature of the risks facing your company in each area and describe the steps you can take, or have already taken, to lessen that risk. Include risks such as changing demographics of the market or sociological trends, gaps in the management team, new government regulation, etc.

Exit Plan

When banks or individuals lend you money, it's clear how they expect to get their money back and make a profit: You are to pay them out of income, with interest. They evaluate your business on the basis of whether they think there's enough profit in your operating budget to pay back the loan.

But how do investors get their money back? Since investors become owners of the company (through their stock holdings), their profit is earned in a different manner than banks and lenders. Some investors may be putting money in for the long-run, expecting to take an active part in the development and operation of the company and getting their reward through the distribution of profits.

Other investors, however, especially venture capitalists, eventually plan to liquidate their investment — to convert their holdings to cash or easily traded stock. Ideally, these investors want to know at the outset how they will get a substantial profit out of their investment. They want to see your exit plan.

Developing an Exit Plan

Considering your potential exit plan benefits you as well as investors. After all, you've devoted substantial time and money of your own to

Priorities

Rate each area's priority for the expenditure of funds, in hierarchical order (1-2-3, with 1 being the highest priority). Describe the specific priorities or amounts in each area.

Priorities	Specifics	Rating
Add Employees	_____	_____
	_____	
Add New Lines	_____	_____
	_____	
Increase Marketing	_____	_____
	_____	
Add Locations	_____	_____
	_____	
Add Capacity	_____	_____
	_____	
Increase Salaries	_____	_____
	_____	
Increase Inventory	_____	_____
	_____	
Increase Profits	_____	_____
	_____	
Retire Debts	_____	_____
	_____	
Increase Reserve	_____	_____
	_____	
Acquire Other Companies	_____	_____
	_____	
Other: _____	_____	_____
_____	_____	_____
_____	_____	_____
_____	_____	_____

this company, and you should have an idea of the way in which you'll reap rewards. Annual income is the major motivation for many entrepreneurs, but ideally your company will have worth beyond its annual profits, and you should eventually benefit from that worth.

A number of options exist for exiting from a company, although venture capitalists may be interested in only two or three of them. Generally, sophisticated investors look for companies that can go public (sell stock that will be traded to the general public on stock exchanges or "over the counter") or that are candidates for acquisition by larger companies. Investors like these exit strategies because they get out of the company cleanly, usually with substantial rewards, based on just one event: either an IPO — an initial public offering (when the stock is first publicly traded) — or the sale of the company.

These two strategies, however, often result in the top management, including the founder(s), either having to leave or having far less control over the company.

Entrepreneurs, on the other hand, often imagine being able to buy out their investors, but this is not usually a realistic option. In companies that are very successful, the investor has little motivation to sell and the amount of money needed to purchase their stock could be prohibitive. In less successful companies, the investors may want to get out, but the entrepreneur is unlikely to have the extra cash necessary to buy them out.

Exit Plan Options — which are briefly outlined near the end of this chapter — describing the major exit strategies and their advantages and disadvantages and then describe your company's exit plan. The disadvantages assume the current management would like to have a continuing role in the company.

Exit Strategies

After reviewing the strategies outlined in the upcoming Exit Plan Options chart, describe your company's exit strategy on the subsequent Development Plan Preparation Form.

Preparing the Development Section of Your Plan

In preparing a business plan for outside investors, the two most important aspects of your Development section are your milestones list and the description of your exit plan. Through these investors get a clear idea of how the company will grow and how they will realize their financial rewards.

For a plan to be used for internal purposes, emphasis should also be placed on the vision of the company's growth. Describing the specific strategies and priorities for expenditure of resources will make your

Milestones

State your specific future objectives and when you plan to achieve each one.

Event	Specifics	Date
Incorporation	_____	_____
Lease Signed	_____	_____
Key Employees Hired:	_____	_____
_____	_____	_____
_____	_____	_____
_____	_____	_____
_____	_____	_____
Initial Financing Secured	_____	_____
Product Design Completed	_____	_____
Market Testing Completed	_____	_____
Trademarks/Patents Secured	_____	_____
Strategic Partnerships Secured	_____	_____
First Product Shipped	_____	_____
Level of Sales Reached ($)	_____	_____
Level of Sales Reached (units)	_____	_____
Level of Employees Reached	_____	_____
Profit Level Reached	_____	_____
Second Product Line Developed	_____	_____
Second Product Line Tested	_____	_____
Second Product Line Shipped	_____	_____
Additional Financing Secured	_____	_____
Debts Retired	_____	_____
Additional Location Opened	_____	_____
Other:_____	_____	_____
_____	_____	_____
_____	_____	_____
_____	_____	_____

plan a useful tool that you can refer to frequently to help in making major decisions.

A Plan Preparation Form is provided for you to outline the Development section of your business plan.

Chapter Summary

The Development section of your business plan shows that you have given careful consideration to how your company will grow over time. By including a milestones chart, you provide a clear timetable of your company's development and allow yourself to be judged by objective measurements. By describing the potential risks your company faces, you display confidence in your ability to overcome such risks. Investors will be interested in how they can recoup the money they have devoted to your company, and they will appreciate that you have considered a realistic exit plan.

"It's easy to get into an investment, but investors want to know, how do we get out? It's not good enough to just say that there will be a public offering, because selling to the public may not be realistic at times. Instead, you have to show you have an attractive business that other businesses will want to own, either because it complements an existing product line or on its own."

Eugene Kleiner
Venture Capitalist

Risk Evaluation

Specify the major risk(s) facing your company in each area, rate the approximate extent of that risk (high-, medium-, or low-risk), and note steps you can take, or have taken, to lessen that risk:

Area	Risks	Rating	Response
Industry	_____	_____	_____
	_____		_____
Market	_____	_____	_____
	_____		_____
Competition	_____	_____	_____
	_____		_____
Product Use	_____	_____	_____
	_____		_____
Costs	_____	_____	_____
	_____		_____
Suppliers	_____	_____	_____
	_____		_____
Distributors	_____	_____	_____
	_____		_____
Sales	_____	_____	_____
	_____		_____
Technology	_____	_____	_____
	_____		_____
Legal/Regulatory	_____	_____	_____
	_____		_____
Management	_____	_____	_____
	_____		_____
Financing	_____	_____	_____
	_____		_____
Cash-Flow	_____	_____	_____
	_____		_____
Other: _____	_____	_____	_____
	_____	_____	_____
	_____	_____	_____

Exit Plan Options

Option	Description	Advantages	Disadvantages
Go Public	Sell shares in the company to the public, traded on a stock exhange or "over the counter."	Stock easily convertible to cash, liquidity; current management stays.	Must be large company: approx. $25 to $50 million; highly regulated; manage ment can be replaced by stockholders.
Acquisition	Bought by another existing company.	Receive cash and/or stock; current management may have continuing role.	Must be appropriate fit for existing co.; management leaves or has new boss.
Sale	Bought by individuals.	Receive cash.	Must find willing buyer; management goes.
Merger	Join with existing company.	Combined resources; current management may stay; may receive stock or some cash.	New partners or bosses; usually little or no cash; less control.
Buy-Out	One or more stockholders buy out the interests of another.	Seller gets cash; others stay in control of company.	Must have sufficient cash; seller must be willing.
Franchise	Sell concept to others to replicate.	Receive cash; current management stays; future potential.	Concept must be appropriate; legally complicated.
Hand Down	Give company to next generation.	Stays in family; current management may continue.	Family tensions; no cash; tax implications.
Close	End operations.	Relatively easy; feeling of being finished.	No financial reward; feeling of loss.

Development Plan Preparation Form

Describe your company's goals for the next five to ten years, in terms of position in the market, sales, number of employees, etc.:_____

_____

_____

_____

_____

_____

_____

_____

Describe the basic strategy you will use to reach those goals, and the priority for the expenditure of funds: _____

_____

_____

_____

_____

_____

_____

_____

Describe the major risks facing your company: _____

_____

_____

_____

_____

_____

Describe the exit plan for your investors: _____

_____

_____

_____

_____

Use this information as the basis of your plan's Development section.

SAMPLE PLAN: Development

Development

Long-Term Goals

States vision of company.

ComputerEase plans to grow steadily over the next 5 years, becoming the premier provider of software training to businesses in the greater Vespucci area. By 1996, the company plans to have a market share of at least 50% of all corporate software training in the Vespucci area. Within 10 years, the company plans to have expanded throughout the Midwest, capturing at least one-third of the share of the corporate software training market in the region.

Strategy for Achieving Goals

To accomplish this, the company plans expansion activities every year, adding both staff and training classrooms. This expansion will be financed primarily from income. As such, the officers of the company have a priority of committing funds from income to growth rather than to the distribution of profits.

Gives priority for expenditure of funds.

The first priority for expansion is the addition of an in-house training staff and a second training classroom, most likely at the current location in downtown Vespucci. The second priority is to enlarge the marketing staff. Third, an additional location within the greater Vespucci area will be established. This is the growth plan for the first three years.

After that, however, to remain competitive, ComputerEase must have a presence and connection beyond the Vespucci area. As the company anticipates that corporate software training increasingly will be marketed on a nationwide basis, ComputerEase must have national connections. To do so, in the immediate future, plans call for becoming a member of a national software training association. However, more formal expansion is also needed.

By year three, the officers of the company will have assessed the nature of that formal expansion. Two options are foremost: to open additional ComputerEase company-run branches in other metropolitan areas or to franchise.

Greater Expansion Plans

The first route — additional company-run locations — will center on the Midwest as the area of expansion. ComputerEase will choose major metropolitan areas based on an assessment of sales potential and the intensity of the competition in each market at the time of expansion. It is estimated that at least one metropolitan area would be added each year from 1996–2000. To fund such expansion, the company will require additional capital, which would ideally be secured from bank financing. In the event that conventional financing is not secured, funds will be sought from investors.

The ComputerEase concept also lends itself well to franchising. Since corporations with offices throughout the United States often prefer to have all their computer training provided by the same company, a franchise operation gives the company greater marketing clout. Moreover, the franchising concept produces additional revenue streams to the company from the franchisees, both from franchise fees and through the purchase of materials and staff training. If the decision is made to franchise, venture capital investment will be sought. Current investors could choose to liquidate their holdings in ComputerEase at that time or convert their holdings to stock in the franchise operation.

Describes potential exit opportunity for investor.

Risks Associated with Expansion

The biggest risk facing the expansion of ComputerEase is timing. Existing software training firms in other parts of the country are well-positioned to establish themselves as nationally-known providers. If they are able to market themselves on a national level, they represent not only potential competition on a national or regional level, but they could possibly enter the local market in direct competition.

Recognizes and acknowledges potential risks.

To prepare for this eventuality, company management is closely following developments, and the company is prepared to enter into agreements with other software training companies. Such agreements include the possibility of merger, acquisition, or the provision of services under the name of the larger company, if necessary.

"Motivating your employees comes from setting a standard of performance you develop over years. A person becomes motivated from exposure to an atmosphere of high expectations, high standards, and being able to see improvement and success over time. Motivation is superficial if you think in terms of a one-time conversation or event. It's more subtle than that; it's a matter of professionality and continually searching for ways to motivate and inspire people, noting improved skills, and reminding people of their role in maintaining a high standard of performance."

Bill Walsh
Former Coach and
President, S.F. 49ers

Chapter 13

The Financials

Numbers are merely the reflection
of decisions you make.

How to Painlessly Deal with Numbers and Financial Forms

People in business usually fall into one of two categories: those who are fascinated with numbers, or those who are frightened by them. If you're in the first category, you are probably delighted to finally reach this section. You may have even skipped previous sections to do this one. If you are one of those in the second category, however, you're probably intimidated by the very prospect of having to fill in the forms encountered in this chapter.

Numbers Represent Your Decisions

Take heart: Numbers are neither magical, mysterious, nor menacing. They merely reflect other decisions you have made previously in your business planning. If you decided to advertise each week in your local newspaper, there's a number attached to that decision. If you projected sales at a certain level, there's a number attached to that decision as well.

Every business decision leads to a number, and taken together, these numbers form the basis of your financial forms. But numbers themselves are not decisions. You cannot pull a number out of thin air because the financial forms you are completing call for a specific figure on a specific line. Rather, your numbers should always be the result of careful planning.

"Anticipate that costs will go up; interest rates will go up; it will take longer than planned for construction. Everything costs more and takes longer than planned. Things go wrong. You can't have wishful thinking in your planning. Assume you've underestimated all costs and build in a cushion. Use a good accountant or bookkeeper, and a good lawyer, and listen to their advice. Get help in those areas in which you aren't familiar."

Martha Johnson
Owner, Suppers
Restaurant

Getting Control of Your Finances

Even if you are not responsible for preparing ongoing financial reports, you should have a working understanding of financial statements so that you can better control your company.

Financial statements provide you with the information you need to make decisions. Many managers mistakenly believe that they are in charge of the big picture, while bookkeepers and bean counters get caught up with mere details. Numbers are not just details: They are the vital signs of any business; you must understand your company's numbers to realistically assess the condition of your business.

Read Your Financial Statements

Get in the habit of reading your financial statements at least monthly, and make sure you understand what you read. Track items such as sales receipts on a daily or weekly basis. Don't wait for reports to come back from the accountants before knowing your cash position. You will find you have more confidence in your decisions if you comprehend the financial implications of each of your choices.

Try to view your financial statements in a relatively dispassionate manner. It is difficult, especially when you own your own business, to keep emotions from clouding your ability to properly examine your financial reports. If you know it has been a bad month, you may be tempted just to ignore that month's cash-flow or income statements. Don't.

Set Policies and Stick with Them

Set financial policies in place and stick with them, in good times and bad. Many businesses, even big companies, get in trouble through inadequate billing and collection procedures. Stay on top of your finances.

If you are establishing accounts for the first time, get professional assistance from an accountant or bookkeeper. A professional can set up your initial books, assist you in understanding financial terms, and give you valuable advice on billing payment, and payroll procedures.

Cash-Basis Accounting

One aspect of your business an accountant will help you decide is whether to set up your books on an accrual basis or a cash basis. Most smaller businesses are generally advised to conduct business on a cash basis, meaning that income and expenses are entered in the books at the time money actually changes hands.

Thus, if you receive a $5,000 order in January, but you don't receive payment until March, the $5,000 credit appears as income only on your March statements. This gives a truer picture of a company's ability to meet its financial obligations than does accrual accounting.

Accrual-Basis Accounting

With accrual-basis accounting, income and expenses are counted at the time they are originally transacted; thus, the $5,000 order would show as income in January. If payment is never made, additional accounting entries would later be made to write off the loss. Larger businesses choose this accounting form to have a better sense of overall profitability.

Using Spreadsheets to Prepare Your Forms

In preparing your plan's financial forms, you probably want to use a computer spreadsheet program. These spreadsheets, which display or "spread" your figures across a number of columns representing months of the year, etc., allow you to change numbers in one or two categories, after which the program automatically refigures all the numbers for you.

Many relatively powerful spreadsheet programs, such as Lotus 1-2-3 or Excel, are widely available and recommended for people with larger businesses and those comfortable with computers. Integrated programs like Microsoft Works often contain spreadsheets along with wordprocessing, database, and communication software. These programs may be easier to use for those new to financial programs.

PSI Research/The Oasis Press offers software for creating a business plan and financial templates to accompany this book. For more information, call 1-800-228-2275.

For maintaining your accounts on an ongoing basis, you can purchase an accounting software program such as *ACCPAC*. Owners of smaller businesses will find a number of less powerful but easier-to-learn accounting packages, such as *QuickBooks*. These programs might not manipulate as many figures or produce such detailed reports, but they are still handy tools.

Using the Abrams Method of Flow-Through Financials

One of the most difficult questions, especially for new businesses, is "Where do I get the figures for my financial forms?"

If you have been filling out the Flow-Through Financial worksheets throughout the previous chapters, you have already compiled many of the figures you need to complete the worksheets in this chapter. For instance, you have already computed your marketing budget in Chapter 9. Likewise, on other worksheets, you have detailed costs of salaries, equipment, and other aspects of your business.

Now just transfer the figures from each of your Flow-Through Financial worksheets (marked with the dollar-sign logo) to their appropriate line(s) on the Financials forms that follow. Refer to the chart on page 206 to see on which form and line each specific figure should be placed.

"In financials, we look for professionalism. Use standard formats. Hire an accountant, not so much as to come up with your numbers but for your forms. We want to see a cash flow analysis as well as everything else in a standard annual report (balance sheet, income statement). You or an accountant should compare your numbers with those of existing companies. If they are very different from those of well-managed companies, they may be unrealistic."

Eugene Kleiner
Venture Capitalist

Abrams Method of Flow-Through Financials

Worksheet	Chapter	Transfer to	Use on Lines
Seasonal Factors	6, pg 73	Cash-Flow Projection	Sales, Collections, Cost of Goods, Operating Expenses
		Income Statement	Sales, Cost of Goods, Marketing
Financial Patterns	6, pg 77	Income Statement	Sales, Returns, Cost of Goods, Commissions, Utilities, Salaries
		Cash-Flow Projection	Sales, Cost of Goods, Operating Expenses
		Break-Even Analysis	
Marketing Vehicles	9, pg 121	Marketing Budget (Chapter 9, pg 130)	
		Income Statement	Marketing
		Cash-Flow Projection	Operating Expenses
Marketing Tactics	9, pg 122	Marketing Budget (Chapter 9, pg 130)	
		Income Statement	Profit Margin, Marketing
		Cash-Flow Projection	Operating Expenses
Monthly Marketing Budget	9, pg 130	Income Statement	Marketing, Travel/Entertainment, Professional Services
		Cash-Flow Projection	Operating Expenses
Monthly Sales Projections	9, pg 132	Income Statement	Sales, Commissions
		Cash-Flow Projection	Operating Expenses
Facilities	10, pg 141	Income Statement	Rent, Utilities, Maintenance
		Cash-Flow Projection	Operating Expenses, Other Expenses
		Balance Sheet	Fixed Assets, Depreciation
Production	10, pg 144	Income Statement	Cost of Goods, Salaries, Employee Benefits, Payroll Taxes
		Cash-Flow Projection	Operating Expenses
Supply and Distribution	10, pg 150	Income Statement	Cost of Goods, Commissions
		Cash-Flow Projection	Cost of Goods, Operating Expenses

Worksheet	Chapter	Transfer to	Use on Lines
Equipment Schedule	10, pg 146	Income Statement	Depreciation, Equipment Rental, Furniture and Equipment
		Cash-Flow Projection	Operating Expenses, Equipment Purchase
		Balance Sheet	Fixed Assets, Depreciation
Order Fulfillment	10, pg 152	Income Statement	Postage and Shipping, Returns and Allowances, Salaries (Customer Service Personnel)
		Cash-Flow Projection	Operating Expenses
Research and Development	10, pg 154	Income Statement	Allot costs to appropriate lines (e.g., salaries, equipment) or create separate R & D line
		Cash-Flow Projection	Operating Expenses
Other Operational Issues	10, pg 157	Income Statement	Insurance, Professional Services, Other (for permits, licenses)
		Cash-Flow Projection	Operating Expenses
Start-up Costs	10, pg 160	Income Statement	First month's operating expenses on appropriate lines
		Cash-Flow Projection	First month's operating expenses (and months for term payments)
		Balance Sheet	Current Assets, Fixed Assets, Current and Long-Term Liabilities (for loans secured to pay costs), or Equity (for investment income)
Compensation & Incentives	11, pg 171	Income Statement	Salaries, Employee Benefits, Payroll Taxes
		Cash-Flow Projection	Operating Expenses
Key Management Personnel to Be Added	11, pg 176	Income Statement and Cash-Flow Projection	Salaries (projections for future months and years)
Staffing Chart	13, pg 214	Income Statement	Salaries, Employee Benefits, Payroll Taxes
Monthly Cash Income Projections	13, pg 216	Income Statement	Gross Sales (unless your business is accrual based)

Types of Financial Forms

For the financial portion of your business plan, the three most important forms are:

- **Income Statement.** Shows whether your company is making a profit.
- **Cash-Flow Projection.** Shows whether the company has the cash to pay its bills.
- **Balance Sheet.** Shows how much the company is worth overall.

Other forms include:

- **Sources and Use of Funds.** Shows where you will get financing for your business and how you will spend the money invested or lent. A potential investor or loan officer will want to see this.
- **Break-even Analysis.** Shows the point at which sales exceed costs and you begin to make a profit. Advisable for internal planning.
- **Assumption Sheet.** Shows those reading your financial statements how you determined the figures used. A good adjunct to other forms.

Time Frames Your Forms Should Cover

Generally, investors want to see financial projections for three to five years in the future, and historical records of the past three to five years for currently operating businesses. If possible, find out what periods of time your lending institution or potential investor wants to see and prepare your forms accordingly. Otherwise, prepare forms to cover the time frames cited below.

- **Income Statements**. First year: monthly projections. Years two and three: quarterly projections. First three to five years: annual projections. Existing businesses: actual annual income statements for the last three years.
- **Cash Flow.** First year: monthly projections. Years two and three: quarterly projections.
- **Balance Sheet.** First year: quarterly projections. Years two to five: annual projections. Existing businesses: current balance sheet and actual balance sheets for last two years.

General Financial Terms

The terms that follow are frequently used in financial forms. If you are in business, you should have a working knowledge of these terms.

Even if you're familiar with financial statements, take a few minutes to update your understanding of these key words; and if you've never produced (or reviewed) a financial statement before, study these terms until you feel comfortable with them.

Accounts Payable. Obligations owed to others; list of outstanding bills.

Accounts Receivable. Obligations owed to your company by others; a list of outstanding invoices.

Accumulated Depreciation. The amount of depreciation a company has already taken in the form of tax deductions; such accumulated depreciation must be accounted for when selling fixed assets.

Assets. Anything the company owns having a positive monetary value.

Current Assets. Assets that can be converted quickly, with relative ease to cash; these assets are designed to be turned over in the normal course of doing business, such as bank deposits, inventory, and accounts receivable.

Fixed Assets (or Property, Plant, and Equipment). Assets that are the ongoing means of doing business; such assets are generally cumbersome to turn into cash; includes buildings, land, and equipment.

Cash. Immediately available money in the form of currency, checks, or bank deposits.

Cost of Goods. Expenses associated with producing and making a specific sale. Companies differ as to which expenses they attribute to cost of goods, but generally items such as sales commissions, direct materials, direct labor, and freight are included.

Current Liabilities. Any bills, debts, or obligations occurring in the ongoing course of business; any debt due within the next year. Includes accounts payable, accrued payroll expenses, and loans and credit lines with less than one year's maturity date.

Debt. An ongoing obligation of the company, such as a bank loan.

Depreciation. The wear and tear on fixed assets — not a cash expenditure, but an ongoing expense of the business as equipment wears down. A tax deduction.

Equity. Ownership of a company, usually distributed by means of shares of stock. A person who owns part of a company is said to have an equity interest in the company.

Fixed Costs. Ongoing expenses or overhead of a business that occur regardless of the amount of sales. These expenses usually include items such as rent, utilities, and salaries.

Gross Profit. Percentage of income your company realizes on each sale before administrative expenses.

Liabilities. Any outstanding obligation or debt of the company.

Long-Term Liabilities. Loans and other debts that come due in more than a year's time. This year's interest payments on such loans, or debt service, are included in Current Liabilities.

Net Profit. Amount of income after deducting all costs of doing business, including administrative overhead and other fixed costs.

Net Worth. Value of a company after deducting liabilities from assets.

Other or Intangible Assets. Aspects of your company that have value not easily interpreted in specific monetary terms or directly convertible to cash; assets such as a popular trademarked name and the good-will a company has built up over time.

Profit. Amount a company earns after expenses.

Pro forma. Financial statements based on projected future performance rather than actual historical data.

Retained Earnings. Net worth amount the company keeps internally for ongoing development of the business rather than distributing to shareholders.

Financial Symbols

The symbols below commonly appear on financial forms:

(   ) Numbers appearing in parentheses are negative numbers; they represent losses.

—- Single lines represent subtotals.

=== Double lines represent totals.

000's This indicates that numbers are expressed in thousands.

Guidelines for Preparing Your Financial Forms

In preparing your financial forms, you will almost certainly have questions as to how to attribute certain expenses for your business. You might wonder whether you should ascribe sales commissions to cost of goods sold or to operating expenses. Accounting practices differ, so follow these guidelines:

When preparing your financial forms, keep these imperatives in mind:

1. **Be conservative.** Avoid the tendency to paint the rosiest picture possible; doing so reduces your credibility.
2. **Be honest.** Experienced financing sources will sense dishonest or manipulated figures; expect to be asked to justify your numbers.
3. **Don't be creative.** Use standard formats and financial terms; otherwise you look inexperienced to financing sources.
4. **Get your accountant's advice.**
5. **Follow the practices used in your industry.**
6. **Choose the appropriate accounting method.**
7. **Be consistent**. Make a decision and stick with it for all your accounts, otherwise you can't compare one year's figures to another.

Staffing Chart

In many companies, the costs associated with employees are often the largest expenses of the business. In any company, labor costs are a critical issue. When planning a business, it's easy to underestimate or overlook labor costs.

Number and Timing

You must first figure out how many employees you will need and exactly when you will need them. It is easy to underestimate this number, anticipating that you will only hire outstanding employees, all of whom will work to maximum capacity. But remember, employees will probably not work as hard or as long as you do, so don't plan your expenses based solely on your own level of productivity.

Some industries, such as those in the service sector, are particularly labor intensive. And in a small business, customers often expect very high levels of personal service, which can mean higher staffing levels. Even if your is a sole proprietorship, you may occasionally need to hire some assistance, and you should plan accordingly.

If yours is a new business, you may want to talk with entrepreneurs in existing businesses about the level and timing of their personnel to help you devise your own projections. If you are changing the direction of an existing business, how will your new needs effect your staffing levels and deployment? Will current employees be able to be trained for new tasks, or will new staff need to be hired?

Not all employees will be hired at once, and not all employees will be permanent. The staffing chart allows you to change the number of workers in each category depending on the actual month(s) they work. You may have seasonal work which requires additional staff for some portions of the year. Timing your hiring can be very important in making certain you are adequately prepared for your workloads. Most people, even those who have been in business for a long time, underestimate the time it will take to hire and train new staff. Allow yourself realistic lead-time for staff recruitment, and don't forget to account for the costs of any temporary help you may need until permanent staff is in place.

Also, it's almost inevitable that you will at some point hire people who do not perform well. There will be costs associated with dismissing employees. These costs may include temporary help to fill their slots while you seek replacement and any severance pay that is required by their contract.

Benefits and Taxes

One of the first things you will need to do is to figure out the benefits that you will need and want to attract and retain qualified staff. These benefits may include health, life, dental, or disability insurance, pension benefits, and paid vacation.

Some employee costs are required by law. Check with your state's department of labor to find out about mandatory benefits, such as workmen's compensation. There will also be payroll taxes, which can add a substantial amount to your total employee costs. You may want to talk with an accountant or lawyer to learn what costs to anticipate with regard to benefits and taxes.

The upcoming Staffing Chart will help you plot out all the labor costs associated with your business. The chart is presented in a monthly format to allow you to reflect the changes in your staffing depending on when you hire new employees, add new divisions, or when you use seasonal or variable labor.

The information in the Staffing Chart transfers to the Salary/Wages, Employee Benefits and Payroll Taxes lines on your Income Statement, page 220.

Cash Projections

An important fact to remember when preparing your financial projections is that you will often not receive full payment at the time of an actual sale or transaction. Projecting cash flow solely on the sales made, rather than cash actually received, will leave you seriously short on money.

Some basis of industries have particularly long lag times between orders and payment. This can be especially true in manufacturing companies. A clothing manufacturer, for instance, may make sales many months before payment is due. Even in retail, you may find that you establish some credit accounts for very large or repeat customers and these customers take longer to pay.

Your business may allow payment terms over a number of months, or the type of work you do may make payment over time a necessity. In almost any company, some customers will be slow payers. While most customers may pay within 30 days, some may take as much as 120 days, and some will never pay at all. For instance, if you make a $10,000 sale in the month of February, you may only receive a deposit of $2500 in February, with the rest paid as partial payments through June. Of course, you can try to reduce the amount of slow or non-payers by requiring larger percentages of payment at the time of sale or delivery or by charging interest on unpaid balances, but it is still necessary to anticipate actual payment patterns in your cash flow projections.

It's also a good idea to differentiate between the income of each product or service line. While it may seem like a bit more work to keep track of each product or service line's income separately, this information will help you make decisions about the long-term direction of your company and better understand exactly where your profits come from.

Complete the upcoming Monthly Cash Income Projections. The information from this form can then be transferred to your income statement. If yours is an existing business, review your past records to determine the average payment pattern to use in this form. If you are new to business, check with others in your industry to see what are typical payment patterns. Be conservative in your projections. It's always better to find out that you have more cash than you anticipated rather than less.

Income Statements

The income statement is also frequently called either a profit and loss statement, P & L, or income and expense statement. This form shows how profitable your company is — how much money it will make after all expenses are accounted for. It does not give a total picture of what your company is worth overall, or its cash position.

A company can be losing money but still be worth a great deal because it owns valuable property, or it can be profitable but still not have enough cash to pay its bills due to cash-flow problems. An income statement does not reveal either of these "hidden" situations.

You read an income statement from top to bottom. The first line accounts for sales. Each subsequent line represents deductions from income. The result is the company's profit (or, possibly, loss).

To prepare an income statement, accumulate detailed information about your sales and expenses. Specific lines on the form should mirror the categories by which you maintain your ongoing accounts. When completing the income statement, refer to the previous list of financial terms. Additionally, note these references:

Gross Sales. Total sales from all product line categories.

Depreciation and Amortization. The value of either fixed assets (depreciation) or intangible assets (amortization) that is allocated as a yearly expense or deemed to be lost each year through use or obsolescence.

Employee Benefits. Items such as health and dental insurance; any other benefits with specific costs associated;

Office Supplies. Usual office or business supplies, rather than the materials necessary to produce the item for sale.

Marketing. Advertising and marketing expenses other than Travel/Entertainment, which may have different tax treatment; transfer this figure from your Marketing Budget worksheet in Chapter 9.

Travel/Entertainment. Costs of necessary business travel and entertainment; auto expenses can go here or on a separate line.

Insurance. Insurance premiums such as those for liability, malpractice, auto, or equipment insurance. Excludes insurance included in Employee Benefits line.

Professional Services. Attorney's, accountant's, and consultant's fees.

Maintenance. Janitorial or cleaning services, regular maintenance programs or service contracts, and repairs.

Complete the historical (if applicable to your business) and pro forma income statements on the next few pages. Document income on a monthly (first year), quarterly (first two to three years), and annual basis (first three to five years). If necessary, adjust the form to meet the needs of your company.

"What kind of numbers do we like to see? The more mature a business is, the more we rely on numbers. For a newer business, the numbers matter less and the words matter more."

Robert Mahoney
Executive Director New England Corporate Banking, Bank of Boston

Staffing Chart

For Year: _____	January	February	March	April	May
Management # Employees					
Salary / Wages					
Benefits					
Payroll Taxes					
Total Costs					
Administrative / Support # Employees					
Salary / Wages					
Benefits					
Payroll Taxes					
Total Costs					
Sales / Marketing # Employees					
Salary / Wages					
Benefits					
Payroll Taxes					
Total Costs					
Operations / Production # Employees					
Salary / Wages					
Benefits					
Payroll Taxes					
Total Costs					
Other # Employees					
Salary / Wages					
Benefits					
Payroll Taxes					
Total Costs					
TOTAL # Employees					
Salary / Wages					
Benefits					
Payroll Taxes					
TOTAL COSTS					

							$ ▶ $$ ▶ $$$
June	July	August	September	October	November	December	TOTAL

Monthly Cash Income Projections

For Year: _____	January	February	March	April	May
PRODUCT LINE #1 SALES **Cash Received**					
Current month sales					
30 days prior sales					
60 days prior sales					
90 days prior sales					
120 days prior sales					
Total Product #2 Cash Income					
PRODUCT LINE #1 SALES **Cash Received**					
Current month sales					
30 days prior sales					
60 days prior sales					
90 days prior sales					
120 days prior sales					
Total Product #2 Cash Income					
PRODUCT LINE #3 SALES **Cash Received**					
Current month sales					
30 days prior sales					
60 days prior sales					
90 days prior sales					
120 days prior sales					
Total Product #3 Cash Income					
PRODUCT LINE #4 SALES **Cash Received**					
Current month sales					
30 days prior sales					
60 days prior sales					
90 days prior sales					
120 days prior sales					
Total Product #4 Cash Income					
TOTAL CASH INCOME					

June	July	August	September	October	November	December	TOTAL
							$ ▶ $$ ▶ $$$

Income Statement: Historical

For Year: _____	January	February	March	April	May
INCOME **Gross Sales**					
Less returns and allowances					
Net Sales					
Cost of Goods					
GROSS PROFIT					
General and Administrative Expenses Salaries and wages					
Employee benefits					
Payroll Taxes					
Sales commissions					
Professional services					
Rent					
Maintenance					
Equipment Rental					
Furniture and Equipment purchase					
Depreciation and amortization					
Insurance					
Interest expenses					
Utilities					
Telephone					
Office supplies					
Postage and shipping					
Marketing and Advertising					
Travel					
Entertainment					
Other					
Other					
Other					
TOTAL G & A EXPENSES					
Net Income before Taxes					
Provision for taxes on income					
NET INCOME AFTER TAXES (NET PROFIT)					

							$ ▶ $$ ▶ $$$
June	July	August	September	October	November	December	TOTAL

Income Statement: Annual by Month

For Year: _____	January	February	March	April	May
INCOME					
Gross Sales					
Less returns and allowances					
Net Sales					
Cost of Goods					
GROSS PROFIT					
General and Administrative Expenses					
Salaries and wages					
Employee benefits					
Payroll Taxes					
Sales commissions					
Professional services					
Rent					
Maintenance					
Equipment Rental					
Furniture and Equipment purchase					
Depreciation and amortization					
Insurance					
Interest expenses					
Utilities					
Telephone					
Office supplies					
Postage and shipping					
Marketing and Advertising					
Travel					
Entertainment					
Other					
Other					
Other					
TOTAL G & A EXPENSES					
Net Income before Taxes					
Provision for taxes on income					
NET INCOME AFTER TAXES (NET PROFIT)					

	June	July	August	September	October	November	December	TOTAL
$ ▶ $$ ▶ $$$								

Income Statement: Annual by Quarter					$ ▶ $$ ▶ $$$
For Year: _____	1st Quarter	2nd Quarter	3rd Quarter	4th Quarter	TOTAL
INCOME **Gross Sales**					
Less returns and allowances					
Net Sales					
Cost of Goods					
GROSS PROFIT					
General and Administrative Expenses Salaries and wages					
Employee benefits					
Payroll Taxes					
Sales commissions					
Professional services					
Rent					
Maintenance					
Equipment Rental					
Furniture and Equipment purchase					
Depreciation and amortization					
Insurance					
Interest expenses					
Utilities					
Telephone					
Office supplies					
Postage and shipping					
Marketing and Advertising					
Travel					
Entertainment					
Other					
Other					
Other					
TOTAL G & A EXPENSES					
Net Income before Taxes					
Provision for taxes on income					
NET INCOME AFTER TAXES (NET PROFIT)					

Income Statement: Annual for Five Years $ ▶ $$ ▶ $$$

	Yr: _____	Yr: _____	Yr: _____	Yr: _____	Yr: _____
INCOME **Gross Sales**					
Less returns and allowances					
Net Sales					
Cost of Goods					
GROSS PROFIT					
General and Administrative Expenses Salaries and wages					
Employee benefits					
Payroll Taxes					
Sales commissions					
Professional services					
Rent					
Maintenance					
Equipment Rental					
Furniture and Equipment purchase					
Depreciation and amortization					
Insurance					
Interest expenses					
Utilities					
Telephone					
Office supplies					
Postage and shipping					
Marketing and Advertising					
Travel					
Entertainment					
Other					
Other					
Other					
TOTAL G & A EXPENSES					
Net Income before Taxes					
Provision for taxes on income					
NET INCOME AFTER TAXES (NET PROFIT)					

Cash-Flow Projections

For almost every business, cash-flow analysis is the single most important financial assessment. After all, if you can't pay your employees, your bills, or yourself, you're not going to stay in business long, and you're certainly not going to sleep very well at night.

The cash-flow projection is not about profit — it's about how much money you have in the bank. It doesn't tell you whether your company will show an overall profit at the end of the year or how many orders you are placing, but instead gives a real-life picture of the money going in and out of your business on a monthly basis.

Cash-flow analysis is particularly important for seasonal businesses, those with large inventories, or those that sell much of their merchandise on credit. You must plan for the slow months and for the long time lag between paying for materials and actually realizing cash receipts.

Maintaining historical cash-flow records gives you an idea of what to expect in certain months of the year and helps you plan future cash management. Get in the habit of keeping monthly cash-flow accounts. Complete the upcoming Cash Flow History worksheet if yours is an existing business.

In preparing these forms, separate out cash you receive from doing business (sales) and the cash you get from taking out loans or receiving investments (financing). This will give you a better sense of where your money is coming from and how much you are relying on credit. Note these items used in your cash-flow analysis:

Cash Sales. Sales made for immediate payment or prepayments.

Collections. Income collected from sales made in a previous period.

Interest Income. Income paid from bank and other interest-bearing accounts.

Loan Proceeds. Income from bank loans and other credit lines.

Cost of Goods. Actual payments made on items in this category. (Cash and accrual accounting methods treat this line differently; consult your accountant.)

Operating Expenses. Actual payments made on items in this category, minus depreciation (as depreciation is not an actual cash payment). Since cash and accrual accounting methods treat this line differently; consult your accountant.

Reserve. Money put into accounts for future, unanticipated expenses.

Owner's Draw. Money paid to owner in lieu of salary in a proprietorship, or money otherwise distributed to owners (except for expense reimbursement). In a corporation it is called a dividend and paid from after-tax income. Since this income to the owner is subject to federal and state taxes, your accountant may suggest that you add a provision for taxes to the income tax line on the cash-flow form.

Net Cash Flow. Money left over after all disbursements have been deducted from all cash received.

Opening Cash Balance. Amount of money in the bank at the beginning of the month being evaluated; should be the same as the previous month's ending cash balance. Complete the following cash-flow analysis, on a monthly basis for the first year (or two) and quarterly for the next year.

Balance Sheet

For those who are new to business, the balance sheet is probably the least understood of the financial forms. In essence, the balance sheet gives a snapshot of the overall financial worth of the company — the value of all its various components and the extent of all its obligations.

The balance sheet accounts for all the company's assets minus all the company's liabilities. The remaining amount (if any) is figured to be the net worth of the company. The net worth is then distributed as either belonging to the owners of the company, equity, or as retained earnings for the company to use. These allotments are listed in the Liabilities category. Once you do this, the amounts in the Assets and Liabilities categories are equal: They balance.

While entrepreneurs rarely view the balance sheet as a planning tool, bankers and investors rely on the balance sheet to give them a fuller picture of the company's value. Only on the balance sheet can one see the worth of existing property and equipment. Some companies own valuable land or buildings that far exceed the income of the actual business; other businesses own expensive machinery. Other companies may be profitable but heavily in debt.

Refer to the General Financial Terms section at the beginning of this chapter for an explanation of the items listed on the balance sheet. Additionally, note that the balance sheet uses the terms:

Inventory. The value of the stock you have on hand; this could include both raw materials and finished products.

Fixtures. The property improvements owned by the business, such as lights, computers, display cases, shelving units.

Accrued Payroll. The amount of money owed personnel for time expended by the date of the balance sheet.

Prepaid Expenses. Payments made for goods or services not yet received.

When completing the balance sheet, you may find you need more help with this form than with any other, especially when trying to figure accumulated depreciation or the worth of inventory. Get help from your accountant or have your accountant prepare the form. But you must still understand it.

Cash Flow History

For Year: _____	January	February	March	April	May
CASH RECEIPTS					
Income from Sales					
Cash Sales					
Collections					
Total Cash from Sales					
Income from Financing					
Interest Income					
Loan Proceeds					
Total Cash from Financing					
Other Cash Receipts					
Total Cash Receipts					
CASH DISBURSEMENTS					
Expenses					
Cost of Goods					
Operating Expenses					
Loan Payments					
Income Tax Payments					
Other Expenses/Equip Purchase					
Reserve					
Owner's Draw					
Total Cash Disbursements					
Net Cash Flow					
Opening Cash Balance					
Cash Receipts					
Cash Disbursements					
ENDING CASH BALANCE					

	$ ▶ $$ ▶ $$$						
June	July	August	September	October	November	December	TOTAL

Cash Flow Projection: Annual by Month

For Year: _____	January	February	March	April	May
CASH RECEIPTS					
Income from Sales					
Cash Sales					
Collections					
Total Cash from Sales					
Income from Financing					
Interest Income					
Loan Proceeds					
Total Cash from Financing					
Other Cash Receipts					
Total Cash Receipts					
CASH DISBURSEMENTS					
Expenses					
Cost of Goods					
Operating Expenses					
Loan Payments					
Income Tax Payments					
Other Expenses/Equip Purchase					
Reserve					
Owner's Draw					
Total Cash Disbursements					
Net Cash Flow					
Opening Cash Balance					
Cash Receipts					
Cash Disbursements					
ENDING CASH BALANCE					

	June	July	August	September	October	November	December	TOTAL
								$ ▸ $$ ▸ $$$

Cash-Flow Projection: Annual by Quarter		$ ▶ $$ ▶ $$$			
For Year: _____	1st Quarter	2nd Quarter	3rd Quarter	4th Quarter	TOTAL
CASH RECEIPTS					
Income from Sales					
Cash Sales					
Collections					
Total Cash from Sales					
Income from Financing					
Interest Income					
Loan Proceeds					
Total Cash from Financing					
Other Cash Receipts					
Total Cash Receipts					
CASH DISBURSEMENTS					
Expenses					
Cost of Goods					
Operating Expenses					
Loan Payments					
Income Tax Payments					
Other Expenses/Equip Purchase					
Reserve					
Owner's Draw					
Total Cash Disbursements					
Net Cash Flow					
Opening Cash Balance					
Cash Receipts					
Cash Disbursements					
ENDING CASH BALANCE					

Balance Sheet

$ ▶ $$ ▶ $$$

Balance Sheet

For Company : _____

For Period:_____ Ending:_____, 19____

ASSETS

Current Assets

Cash _____

Accounts Receivable _____

Inventory _____

Prepaid Expenses _____

Total Current Assets _____

Fixed Assets

Land _____

Buildings _____

Equipment _____

Furniture _____

Fixtures _____

Less Accumulated Depreciation _____

Total Fixed Assets _____

Other Assets _____

TOTAL ASSETS _____

LIABILITIES

Current Liabilities

Accounts Payable _____

Accrued Payroll _____

Taxes Payable _____

Short-Term Notes Payable _____

Total Current Liabilities _____

Long-Term Liabilities

Long-Term Notes Payable _____

Total Long-Term Liabilities _____

Net Worth

Shareholders' Equity _____

Retained Earnings _____

Total Net Worth _____

TOTAL LIABILITIES AND NET WORTH _____

Include in the Financial section of your business plan.

Since much of the information on balance sheets does not change very quickly, you can prepare balance sheets primarily on a quarterly or annual basis (unless, of course, your potential funding sources wants monthly projections).

Sources and Use of Funds

If you are seeking outside financing, either through loans or investors, those contemplating giving you money will naturally want to know what you're going to do with the money you raise. They will also want to see what other sources of money you have, if any, and whether you have contributed any of your own funds.

To provide such information, it is best to devise a one-page description of the sources and use of funds. This can go in the business plan itself or can be sent with the cover letter to potential financing sources. It should tell a potential investor that you have specific plans for the money you raise, that you are not taking on debts or giving up equity thoughtlessly, and that you will use funds to make your business grow.

A clear "Sources and Use of Funds" statement is particularly beneficial if you are applying the funds to business expansion rather than offsetting operating deficits (which investors notoriously dislike); have arranged much of your financing already (which shows other people believe in your company); or are committing significant personal funds (which shows you believe in the project enough to take substantial personal risk).

In preparing the Sources and Use of Funds statement, consider the following issues and terms:

Funding Rounds. The number of development stages at which you will seek financing from the investment community.

Total Amount. Amount of money sought in this round of financing, from all funding sources.

Equity Financing. Amount you will raise by selling ownership interest in the company; you don't need to list total stock outstanding.

Preferred Stock. Outstanding stock for which dividends will be paid. before other dividends can be paid for common stock or before other obligations of the company are paid; investors often want preferred stock.

Common Stock. Stock for which dividends are paid when company is profitable and has paid preferred stock dividends and other obligations.

Debt Financing. Amount of money you will raise by taking out loans.

Long-Term Loans. Loans to be paid back in more than a year's time.

Mortgage Loans. Loans taken out with property as collateral.

> "A sure killer for a proposal is a plan that shows improper use of funds. If all the funds aren't going to build the business, we're not interested in financing it."
>
> **Ann Winblad**
> *Venture Capitalist*

Sources and Use of Funds

$ ▶ $$ ▶ $$$

Complete the following form to describe how much money you are seeking and how you will use the funds raised. Be as specific as possible: If you know what equipment you are going to buy, list it; if you have a loan from the First State Bank, state the name of the lending institution, amount and terms.

Number of funding rounds expected for full financing: _____

Total dollar amount being sought in this round: _____ _____

Sources of Funds

Equity Financing:

Preferred Stock: _____ _____

Common Stock: _____ _____

Debt Financing:

Mortgage Loans: _____ _____

Other Long-Term Loans: _____ _____

Short-Term Loans: _____ _____

Convertible Debt: _____ _____

Investment from Principals: _____ _____

Uses of Funds

Capital Expenditures:

Purchase of Property: _____ _____

Leasehold Improvements: _____ _____

Purchase of Equipment/Furniture: _____ _____

Other: _____ _____

Working Capital:

Purchase of Inventory: _____ _____

Staff Expansion: _____ _____

New Product Line Introduction: _____ _____

Additional Marketing Activities: _____ _____

Other Business Expansion Activities: _____ _____

Other: _____ _____

Debt Retirement: _____ _____

Cash Reserve: _____ _____

Submit this with the Financial section of your business plan.

Short-Term Loans. Bridge loans, credit lines, and other loans to be paid back in less than a year.

Convertible Debt. Loans that are later convertible to stock at the funder's option, giving both the security of a loan and the potential of stock.

Investment from Principals. Amount of money that you or other key employees are contributing to the company, this can be in the form of cash or property.

Capital Expenditures. Purchase of necessary equipment or property.

Working Capital. Funds to be used for the ongoing operating expenses of the business.

Debt Retirement. Funds used to pay off existing loans or obligations.

Assumption Sheet

Financial forms are merely meaningless numbers unless they are based on decisions. Your potential financing sources want to see the key decisions on which you based your figures. Of course, they could read the entire business plan and discern most of those decisions, but they want to save time by having the information all in one place.

It is good discipline for you, as well, to learn to develop an assumption sheet whenever you do financial projections. Otherwise, you can be too easily tempted to write down figures that look good on paper but have little to do with reality.

If you have worked through the business planning process, putting together an assumption sheet should be a relatively easy task. You have already asked yourself most of the questions called for on this form and have the answers available to you.

An assumption sheet should list purely straightforward information; it does not require substantial detail or explanation. You do not even need to use sentences, just provide the data in each category. (You can use the first sentence, as written on the worksheet, on your own assumption sheet.)

Complete the upcoming assumption sheet and include a finished sheet at the conclusion of your financial forms in your business plan.

Break-Even Analysis

Finally, you want to determine how much income you must earn to pay your expenses — at what point you break even. At the break-even point you are neither making a profit nor losing money; you have just covered the cost of staying in business and making your sales. Most people new to business assume their break-even point is when sales equal the amount of fixed expenses: rent, telephone, insurance, etc.

Fixed expenses are easy to determine, since they are in place from the time you first open your doors, and they remain relatively stable regardless of the amount of sales.

But because almost all sales have some costs associated with them, you must also figure the variable cost of sales into your break-even analysis; otherwise you do not have a true picture of your cost of doing business.

For instance, if you are a florist and your fixed expenses are $20,000 a month, it's not just enough to make $20,000 in sales: You would still be losing money. You must pay for flowers, vases, delivery, commissions to floral wire services, etc., before you earn income on a sale. If these costs amount to an average of 30% of the cost of each sale, at $20,000 in income, you're still $6,000 in the hole ($20,000 in fixed expenses plus $6,000 in costs of goods).

The total cost of goods keeps rising as your sales rise; unlike your fixed costs, the figure keeps changing and is harder to pin down. But your gross profit margin — the average percentage you earn on each sale after direct costs are deducted — stays basically the same. (As you sell greater amounts, you may be able to increase your profit margin by receiving volume discounts; for the purpose of this exercise; however, you can assume a stable gross profit margin.)

To determine an actual break-even point, you must know your:

- Fixed Expenses
- Gross Profit Margin (average percentage of gross income realized after cost of goods).

Then, to figure the amount of total sales needed to break even, you work the equation:

Fixed Expenses = Total Sales x Gross Profit Margin (GPM)

or, saying the same thing:

$$\frac{\text{Fixed Expenses}}{\text{GPM}} = \text{Total Sales to Break Even}$$

In the above example of the florist, we know:

- Fixed Expenses = $20,000
- Gross Profit Margin (GPM) = 70% (since cost of goods is 30%)

So, the numbers would look like:

$$\frac{20,000}{.70} = \text{Sales to Break even}$$

Doing the arithmetic, we see that this florist must make $28,571 to reach the break-even point.

A break-even analysis is an important tool for your internal planning. However, it is not necessary for you to include a break-even analysis in a business plan submitted to outside funding sources. (Of course, there is nothing wrong with including it if you wish.)

Complete the worksheet below to figure your own break-even point.

Break-Even Analysis

Monthly Total Fixed Expenses (FE): $_____

Gross Profit Margin, in percentage terms (GPM):_____ %

Divide:

$$\frac{\text{FE: } \$ \underline{\qquad\qquad}}{\text{GPM:} \underline{\qquad\qquad}\%} = \$ \underline{\qquad\qquad\qquad}$$

(Sales to Break Even)

Chapter Summary

The financial portion of your business plan will consist mostly of the actual financial projections. You should include the following forms:

- Income Statement
- Cash-Flow Analysis
- Balance Sheet
- Sources and Use of Funds
- Assumption Sheet

Additionally, you will want to do a break-even analysis for your internal planning.

It is advisable to get professional help in putting together your financial forms and setting up accounts. Set good financial procedures in place from the beginning of your business and stick to them. If yours is an existing business, review your procedures to make sure you have adequate control of billing and payments.

Get in the habit of reviewing your financial statements regularly and understanding what you read. Don't leave the finances entirely up to others and don't be intimidated by numbers.

Assumption Sheet

The figures on the previous financial forms are based on the following assumptions:

Sales Product Line	Year $	Units	Year $	Units	Year $	Units	Annual Growth Rate %
___	___	___	___	___	___	___	___
___	___	___	___	___	___	___	___
___	___	___	___	___	___	___	___
___	___	___	___	___	___	___	___
___	___	___	___	___	___	___	___
Total	___	___	___	___	___	___	___

Describe the projected increase/decrease in selling price of each product line/service. _____

_____

_____

Personnel/Management

Describe the number of employees and assumptions regarding total payroll projected in the financial forms. ____

_____

Describe key management positions to be added and timing._____

_____

_____

Gross Profit Margin

List the projected gross profit margin for each product line or service.

_____

_____

_____

Describe any major changes in cost of goods that are projected to affect gross profit margin.

_____

_____

_____

Continued on next page

Assumption Sheet (continued)

Key Expenses

Describe the timing and costs of key projected expenses.

Plant Expansion or New Branches _____

_____

Major Capital Purchases _____

_____

Major Marketing Expenses _____

_____

Research and Development _____

_____

Other Key Expenses _____

_____

Financing

Describe any financing debt (loans) that are projected to be added or retired.

_____

_____

_____

Describe the interest rates assumed to be in effect for these financial projections.

_____

_____

Other

Describe any other major developments that are assumed in creating your financial projections (such as strategic partnerships, competitive situation, etc.).

_____

_____

_____

_____

_____

SAMPLE PLAN: Income Statement Three-Year Projection

Income Statement

	1993	1994	1995	
INCOME				
Gross Sales	**$233,000**	**$493,875**	**$818,615**	
Less returns and allowances	0	0	0	
Net Sales	**233,000**	**493,875**	**818,615**	*Shows increasing profit margin.*
Cost of Goods	38,870	62,133	86,610	
Gross Profit	**194,130**	**431,742**	**732,005**	
OPERATING EXPENSES				
General & Administrative Expenses				
Salaries and wages	95,000	176,800	233,600	
Employee benefits	6,600	15,000	21,600	
Payroll Taxes	6,095	15,000	20,000	
Sales Commissions	9,610	61,360	82,920	
Professional services	7,550	5,000	6,000	*Includes sales personnel salaries in General & Administrative expenses.*
Rent	10,500	39,600	42,000	
Maintenance	600	2,400	4,500	
Equipment Rental	11,750	48,000	48,000	
Furniture and Equipment purchase	410	500	0	
Depreciation and amortization	2,000	4,000	4,000	
Insurance	3,400	4,200	5,500	
Interest Expenses	1,375	1,500	0	
Utilities	3,950	6,200	7,500	
Office supplies	3,395	5,000	6,000	
Postage and Shipping	2,505	3,600	5,000	
Marketing and Advertising	20,050	30,000	45,000	
Travel	1,500	2,595	4,570	
Entertainment	865	1,805	3,430	
Bad debts and doubtful accounts	0	0	4,000	
TOTAL OPERATING EXPENSES	**187,155**	**422,560**	**543,620**	
Net Income before Taxes	6,975	9,182	188,385	
Provision for taxes on income	1,046	1,377	56,720	
NET INCOME AFTER TAXES	**5,929**	**7,805**	**131,665**	

SAMPLE PLAN: Income Statement Annual

Income Statement

Year: 1993 (Actual through 8/31/93)

	Jan	Feb	Mar	Apr	May
INCOME					
Gross Sales	$0	$2,000	$2,000	$5,000	$12,000
Less returns and allowances	0	0	0	0	0
Net Sales	0	2,000	2,000	5,000	12,000
Cost of Goods	0	324	324	812	1946
Gross Profit	0	1,676	1,676	4,188	10,054
OPERATING EXPENSES					
General & Administrative Expenses					
Salaries and wages	2,500	3,700	5,700	6,200	7,700
Employee benefits	275	275	510	510	510
Payroll Taxes	210	310	505	505	505
Sales Commissions	0	0	0	0	350
Professional services	2,500	250	2,000	200	200
Rent	0	0	0	0	0
Maintenance	0	0	0	0	0
Equipment Rental	250	250	250	250	250
Furniture and Equipment purchase	0	0	0	410	0
Depreciation and amortization	2,000	0	0	0	0
Insurance	400	0	0	200	0
Interest Expenses	0	125	125	125	125
Utilities	350	110	225	310	280
Office supplies	450	125	215	185	125
Postage and Shipping	210	80	310	65	450
Marketing and Advertising	3200	1,800	4,000	1,500	1,500
Travel	55	150	100	150	0
Entertainment	0	0	110	320	195
Bad debts and doubtful accounts	0	0	0	0	0
TOTAL OPERATING EXPENSES	12,400	7,175	14,050	10,930	12,190
Net Income before Taxes	(12,400)	(5,499)	(12,374)	(6,742)	(2,136)
Taxes on income	0	0	0	0	0
NET INCOME AFTER TAXES	(12,400)	(5,499)	(12,374)	(6,742)	(2,136)

Includes materials and freight in Cost of Goods.

Includes variable labor in Salaries & Wages.

Purchased $10,000 in Furniture and Equipment and depreciated it over five years; entered on Depreciation line.

	June	July	Aug	Sep	Oct	Nov	Dec	TOTAL
	$16,000	$20,500	$28,000	$34,200	$41,800	$50,000	$21,500	$233,000
	0	0	0	0	0	0	0	$0
	16,000	20,500	28,000	34,200	41,800	50,000	21,500	$233,000
	2,595	3,449	4,741	5,691	6,926	8,400	3,662	$38,870
	13,405	17,051	23,259	28,509	34,874	41,600	17,838	$194,130
	8,400	7,300	10,900	10,100	11,100	12,100	9,300	$95,000
	510	510	700	700	700	700	700	$6,600
	505	505	610	610	610	610	610	$6,095
	750	775	1,235	1,500	1,850	2,200	950	$9,610
	200	200	1,200	200	200	200	200	$7,550
	0	0	2,100	2,100	2,100	2,100	2,100	$10,500
	0	0	120	120	120	120	120	$600
	250	250	2,000	2,000	2,000	2,000	2,000	$11,750
	0	0	0	0	0	0	0	$410
	0	0	0	0	0	0	0	$2,000
	0	200	1,000	350	550	350	350	$3,400
	125	125	125	125	125	125	125	$1,375
	330	275	510	420	410	380	350	$3,950
	85	110	1,100	250	250	250	250	$3,395
	85	260	60	410	75	300	200	$2,505
	300	1,500	1,750	2,000	250	2,000	250	$20,050
	25	100	0	150	150	150	150	$1,180
	200	75	85	50	50	50	50	$2,365
	0	0	0	0	0	0	0	$0
	11,765	12,185	23,495	21,085	20,540	23,635	17,705	$188,335
	1,640	4,866	(236)	7,424	14,334	17,965	133	$5,795
	0	0	0	0	0	0	1,046	$1,046
	1,640	4,866	(236)	7,424	14,334	17,965	(913)	$4,749

Cash-Flow Projection

Year: 1993

	Jan	Feb	Mar	Apr	May
CASH RECEIPTS					
Income from Sales					
Cash Sales	$0	$2,000	$2,000	$5,000	$12,000
Collections	0	0	0	0	0
Total Cash from Sales	**0**	**2,000**	**2,000**	**5,000**	**12,000**
Income from Financing					
Interest Income	0	0	0	0	0
Loan Proceeds	15,000	0	0	6,000	10,000
Total Cash from Financing	**15,000**	**0**	**0**	**6,000**	**10,000**
Other Cash Receipts	20,000	0	10,000	0	0
Total Cash Receipts	**35,000**	**2,000**	**12,000**	**11,000**	**22,000**
CASH DISBURSEMENTS					
Expenses					
Cost of Goods	0	900	900	2,300	4,950
Operating Expenses	10,400	6,550	13,425	9,805	9,215
Loan Payments	0	125	125	125	125
Income Tax Payments	0	0	0	0	0
Other Expenses/Equip Purchase	10,000	0	0	0	0
Reserve	0	0	0	0	0
Owners Draw	0	0	0	0	0
Total Cash Disbursements	**20,400**	**7,575**	**14,450**	**12,230**	**14,290**
Net Cash Flow	**14,600**	**(5,575)**	**(2,450)**	**(1,230)**	**7,710**
Opening Cash Balance	0	14,600	9,025	6,575	5,345
Cash Receipts	35,000	2,000	12,000	11,000	22,000
Cash Disbursements	(20,400)	(7,575)	(14,450)	(12,230)	(14,290)
Ending Cash Balance	**14,600**	**9,025**	**6,575**	**5,345**	**13,055**

Enters investment from S. Connors as Other Cash Receipts.

Operating Expenses is total of G & A and Sales Expenses minus depreciation.

Shows $10,000 Equipment and Furniture payment as January cash disbursement.

Cash disbursements deducted from opening cash balance and cash receipts.

	Jun	Jul	Aug	Sep	Oct	Nov	Dec	TOTAL
	$12,000	15,500	19,800	20,000	30,800	35,000	15,500	**$169,600**
	4,000	5,000	8,200	14,200	11,000	15,000	6,000	**$63,400**
	16,000	**20,500**	**28,000**	**34,200**	**41,800**	**50,000**	**21,500**	**$233,000**
	0	0	0	0	0	0	0	**$0**
	0	0	4,000	0	0	0	0	**$35,000**
	0	**0**	**4,000**	**0**	**0**	**0**	**0**	**$35,000**
	0	0	0	0	0	0	0	**$30,000**
	16,000	**20,500**	**32,000**	**34,200**	**41,800**	**50,000**	**21,500**	**$298,000**
	6,750	6,690	10,445	11,120	14,000	17,500	7,825	**$83,380**
	7,690	9,185	17,035	15,460	13,565	15,310	13,430	**$141,070**
	125	125	125	125	125	5,125	10,125	**$16,375**
	0	0	0	0	0	0	0	**$0**
	0	0	0	0	0	0	0	**$10,000**
	0	0	0	0	0	5,000	5,000	**$10,000**
	0	0	0	0	0	0	0	**$0**
	14,565	**16,000**	**27,605**	**26,705**	**27,690**	**42,935**	**36,380**	**$260,825**
	1,435	**4,500**	**4,395**	**7,495**	**14,110**	**7,065**	**(14,880)**	**$37,175**
	13,055	14,490	18,990	23,385	30,880	44,990	52,055	0
	16,000	20,500	32,000	34,200	41,800	50,000	21,500	**$298,000**
	(14,565)	(16,000)	(27,605)	(26,705)	(27,690)	(42,935)	(36,380)	**($260,825)**
	14,490	**18,990**	**23,385**	**30,880**	**44,990**	**52,055**	**37,175**	

SAMPLE PLAN: Balance Sheet

Balance Sheet

For ComputerEase, Inc.

For Year Ending: December 31, 1993

ASSETS

Current Assets

Cash	52,175	
Accounts Receivable	18,000	
Inventory	2,100	
Prepaid Expenses	780	
Total Current Assets		**$73,055**

$10,000 in Equipment and Furniture shows as company asset minus depreciation taken as expenses.

Fixed Assets

Land	0	
Buildings	0	
Equipment	7,000	
Furniture	3,000	
Fixtures	0	
Less Accumulated Depreciation	(2,000)	
Total Fixed Assets		**$8,000**

Other Assets 0

TOTAL ASSETS **$81,055**

LIABILITIES

Current Liabilities

Accounts Payable	8,675	
Accrued Payroll	3,050	
Taxes Payable	295	
Short-Term Notes Payable	5,000	
Total Current Liabilities		**$17,020**

Short-Term loan from S. Connors due in less than one year.

Long-Term Liabilities

Long-Term Notes Payable	15,000	
Total Long-Term Liabilities		**$15,000**

Long-Term loan from L. Silver due in more than one year.

Net Worth

Shareholders' Equity	49,035	
Retained Earnings	0	
Total Net Worth		**$49,035**

Owners' interest in company is valued at $49,035 at end of year.

TOTAL LIABILITIES AND NET WORTH **$81,055**

SAMPLE PLAN: Sources and Use of Funds

Sources and Use of Funds

Total Dollar Amount Being Sought: $80,000 in equity financing in return for 20% of the stock in the corporation. The company prefers that this entire amount be secured from only one investor.

Funding Rounds: ComputerEase expects only one funding round for full financing. If the company were to later become a franchise, another funding round would be considered at that time.

USE OF FUNDS

Capital Expenditures

Leasehold Improvements	$5,000
Purchase of Equipment and Furniture	15,000
Total Capital Expenditures	**20,000**

Working Capital

Purchase of Inventory	5,000
Staff Expansion	25,000
Additional Marketing Activities	15,000
Other Business Expansion Activities	15,000
Total Working Capital	**60,000**

TOTAL USE OF FUNDS	**$80,000**

SAMPLE PLAN: Assumptions

Assumptions

The figures on the previous financial forms are based on these assumptions:

SALES BY LINE ($ expressed in 000's)	1993 $ / Units	1994 $ / Units	1995 $ / Units	Growth Rate 1994–93
Training Center classes (Corporate)	45.5 / 11	171 / 38	333.2 / 68	80%
On-Site (Corporate)	166.7 / 38	232.9 / 45	330.2 / 58	30%
Center classes (Saturday)	20.8 / 17	90 / 60	155.3 / 90	50%

These sales figures reflect price increases of 10% annually for corporate training center classes; 15% in 1994 and 10% in 1995 for corporate on-site training classes, and 10% in 1994 and 15% in 1995 for Saturday classes.

Personnel

The staff size of the company (two FT professionals and one PT support) will stay constant for the remainder of 1993. Total payroll projected for 1993 is $62,200. In 1994, the payroll increases to $151,800 (four FT professionals, one FT support, one PT support). In 1995, the payroll is projected at $195,600 (4 FT professionals, one PT professional, and two FT support).

Expansion

Figures in these projections assume opening a second Training Center classroom 1/1/94. Direct costs associated with expansion include leasehold improvements, equipment/furniture, and marketing. Additional operating costs include equipment rental and addition of a staff trainer. This expansion increases capacity in corporate training classes by 100%.

Financing

To date, ComputerEase has been financed by a $30,000 investment from Scott E. Connors; a $15,000, 10% interest-only loan from l. Silver (Mr. Connors' sister-in-law), due 12/31/93; and a $20,000 n0-interest loan from Mr. Connors, principal due on or before 3/31/94. Projections call for the retirement of$15,000 of the Connors loan in 1993, with the remainder by 3/31/94, and the remainder of the Silver loan when due. The 1994-95 financial projections assume securing an additional $80,000 of investment income by 1/1/94.

Chapter 14

The Plan's Appendix

It's not over till it's over,
and even then it's not over.

Use an Appendix to Reinforce Your Plan's Content

One of the frustrations of developing a business plan is that you are limited in how much information you can include. You may be excited about your product's new packaging, a contract from a large customer, or positive market research results, but you should not go into great detail about these items in the business plan itself. Such details make the document too long.

Instead, your plan's Appendix is the proper place to provide information that supports, confirms, and reinforces conclusions you reach in the plan. An Appendix is where you give greater details about particular aspects covered in the plan, and you can include very specific details regarding market research, technology, location, etc. An Appendix is not the place, however, for any data that is essential to understanding your business. Essential information goes in the plan itself.

"If you have a lot of appendices, put them in a separate binder, so the plan itself stays small."

Ann Winblad
Venture Capitalist

Guidelines

If you choose to include an Appendix, follow these guidelines:

1. Your plan must stand on its own; many people do not read appendices, especially on the first perusal of a business plan.

2. You don't have to include an Appendix at all; add one only if you believe the additional information is compelling (in the case of a

plan for outside financing) or can be used for reference (in the case of internal plans).

3. Do not put totally new information in the Appendix; the material in the Appendix should be referred to in the plan itself.

4. Keep it short. The Appendix should be no longer than the plan itself. If your plan and Appendix are both fairly long, consider putting the Appendix in a separate binder.

Remember, your plan must not seem overly long or intimidating to the reader, so give the same careful consideration to what you put in your Appendix as you give to what you put in the plan itself.

Appendix Content Options

The kinds of information described below are appropriate for inclusion in an Appendix. Notice that this material all supports information already in your plan.

Letters of Intent/Key Contracts

One of the very best items that can be included in an Appendix is a copy of a letter of intent to purchase or a contract from a key customer, especially for a new business. This immediately shows that the business has a source of income and that customers are interested in the product or service.

Endorsements

Letters, articles, or other information from credible sources, particularly customers, reinforce the sense that the company is capable and the product or service desirable. Laudatory newspaper or magazine articles about the company are appropriate and convey the message that the company is well-established.

Photos

Photos generally do not belong in the body of the business plan; so if photos of your product, location, display cases, etc., are useful, include them in the Appendix. In most cases, avoid photos of management personnel.

List of Locations

If your company has numerous locations — stores, branch offices, plants — a complete list can go in the Appendix rather than in the plan.

Market Research Results

If you conducted extensive market research as part of your business planning process, you may want to include detailed descriptions of your findings in the Appendix. You can also include information from city or county planning departments or other government agencies that give additional details about the nature of your market.

Resumes of Key Managers

If the resumes of your key managers are particularly impressive, consider including them in your Appendix; otherwise, the description in your Management section should suffice.

Technical Information

If your company is using or developing new technology, and the readers of your plan are knowledgeable in those areas, more detailed descriptions of your technology can be placed in the Appendix rather than in the business plan. You may also want to include technical drawings.

Manufacturing Information

If yours is a manufacturing business, you may want to include a detailed description of the manufacturing process or a flow chart describing the process.

Marketing Material

You can include nonbulky marketing material, such as a brochure or leaflet. For cumbersome marketing materials, such as packaging, use a photograph.

Work Schedule

You can include a work schedule describing how you utilize employees; such a schedule is useful when the company has more than one shift.

Floor Plan

Especially if yours is a retail or manufacturing business, you may want to include a floor plan showing the layout and use of space.

Other Information

You can also include other information derived from the business planning process, such as:

- Competitive Analysis (see Chapter 8).
- Marketing Budget (see Chapter 9).
- Equipment Schedule (see Chapter 10).

Any other information that you believe supports and reinforces information in your plan can be included in the Appendix.

"The only kind of market research that impresses me is to see what you've learned from testing your product in the real world and to get a list of those companies already using the product."

Ann Winblad
Venture Capitalist

Chapter Summary

Use an Appendix to provide information that is too extensive to be included in your business plan itself. Remember, if you are submitting your business plan to outside financing sources, the Appendix is likely to be reviewed only by those who have already read the plan and decided that it warrants further examination. If readers lose interest in your plan itself, the Appendix will go untouched. If after reviewing your plan, however, they are still interested in your business, the Appendix becomes a subtle marketing tool. So be certain to use it only for information that reinforces the sense that yours is a well-conceived, well-run business.

Putting the Plan to Work

Section III

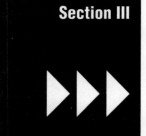

Chapter 15

Internal Planning for Existing Businesses & Corporations

Planning isn't just what you do to go into business;
it's what you have to do to stay in business.

If You Have an Existing Business

While the entire business planning process described in this book is aimed at both new and existing businesses, companies already in operation have the ability, and need, to examine key operating and financial activities more closely. This in-depth analysis particularly benefits those companies undertaking the business planning process for internal planning purposes rather than as a method of securing outside funding.

Ongoing internal planning is a must for any business; it enables you to stay competitive. A thorough planning process forces you to look closely at the dynamics of the current market situation rather than rely on old assumptions.

Internal planning provides you with the opportunity to examine ways to keep costs down and increase your profitability. In the constant or day-to-day business, taking the time to think about what you do and in which direction your company is headed gives you more control and better information on which to base crucial business decisions.

The Purpose of Internal Planning

When undertaking your internal planning process, you must first assess the goals and purpose of the process for your company.

Generally, internal planning can take one of three forms:

- **Evaluating.** To provide information on company performance.
- **Goal Setting.** To establish annual or periodic objectives.
- **Problem Solving.** To address a particular issue or concern.

These types of plans differ only in their objectives and scope; the process in each case is relatively similar. All three plans require that you assemble or develop sufficient information to enable you to evaluate and assess current company conditions; obtain necessary personnel to be involved in the evaluation of the data compiled; and have the ability to bring an honest and critical eye to the examination of your company's situation.

The Evaluational Plan

An evaluational plan provides management with the information needed to make decisions. Data gathering and assessment, rather than the recommendation of specific actions or the setting of specific performance objectives, are emphasized in this type of plan.

Such a plan particularly benefits a company that has not made a close examination of its operations or the market conditions for some time, or it may be used annually by a company that wants to do an in-depth analysis of these factors on a regular basis. An evaluational plan might be the most appropriate type for a company in which all decisions are made at upper levels of management only, and the input of middle management and staff is given relatively little weight.

The Goal-Setting Plan

Probably the most widely used type of corporate business plan is that with the purpose of annual or periodic goal setting.

The function of this plan is not only to evaluate current and past conditions within the company and its environment, but to establish the specific, measurable objectives which departments and/or individuals are expected to achieve.

Some of the areas in which specific objectives may be set include:

- Total Revenues
- Sales per Employee
- Revenues per Customer
- Profit Margin
- Inventory Levels
- Production Time
- Collection Activity

Many companies set performance objectives in these and other areas annually, based on past performance and projections of future conditions. Performance objectives should be:

- **Measurable.** With specific numbers or dollar figures attached rather than merely subjective qualities or quantities.
- **Reasonable.** Based on a fair assessment of current and past activity and a temperate projection of future conditions rather than on an unreachable ideal.
- **Time Specific.** Delineating a clear time frame in which the objectives are to be achieved.
- **Motivational.** Neither impossible to reach nor too easily accomplished, either of which will reduce employee motivation.

The Problem-Solving Plan

Another option for internal planning is to narrow the planning process to a few key issues to be addressed. This type of problem-solving process focuses on the top priorities for operational improvement rather than on an overall evaluation of company performance. Planning for problem solving, however, should not take the place of more comprehensive planning; you still need to look at your complete operations. But it offers you a method of focusing resources and creativity on one or two areas in order to make significant gains in performance.

A problem to be solved can be assigned to a department or division, but often it is advisable instead to assemble a task force to tackle the issue. Such a task force allows management to bring together staff across divisional or departmental lines.

Keep in mind that to a large extent whom you choose to participate in the task force will determine the outcome. If the task force is composed only of staff members who have been with the company for 20 or more years, it is unlikely you will come up with fresh approaches to the problem. If the members are too inexperienced, on the other hand, they will neither have the necessary knowledge of the realities of the business nor will their recommendations be viewed with much authority.

The problem-solving process consists of:

- **Defining the Problem.** Either management or staff may delineate the areas of concern or challenges.
- **Assembling the Team.** Limit the number of people involved and bring together only those whose contribution will move the process forward; choose team members more for their intelligence, attitude, and knowledge than for job title or data access.
- **Considering Solutions.** Persistent problems often require creative solutions; be willing to make changes to achieve results.
- **Recommending Specific Activities.** Suggest the changes or enhancements necessary to solve the problem.

"Each major marketing division and each staff department must come up with a strategic plan and an annual plan. The strategic plan focuses on the critical issues for the next three years: issues such as declining demographics, product substitutions, discount competition, increased supply prices. It addresses the business environment, the customers, the competitors, the suppliers, and other key issues. There are very few financial schedules. The annual plan starts from the bottom up, and it is very specific. It must make sure all the strategic objectives are being addressed and includes: profit/loss statement; cash-flow analysis; capital spending; inventory analysis, including turnover by product line and mark-downs; and lead time analysis for reaching particular objectives. Both the strategic plan and the annual plan are done every year, but not at the same time."

George James
Sr. V.P. & CFO
Levi Strauss & Co.

Large Corporations

Many, if not most, larger corporations now develop business plans annually on either a company-wide, divisional, or departmental level. *The Successful Business Plan: Secrets and Strategies* serves as a guidebook for developing an overall corporate or divisional business plan, enabling you to evaluate all aspects of your company or division. For departmental or smaller-unit planning, some sections may require modification to accommodate specific circumstances or may not be applicable at all.

As you work through the book, utilize the described process and worksheets but adapt the material to your specific situation and needs. While the term "you" is used throughout the book, particular actions might be carried out by a subordinate, research department, or other members of the planning team. Nevertheless, the person making the final decisions should be sufficiently informed about the planning process and have access to raw data enabling him or her to competently evaluate the action plans recommended by others.

If yours is a particularly large or complex business, you may want to separate your business plan into two sections, one containing the specific financial performance objectives and the other examining more strategic and long-term issues facing the company.

Bottom-Up/Top-Down

The business planning process in large corporations is most successful when conducted as a cooperative effort between those on the top of the decision-making ladder and those who actually carry out the decisions. A one-way planning process without the involvement of both management and staff leads to a company-wide lack of commitment to the plan and inevitably undermines its effectiveness.

In establishing and participating in the business planning process, management has these responsibilities:

- Clearly communicating the specific goals and importance of the planning process.
- Establishing the time frame for completion and execution.
- Assembling the appropriate personnel and making time available for them to participate.
- Bringing in additional outside expertise if necessary.
- Making available the necessary resources for the planning process.
- Being open and responsive to results and recommendations of the plan.

Likewise, staff has certain responsibilities in the process:
- Identifying areas of concern and specific problems.

- Defining the resources and outside expertise required for the planning process.
- Providing the necessary data and information.
- Honestly and diligently evaluating the data gathered.
- Viewing the planning process as necessary and beneficial.
- Realizing the limitations of their roles in decision making.

Ratio Analysis

You may be surprised by how much you can learn about your company and its profitability from a few relatively simple calculations. Even if you think "number crunching" is only for bleary-eyed accountants, you will discover that figures are vital business tools. Particularly useful are the key ratios indicating how one activity or figure relates to another.

For instance, the key ratio of return on equity compares total net profit after taxes to the total amount of money invested in the company. Dividing profit by the amount of equity allows you to see exactly how much each invested dollar earned. This is a vital number for your business as it shows how effectively you used the money you had to spend. The return-on-equity ratio is particularly important for investors who want to know how efficiently the money they invested is being used to create profits.

When evaluating these ratios and using them as a planning tool, you want to look for ways to increase productivity by decreasing the amount of assets necessary to generate sales, reducing your debt, and increasing the amount of profitability made on each sale.

The principal value of computing ratios for your company is in comparing them from one time period to another. In this way, you can assess the progress your company is making in controlling costs and increasing profitability and the trends you see developing in these areas.

Another important way to utilize this information is to compare these key ratios in your company with the ratios of other similar companies in your industry. These figures are available in financial publications such as the annual review by Dun & Bradstreet, the *Almanac of Business and Industrial Financial Ratios,* published by Prentice-Hall, and from industry trade associations. A comparison of your ratios with those of other leading companies will give you a better sense of your company's performance and competitive position.

The Key Ratios Analysis worksheet located later in this chapter shows how to calculate many of the most important measurements of your business. The ratios included on this worksheet help you better understand the profitability of your company and specific operations, how

"Each division is given a great deal of latitude in what their plans are like. We have just a few ground rules: The plan has to reach a minimum stated rate of return. We have no imperative for growth, just for profitability. If growth threatens the rate of return, then don't grow; and we need to understand the cash flow implications, and we need to see how working capital and fixed assets are affected."

George James
Sr. V.P. & CFO
Levi Strauss & Co.

well your company manages the assets it has at its disposal, and your cash-flow situation. A brief discussion of the four ratios you will find on the Key Ratios Analysis worksheet is provided below.

Liquidity Ratios

Liquidity ratios show the extent of the readily available assets, indicating your company's ability to meet short-term debts. Generally, you want to try and increase liquidity and decrease amounts tied up in inventory. Specific types of liquidity ratios include:

- **Current.** How capable the company is to cover short-term debts with short-term assets. (Be certain to use current rather than total assets and liabilities from balance sheets.)
- **Quick or "Acid Test."** How well the company could cover short-term debts without selling inventory; this ratio should always be greater than one.
- **Inventory to Net Working Capital.** How much of the company's cash is tied up in inventory.

Profitability Ratios

Profitability ratios show how much the company has earned and the profits made on sales. Your goal is to have the percentages as high as possible. Profitability ratios include:

- **Profit to Sales.** Relationship of total sales to actual profitability after all expenses.
- **Return on Equity.** Profitability in comparison to the investment of stockholders.
- **Return on Assets.** Profitability in comparison to both investment and loans; how productive the company's total assets are in producing profit.
- **Gross Profit Margin.** Income after the direct costs of sales are deducted.
- **Net Profit Margin.** Income after all expenses are deducted.
- **Earnings per Share.** Amount of income expressed in terms of each share of common stock held.

Debt Ratios

Debt ratios show the extent of the company's debt and its capacity for engaging in additional borrowing; generally, the lower the percentages, the stronger the company's financial position. Debt ratios include:

- **Debt to Assets.** How much the company has relied on borrowing to finance its operations.
- **Debt to Equity.** How much the company owes creditors in comparison to the value owned by stockholders.

Activity Ratios

Activity ratios show how productively the company uses its assets, and how much value the company gets for the inventory or other assets it maintains. The greater the ratio value, the further each dollar goes (except with the Average Collection Period, which ideally is a low figure). Activity ratios include:

- **Inventory Turnover.** Dollar value of the inventory it takes the company to generate sales.
- **Inventory Utilization.** Average amount of money the company has invested in inventory.
- **Inventory Units Turnover.** How much inventory the company has on hand in relation to inventory sold.
- **Fixed Asset Utilization.** Amount of plant and equipment used to generate sales.
- **Total Asset Utilization.** Amount of all assets required to generate the company's sales.
- **Average Collection Period.** Length of time that the company's income is tied up in accounts receivable.

Key Customers

In most businesses, the "80-20 rule" applies to revenues. This rule states that 80% of your income comes from 20% of your customers. This means that a relatively small number of customers are often crucial in determining your success.

In most cases, this 20% is composed of actual individual customers. However, in some cases, it may be a specific type of customer who makes up the bulk of your business.

If indeed your business is dominated by a few key customers (or types of customers), you should take a careful look at their buying patterns and motivation. These customers are vital to your ongoing financial well-being; you want to gain as much insight into their purchasing behavior as possible.

Additionally, you can gain a much better understanding of your customers by examining the significant customers you have recently gained and the important customers you have recently lost. This type of examination of trends in your customer base gives you a sense of how the market views your company and the future direction of your company's sales.

The Key Customer Analysis worksheet, which follows the Key Ratio Analysis worksheet, assists you in evaluating the activity of your key customers.

Key Ratio Analysis

Liquidity Ratios

$$\text{Current} = \frac{\text{Current Assets}}{\text{Current Liabilities}}$$

$$\text{Quick or "Acid Test"} = \frac{\text{Current Assets} - \text{Inventory}}{\text{Current Liabilities}}$$

$$\text{Inventory to Net Working Capital} = \frac{\text{Inventory}}{\text{Current Assets} - \text{Current Liabilities}}$$

Profitability Ratios

$$\text{Profit to Sales} = \frac{\text{Net Income after Taxes}}{\text{Sales}}$$

$$\text{Return on Equity} = \frac{\text{Net Income after Taxes}}{\text{Equity}}$$

$$\text{Return on Assets} = \frac{\text{Net Income after Taxes}}{\text{Average Total Assets}}$$

$$\text{Gross Profit Margin} = \frac{\text{Sales} - \text{Cost of Sales}}{\text{Sales}}$$

$$\text{Net Profit Margin} = \frac{\text{Net Income after Taxes}}{\text{Sales}}$$

$$\text{Earnings Per Share} = \frac{\text{Net Income after Taxes}}{\text{Number of Common Shares Outstanding}}$$

Debt Ratios

$$\text{Debt to Assets} = \frac{\text{Total Debt}}{\text{Total Assets}}$$

$$\text{Debt to Equity} = \frac{\text{Total Debt}}{\text{Total Equity}}$$

Activity Ratios

$$\text{Inventory Turnover} = \frac{\text{Cost of Sales}}{\text{Ending Inventory}}$$

$$\text{Inventory Utilization} = \frac{\text{Cost of Goods Sold}}{\text{Average Inventory at Cost}}$$

$$\text{Inventory Turnover in Units} = \frac{\text{Total Number of Units Sold}}{\text{Average Number of Units in Inventory}}$$

$$\text{Fixed Asset Utilization} = \frac{\text{Sales}}{\text{Average Net Fixed Assets}}$$

$$\text{Total Asset Utilization} = \frac{\text{Sales}}{\text{Average Total Assets}}$$

$$\text{Average Collection Period} = \frac{\text{Accounts Receivable Annual Sales}}{360}$$

Key Customer Analysis

Describe purchasing patterns and motivations of past, current, and new customers.

Key Current Customers

Customer	Products/Services Purchased	Number of Units Purchased	Sales $ This Year	Sales $ Last Year	Sales $ Prior Year
1.					
2.					
3.					
4.					
5.					
6.					

Major New Customers

Customer	Reason for Purchase	How Was Sale Secured	Sales $ This Year	Sales $ Last Year	Sales $ Potential
1.					
2.					
3.					
4.					
5.					
6.					

Major Lost Customers

Customer	Products/Services Purchased	Reason for Loss	Potential for Regain	Last Annual Purchase $	Previous $ High Annual
1.					
2.					
3.					
4.					
5.					
6.					

Touching Base with Your Plan

In corporate business planning, a natural tendency exists to spend a great deal of time and energy putting together a business or annual plan, and then once the planning process is finished, forget the conclusions reached and go back to business as usual. This not only wastes a great deal of resources, it creates a high level of cynicism about the importance and value of the planning process.

To make your business plan a meaningful working document, schedule periodic evaluation meetings to get back in touch with the plan. Perhaps once a month at a staff meeting, the plan can be reviewed and progress assessed. At the very least, the plan should be reviewed quarterly with both management and staff participating in the evaluation. Don't let your business plan gather dust; use it.

Chapter Summary

Existing businesses require business planning as much as start-up enterprises. Planning is a necessity for any company aiming to improve its operations, increase its profitability, or maintain or enlarge its market share. Planning is a regular part of your business, not a once-in-a-business or once-in-a-decade undertaking. Long-term success depends on proper planning: It's the only way to keep up with the competition.

"Retail business is people business. You have to love people and love your customers. Management has to set the example for the salespeople."

Nancy Glaser
President, Golden
Gate Chips

Chapter 16

Considerations for Retailers

Customers expect the best.

What You Need to Know if You're a Retailer

Retail enterprise is on the front line of business trends, and retail is perhaps the most vulnerable sector of the U.S. economy. In retail businesses, consumer rather than business-to-business purchases make up the bulk of income.

Consumers are often fickle customers, and you may find that the merchandise they bought in great quantities last month (and for which you have placed a large reorder) suddenly doesn't sell at all. Consumers are more immediately affected by economic fluctuations than are business customers, and retail operations are often the first to feel the strength or weakness of consumer confidence.

Retail Trends

Retail shopping has changed dramatically over the last 20 years. Shoppers once preferred large metropolitan or suburban department stores offering a broad range of both apparel and household merchandise, appealing to middle-class shoppers. They tolerated mid-range prices and house brands. Stores such as Sears, Montgomery Ward, and J.C. Penney were the dominant examples of this type of retail operation. Consumers supplemented their department store shopping with purchases from local merchants who were able to provide greater convenience at prices only slightly higher than department stores charged.

Shoppers are now far more demanding. They want greater selection and more competitive prices than this general department store/neighborhood merchant model can provide. As a result, retail has begun to polarize at both ends of the cost spectrum and only stores with distinct personalities and images can survive.

Some department stores have evolved into discount stores to adjust to this change (most notable is Sears). But the model is now more that of the superstore or warehouse store with deeply discounted prices, exemplified by The Price Club or Wal-Mart, or the boutique retailer offering unique products and substantially greater customer service than superstores can provide. The superstore concept now dominates the sale of electronics, office supply, home building supplies, and many other product lines. It is also a major force in general merchandise sales.

The other prominent trend in retail has been the increasing domination of franchise and large-chain operations in industries that were previously the exclusive domain of the neighborhood merchant. Local pharmacies are a vanishing species, having been replaced by larger drugstore chains. The corner bakery is now most likely a La Petite Boulangerie or Mrs. Fields.

Options for Retailers

How does the entrepreneur compete in this retail environment? Three options exist. First, you can think big: Position your company and seek the necessary financing to become either a superstore or franchise operation. Second, you can buy a franchise outlet. Third, you can develop a "boutique" orientation, offering customers something uniquely different and substantially more personal than the large or franchise stores can.

Making a Difference in Retail

Today, more than ever, the keys to successful retailing are buying, merchandising, salesmanship, and customer service.

Buying

Perhaps no aspect of retail operations is as crucial as the careful and selective buying of merchandise. Retail buying is a critical skill, virtually an art form. Many first-time retail operators fail to understand the complexities of buying, imagining that buying will be the most enjoyable part of their operations. If you have no experience in buying for retail, either find a partner or key employee who has such experience or delay opening your own business until you have developed sufficient knowledge.

Buying is usually accomplished by:

- Sales representatives calling upon buyers.
- Buyers attending trade shows.
- Buyers purchasing through catalogs.
- Buyers purchasing directly from the manufacturer.

Whenever possible, purchase directly from the manufacturer, which will result in your getting the lowest price possible as you have cut out the intermediary sales representative. This option is rarely available to small operations, however. An option for small enterprises is to use a buying office, which will buy for you, charging a percentage of your overall sales. For a list of such services, contact a trade association or the U.S. Small Business Administration.

When buying, pay particular attention to these factors:

- Nature and Quality of Merchandise (as it relates to your store)
- Price
- Quantities Required
- Reorder Availability
- Delivery Times
- Seasonality
- Payment and Return Policies

Small operations often find themselves in a bind, having to pay more for the smaller quantities they need and being offered the most limited credit options. Try to negotiate discounts based on other factors, such as delivery times or methods, early payment, or total purchase from vendor rather than purchase in one product line.

Buy quantities carefully. Most products have limited shelf lives: Summer sportswear must be marked down in autumn, and this year's fax machine will soon be replaced with a less expensive model having more features. On the other hand, the shopper who wants a bathing suit today will probably not wait to buy from you in two weeks, which is when you expect your next delivery. You're stuck with merchandise if you buy too much; you lose sales if you buy too little. That's why buying is an art.

Merchandising

Once a customer enters your store, how much will he or she buy? You can increase both the likelihood and average amount of purchase by carefully merchandising your products. Merchandising includes all aspects of the company's presentation to the customer — from product displays, to store decor and fixtures, to the music playing in the background, to the way the salespeople are dressed. You want to send a

> *"Retail is an intensely personal business, and service is the key to retail success. You must have the right pricing and product mix for your market. But what keeps people coming into your establishment is service and the consistency of quality."*
>
> **Nancy Glaser**
> **President, Golden**
> **Gate Chips**

message about your products even before the customer talks to a salesperson or looks at a price tag.

A tried-and-true method of merchandising is to bring people as far back into the store as possible. As you shop, notice that sale items and staple commodities are located in the back of each store. Management knows that many customers come in looking for these products, and the goal is to make the customer walk past the nonsale or rotating merchandise first. The longer customers stay in the store, the more likely they are to buy.

Capture Customers' Attention

If your store is in a mall or shopping street with casual foot traffic, your window displays and merchandise displays located at the front of the store must entice customers to come in and shop. Once customers enter your store, your displays and decor must create an atmosphere which makes them feel comfortable, encourages them to stay, and motivates them to buy.

Customers want to feel excited about their purchases, particularly when buying impulse or nonstaple items. Shopping is a recreational activity as much as a necessity, so make shopping in your store a pleasurable experience. No matter what, keep your retail space CLEAN. Nothing discourages sales more than a dirty store, with the possible exception of a surly salesperson.

Here are some helpful merchandising hints:

- Rotate and restock your merchandise frequently.
- Keep your store visually interesting.
- Have the appropriate merchandise displayed for the current season.
- Keep your merchandise fresh; remain aware of current styles.
- Provide discounts for quantity purchases (e.g., 10% off 3 or more).
- Place small impulse items at the check-out point.

Salesmanship

In retail operations, sales personnel are the pivotal force in increasing sales, yet all too often they are hired thoughtlessly, with far more emphasis given to the employee's willingness to work for low hourly wages than to the individual's sales ability. But every interaction a salesperson has with a customer is an opportunity to increase sales; if you are using untrained or incapable salespeople, you're undoubtedly losing revenue.

The components of an outstanding sales force include:

- Wise hiring and prudent firing.
- Regular, meaningful training.

- Recognition and financial incentives for success.
- Employees who know and appreciate the merchandise.
- Management that respects the sales force.

Sales techniques that successful retail salespeople utilize include:

- Greeting customers and making them feel welcome.
- Asking specific rather than general questions to help customers find what they are looking for.
- Suggesting accessory items to go along with a customer's intended purchase.
- Suggesting specials or promotional items.
- Offering alternative suggestions if customers can't find what they want.

Customer Service

Customer service is an increasingly important aspect of retail sales. Customers will no longer put up with bad service; they demand excellent treatment in exchange for the dollars they spend in an establishment. Even in large discount stores, customers expect to have the ability to return items, to have questions answered politely, and to have employees treat them with respect.

Make certain you are offering a complete program of customer service, from the attitude you show to customers when they are in your shop to the support you give them after purchase.

Shrinkage

A major problem in retail operations is theft, both from shoplifters and from employees. Establish security procedures that reduce the amount of shrinkage you experience. Sometimes this means that small, expensive merchandise is kept in locked display cases; overall, some kind of technological security system may be put in place.

Choose a security system carefully; you don't want your customers to feel they are in a police state, but you want to discourage the army of professional thieves from targeting your store. Make sure your security system is appropriate for your type of shop, merchandise, and clientele: An electronics store in an urban setting can post a uniformed guard at the door, check every customer's purchase, and few people will be offended. That same system in a suburban boutique would discourage customers from returning.

Chapter Summary

These are the issues most likely to be foremost on the minds of potential funders of retail businesses:

"We strive for consistency and quality in the way a customer is treated when they walk in a store. We constantly remind salespeople that their job is to enable the customer to have an experience that will make them satisfied and happy, so the customer will want to come back. It's easy to give the customer a happy experience. The rules are simple: smile; know the product; take care of even whimsical requests; make sales suggestions; offer samples; if there's a problem, make it right; make the customer feel as if they're coming to your home."

Charles Huggins
President, See's Candies

- Has the entrepreneur chosen the right location? In retail, location is almost always an essential ingredient for success. The location must be appropriate for the retail concept and provide a market sufficient to sustain the business' profitability.

- Is the retail concept clear? Retail operations now must have distinct personalities. Customers want to know what they can expect immediately when they walk in a store. The entrepreneur must be able to articulate a clear definition of the nature of the merchandise, price points, and customer base.

- Are the profit margins sufficient? Has the company priced its merchandise high enough to account for all expenses and overhead? Will the market support this pricing level?

- Is the management experienced? Retail attracts many novice entrepreneurs, and investors are properly wary of inexperienced management. What expertise specifically related to retail does the management bring?

- Can the operation be franchised or duplicated? What potential exists for the company to grow into a much larger operation?

When finalizing a business plan for your retail business, place special emphasis on those areas that have the most impact on retail success, using the questions above as a guide.

Chapter 17

Considerations for Manufacturers

It's not only what you make;
it's what you do with what you make.

All Manufacturers Face Similar Challenges

Whether your company is a large automobile maker with thousands of employees or a small operation producing handmade jewelry, you have to deal with similar manufacturing concerns. When you take raw materials and fabricate them into a finished product, regardless of the size or the amount of that product, you face certain challenges in improving your production process so that it increases productivity and profitability while maintaining quality.

Manufacturing can be conducted on either a continuous or intermittent production basis. The continuous method produces goods in a veritable constant stream: The production equipment is operated without interruption for long periods of time producing the same product over and over. With intermittent production, on the other hand, the production line may be stopped frequently or interrupted to make changes in the production process. Merchandise is produced in smaller quantities, with more product variation, and the production equipment or layout may have to be adapted to accommodate different product manufacturing requirements.

Generally, continuous production reduces the cost of each unit produced since there is less unutilized downtime due to the production change overs. Intermittent production is used for merchandise made to order, unique products, and smaller quantities. Products made through an intermittent process cost more to produce and must be priced higher

"We use the Andon system, a series of cords or buttons that allow employees to shut down the production line when they see a problem. Each team member is responsible for quality all through the process. Our inspection system exists to validate our system of producing quality throughout the process rather than to find problems at the end of the production line."

Michael Damer
New United Motor
Manufacturing Inc.

than mass-produced products to cover the nonproductive time of the equipment and staff.

Trends in Manufacturing

Technological changes and foreign competition are revolutionizing manufacturing. Today it takes far fewer workers to make the same product as years ago. The products themselves have changed, often utilizing new materials and new technology. Competition has become far more intense, with foreign competition at all levels of the marketplace. A manufacturer, even a small manufacturer, must be positioned to respond to a constantly changing economic environment.

Quantum Technological Changes

It used to be that manufacturing changed slowly and incrementally, with products and equipment evolving through sequential, small improvements. Now, however, changes tend to be revolutionary as much as evolutionary, and manufacturers are faced with an explosion of new technology and materials developed through chemical processes.

These changes often substantially reduce production costs and create intense competitive pressures. Thus, the compact disc player you manufacture today to sell at $300, tomorrow will likely be faced with a competing product offering more features at a lower price. With such a scenario, your product becomes almost impossible to sell profitably.

Improved Information Systems

Bar coding and optical scanning now allow manufacturers to track inventory and sales on a constant basis. Companies such as Levi Strauss & Co. now get electronic data instantaneously and directly from retailers, providing immediate information on inventory. This allows the company to know exactly how many units must be produced to replace those units sold, facilitating faster production time and reducing excess inventory.

Changing Organization of the Production System

Influenced by foreign management techniques, U.S. production systems are changing to give production workers more input into designing the production process. Those who actually work on the front line of production increasingly shape the methods they use to manufacture goods. This trend is profoundly affecting the nature of management-labor relations.

Demand for Quality

Consumers no longer tolerate inadequate goods. They place great importance on quality when making their purchasing decisions, forcing manufacturers to maintain higher standards. Thus, quality control must become an integral part of the production process, and companies must take steps to ensure that very little of their merchandise falls below their high standards of quality.

Strategies in Manufacturing

Production Planning

You can substantially increase your manufacturing productivity and maximize your profit margin through careful production process planning. Many companies, especially smaller enterprises, give relatively little thought to the production process. They pay attention to the specific tasks that need to be accomplished and neglect the overall production system. As a result, they often experience short or excess inventories, underutilized plant capacity, or delays in shipping product.

Every manufacturer, no matter how small, should have a production manual. This manual should indicate the lead time necessary for the purchase and delivery of inventory, the maximum and minimum inventories of both raw material and finished goods to be maintained at various times of the year, and the labor requirements and labor deployment schedules. It should also indicate the planned utilization of equipment.

Careful Inventory Control

Inventory represents money sitting around. Every piece of raw material or finished good waiting in a warehouse ties up capital, making it unavailable for more productive uses. You must minimize your inventory levels. At the same time, there are also costs associated with having too little inventory. Without materials, you may have employees unable to do their jobs; without finished products, you may not be able to fill orders.

The goal is to keep inventories as low as possible while still being able to maintain production and meet demand. Inventory management is a crucial aspect of manufacturing. Work closely with your suppliers to reduce the amount of time necessary for delivery of goods and to lower the minimum quantity for orders while maintaining quantity discounts. Ask vendors to warehouse your purchased materials for you, thus reducing your overhead costs.

Examine how you move materials around your production plant. Many companies never address this issue adequately and find themselves faced with virtual chaos on the plant floor. Improper materials handling results in loss of goods, longer production time, and increased safety hazards. Examine the locations where materials are stored. Observe how they move from one part of the production system to

"Jidoka is one of our basic philosophies. It is the principle of guaranteeing quality in the process itself. Don't allow defective parts to go from one manufacturing process to the next; don't wait for the end product to be manufactured and only then find the defect. Each team on the production line must think of the next stop as its customer, and they are the customers for the previous stop. Therefore, it's their job to make sure they are both receiving and producing quality."

Michael Damer
New United Motor
Manufacturing Inc.

"Just-in-time inventory management aims not at producing a steady stream of products to sell, but at replenishing those products which have already been sold. At each job station, we have only 1 1/2 hour of inventory; our safety stock of inventory is only 3 days. Inventory from California suppliers is only 1 day. This helps insure quality, because if we see a problem with a part, it can be caught quickly and without huge quantities involved. It improves safety, since each work station is less cluttered. It reduces costs since we have less money in inventory and less rework is required. Parts aren't replenished until they are used. This is a 'just-in-time' rather than a 'just-in-case' system of inventory management. This system requires: 1) employees managing the information system right; 2) good relationships with suppliers, so we know we can get parts on time; and 3) good quality from suppliers, because we cannot have many rejects."

Michael Damer
New United Motor
Manufacturing Inc.

another and how finished goods are prepared for shipping. Even large companies find themselves with bottlenecks of goods unable to be finished or shipped due to inadequate attention to the manner in which materials are distributed internally.

Subcontracting

Subcontracting can be an attractive option for manufacturers, as a means of reducing costs and increasing capacity utilization. You can use subcontracting both ways: to have subcontractors work for you to fabricate components of your finished product or for you to act as a subcontractor for other manufacturers. Using subcontractors yourself reduces the cost of maintaining equipment, inventory, and labor. Subcontracting out to others is an attractive way to use the equipment and labor you already have in place to produce more product than you are able to currently sell, and it gives you access to additional distribution outlets.

Companies of any size can take on subcontracting work. Even large automobile manufacturers produce components, such as windows, for other manufacturers. Consider the alternative uses to which you can put your production plant. Can you utilize your excess capacity to produce something for another company?

Joint Venturing

Manufacturers are in a good position to create partnerships with other companies for the production and sale of products. Since manufacturers have links to both ends of the production system — raw materials at one side and distributors or retailers at the other — they have numerous opportunities for developing strategic relationships to help finance expansion activities.

Thus, a vendor of raw materials may be willing to help underwrite the costs of research and development of a new product incorporating those materials. Or a major retailer may see the value of a new product and work with the manufacturer to create it. Consider entering into joint ventures with suppliers, customers, distributors, and retailers to finance new products or the marketing of existing products in new ways.

Adding Perceived Value

The same products from two different manufacturers may be very similar in terms of purpose, functions, and production costs, and yet differ widely in price. One company may be able to command higher prices for its products by adding perceived rather than intrinsic value to its merchandise.

A "brand name" is perhaps the most widely used method of adding perceived value. Customers are more comfortable buying products from companies they know, believing that the product is more likely to be of good quality, and the company more willing to stand behind its merchandise. The costs of developing a brand-name product are substantial, however, as it usually requires large advertising and promotion budgets.

A less expensive way of adding perceived value is through improved product design. Two telephones may work identically, but the one with the sleeker, more modern appearance may be more appealing to customers and leave them with the impression that the internal technology is superior. A specialist in product design can increase the perceived value of your merchandise, and you may only have to pay a one-time charge for these services, which makes each unit you produce more valuable. Finally, attractive packaging may convey added value. Consider the ways that you can increase the perceived value and thus, the price of your products, especially via those methods that require relatively little investment.

Chapter Summary

When assembling a complete business plan for your manufacturing business, place special emphasis on areas having the greatest impact on the success of such businesses. These questions are likely to be foremost on the minds of potential funders of manufacturing businesses:

- How substantial are the barriers to entry for new competition? Since manufacturing companies usually require large amounts of initial investment, funders want to ensure that your company is sufficiently protected from competition so it will be able to gain an adequate market share to be profitable. Some barriers to entry you can stress in your business plan to reassure investors include patents, special expertise required to produce your product, engineering difficulties, large initial capital outlay, and lack of access to distribution systems.

- Does your company depend on key production personnel for its success? If so, what contractual or other arrangements has the company made to ensure that these key employees will stay with the business and will not enter into competition? What contingency plans has the company made if these employees become unavailable?

- What steps has the company taken to reduce production costs? How has your company organized its inventory, equipment, and labor utilization to maximize profitability? Have you brought in experts on production design and scheduling to assist in the development of a well-organized production process?

- Does your management understand production? Many entrepreneurs who establish manufacturing companies understand the product but not how to produce it on a mass, profitable basis.

- How will your company remain competitive in the coming years? What emphasis do you place on research and development? Are the research and development budget and staff adequate? What new products does the company have under development? How often do you plan to introduce new products? What other steps is your company taking to enhance its product line in the future?

Tailor your business plan to respond to these questions. Make certain they are answered thoroughly, because they represent the issues having the greatest impact on the future success of any manufacturing enterprise. Addressing these concerns increases the impact of your completed business plan with potential funding sources and helps ensure the viability of your company for the long term.

Chapter 18

Considerations for Service Businesses

When you sell a service,
you sell yourself.

Many Types of Service Businesses

Service businesses comprise the most diverse sector of the economy. Neither retail nor manufacturing can match the service sector in the breadth of companies that fall under its rubric.

Accountants, aerobics studios, and airlines all are considered service businesses. As little as a physician and a pipefitter may appear to have in common, they are both service providers.

This diverse sector includes many unrelated industries. Some service industries are aimed primarily at the corporate market, providing essential business services; others focus on personal services and home and auto maintenance.

A wide variety of additional industries come under the service category, such as transportation, entertainment, insurance, and construction.

Common Factors of Service Businesses

While service industries may vary greatly in the nature of the particular service provided, these industries are characterized by a number of features that define "service."

If yours is a service business, notice how these factors apply to your company.

Intangible Product

Unlike manufacturers or retailers, service businesses sell an essentially nonmaterial product. Customers buy a process, advice, or result, rather than a tangible item.

Consider what customers actually receive in tangible terms when they hire an attorney, go to a film, or pay for an exercise class, and you realize that very little of the worth of the service is conveyed in tangible form. With an attorney, it is not the piece of paper on which a contract is written that has value, but the knowledge the attorney brings to the task of drawing up the contract. At the movies, it is not the screen or the seats that interest the customers but the images and story projected on the screen, which disappear completely after two hours. And at the exercise class, it is the customers who actually do the work; they are paying for motivation, encouragement, and instruction.

Subjective Judgment of Quality

Because services sell only intangible products, few objective criteria exist by which to judge quality. Most judgments about the quality of services are subjective, based on the opinion of the service receiver. Which exercise teacher is best, the one who makes you work the hardest or the one who lets you go at your own pace? Which movie is better, the action-packed police drama or the romantic love story? These are completely subjective evaluations.

The few objective measures that can be used to judge service quality are usually not known by the consumer. For example, with an attorney, even though other lawyers might be able to tell if key provisions were included or omitted in a contract, most clients using legal services are not sufficiently knowledgeable to be able to judge the quality of the attorney's work. They only know whether or not their lawyer has inspired their trust.

Relatively Few Barriers to Entry

Generally, it is easy to start a service business because physical inventory and equipment play such a small part in the value of the product. It costs far less to start an accounting practice than to open a production plant. While specific expertise may be needed by the accountant, this expertise is widely available and nonpatentable. Little or no protection is offered to service providers to keep them from facing new competition.

Perishable "Product"

Most service providers sell their time, and time is the most perishable commodity of all. A hairdresser has only so many hours during the day to sell; if that time is not booked with clients, then the hairdresser loses money that can never be regained. An airline offers a seat on a plane; if the plane takes off half full, the income from the other seats is lost forever. In your service business, note the ways in which your "product" has a limited time during which it can be sold.

Significant Time Lapse Between Use

Some services are used on a continuing or regularly recurring basis, such as janitorial, child care, barbers, or bookkeeping. But most service businesses are used by customers intermittently, in response to particular needs. Thus, a small business may use an attorney only a few times over twenty years; a customer may hire an interior decorator once every five to ten years; and vacation travelers may use an airline only once a year.

Quality Depends on the Actual Service Provider

When you buy a laser printer from a computer store, you depend more on the manufacturer than on the retailer for quality. But when you go to an accounting firm, the individual accountant who actually does your work is as important, or more important, than the reputation of the overall accounting firm itself. The person performing the service generally determines the quality of the service provided.

Trends in Service Businesses

The nature of service businesses is changing in response to economic, sociological, and technological developments. As customers spend a higher percentage of their disposable income on services, they become more demanding about the quality of those services. As the economy becomes more service industry-intensive, competition becomes keener. In recent years, the trends described below have characterized the service sector.

Speed

Customers demand an increasingly faster delivery of services. The customer used to getting eyeglasses within an hour, photo processing in thirty-seven minutes, and letters instantaneously by fax, is going to be frustrated by waiting three weeks for a doctor's appointment and then spending an hour in the waiting room. Service providers must accommodate consumers' faster pace of life.

Franchising

Making "brand names" out of service providers through franchise operations is a rapidly increasing trend. Franchises have developed in service industries, such as real estate sales and hair salons. They have even developed in professional service fields, such as medical, legal,

"Monthly, we have our trainers meet with our sales staff. Our trainers are the engine of this company, not just the product. The trainers spend more time with the client than the sales rep. They're in a better position to know what clients want, to point out the advantages of our company to the clients, and to let them know the benefits of advanced training. In a service business, the employees providing the service are also your best sales representatives."

Charles Orr
President, Productivity Point International

and dental services. This trend will continue, bringing national or regional advertising budgets into the competition for services. For comprehensive information on franchising, refer to *Franchise Bible*, published by The Oasis Press.

Increased Integration

Service providers are learning that their customers prefer the convenience of "one-stop shopping" and are including a broader range of related services under one roof. Moreover, they are adding products to augment their service line. Some service businesses actually find that the retail products produce greater profits than the services themselves.

Strategies for Improving Your Service Business

You can take a number of steps to make your service business more competitive in light of the factors and trends affecting the service sector. These steps are equally applicable whether yours is a small, one-person operation or a company with hundreds of employees.

Make Your Product More Tangible

Since services are inevitably intangible, customers have a hard time understanding what they are buying. By making your services seem more concrete, you increase the comfort level of the consumer. Consider selling "packages" of services.

For instance, an attorney might offer a "small business startup" package, that covers incorporation, a trademark search, lease review, and writing a standard personnel contract. In this way, clients know exactly what they get for their money; with an hourly fee, clients are more likely to be nervous about using a lawyer.

Develop a Distinct Image

Take steps to distinguish yourself from the competition. Identify the qualities that are unique or central to your company and emphasize those in your marketing and sales activities. In particular, show how your people make your company. Don't scrimp on your marketing budget.

Cultivate Referral Sources

Since consumers usually are unable to distinguish among competitors themselves, they often rely on recommendations from others. Identify those individuals or firms that are likely to be good sources of ongoing customer referrals and develop a program to cultivate and communicate with them.

Stay in Touch with Your Customers

Because your customers may not deal with you for long periods at a time, they may forget about you. This means they are less likely to refer other customers to you and may not return to you even if they were pleased with the service they received. Customer-based marketing is an essential part of a service business. Send newsletters, direct mail, and business greeting cards, or use other methods to stay in touch with your customers.

Encourage Timely Purchases

Since you are selling a perishable commodity, your time, you need to encourage customers to purchase your services in a timely fashion. Special promotions, limited time offers, and discounts during slow periods should be considered.

Stress Quality Control and Employee Training

Unlike a retail or manufacturing operation where the customer's primary interest is in the product, in your service business the employee who provides the service is key. Thus, it is crucial that you establish standards of performance that every employee is expected to maintain and quality-control checks to make certain that the standards are being met.

Find Ways to Use Excess Capacity

How will you deploy your staff during slow periods? If you are paying for an employee, and the employee has nothing to do, you are wasting the excess capacity of your service company. Use your service employees for marketing or other business activities in slow times, and consider ways of subcontracting work from other service providers if appropriate.

Chapter Summary

When putting together a completed business plan for your service business, emphasize the areas that most determine success in service industries. These are the questions most likely to be foremost in the minds of potential service business funders:

- Is there really a strong enough market for this service at the prices necessary to be profitable?
- Does the staff possess the technical expertise or skill necessary to provide this service effectively? Will new staff require significantly high levels of expertise?
- Since labor is a proportionately higher percentage of the cost of a service business (rather than inventory or raw materials), what steps has management taken to control labor costs?

- Have sufficient funds been budgeted for an effective marketing plan and is the plan well conceived?
- Has management taken steps to ensure adequate quality control to maintain a high level of service?
- Does the service business have the potential to become a franchise operation or to open more locations? How does it get to be bigger than just a small business?

As you work through your business plan, be certain to provide the details necessary to answer the questions listed above. Expand the marketing and employee training and utilization sections of your plan; other sections of operations may be less important.

Chapter 19

Sending Out Your Plan & Looking for Money

It's not just what you've got;
it's what you do with what you've got.

Using Your Plan

Now that your plan is complete, or almost complete, it's time to put it to use. Ideally, this book has helped you work through the process of developing your plan and improved your understanding of the forces that affect your business success. If you now do nothing more than put the written document on the shelf and never look at it again, you will still have already reaped major benefits.

But a business plan is a working document, and you probably have a specific idea of how you intend to use it. Most likely, you want to utilize your business plan as 1) a tool for raising funds (either investments or loans); 2) an internal reference document to guide your company's development; or 3) both.

Whether intended for internal or external use, your business plan must be made presentable for others. You must consider how you can best distribute the plan for maximum impact and how to make the finished plan an effective instrument for achieving your aims.

Preparing Your Plan for Distribution

Before you prepare your plan for either internal or external distribution, refer back to Chapter 3, "Making Your Plan Compelling." Now is the time to edit and proofread your plan; see how you can make the language more concise and clear. Have someone else edit and proofread

"Who you know is impor-
tant. It makes a lot of
sense to have first class
consultants. Find out
who are the good small
business attorneys and
accountants in town and
hook up with them.
Then you can believably
say, 'I've found the best
law firm, the best
accountant, and now
I'm looking for the best
bank to complete my
team.'"

Robert Mahoney
Executive Director
New England Corporate
Banking, Bank of Boston

the plan as well. Make sure you have incorporated the suggestions in Chapter 3 regarding layout, typefaces, desktop publishing, and the use of bullet points, graphs, and charts.

Once you are confident that your plan is easy to read and visually stimulating, you can apply the final touches to prepare it for distribution.

Cover Sheet

The very first page in your plan should be a simple cover sheet (different from the cover letter). When binding your plan with a clear front cover (which is recommended), your cover sheet then becomes, in effect, your plan's cover. As such, it should make a positive first impression. It must be uncluttered and businesslike. On your cover sheet, include this information:

- The words "Business Plan."
- The name of your company.
- The date.
- A copy number.
- A disclaimer or confidentiality statement.
- The name, address, and phone number of the contact person (for external distribution).
- The name of the division or department and contact person (for in-house corporate plans).
- The company logo, if desired.

This sounds like a lot, but it's not. You should be able to put all this information on a cover sheet and still leave attractive white space on the page.

Page Numbers

Both you and your readers will find that page numbers make it easy to refer to specific information when discussing your plan. Rather than numbering the pages consecutively from start to finish (page 1, 2, 3, etc.), a better method is to number pages by section and page. Thus your Executive Summary would be 1-1, 1-2, 1-3, etc.; the next section 2-1, 2-2, 2-3, etc.; the next section 3-1, 3-2, 3-3, etc.; and so on. This pagination method enables you to update or make changes in one section without having to reprint the entire plan. Of course, if you change the order of sections to tailor your plan for specific readers, you have to renumber the plan.

Table of Contents

Any plan more than 10 pages benefits from a Table of Contents. Place it at the beginning of your plan, immediately after your cover sheet and before the Executive Summary. Title your Table of Contents

"Contents," and simply list the sections and page numbers on which each section starts. If you want to draw attention to particular portions of certain sections, do so by using subheadings for those sections in the Table of Contents, but don't get carried away. After all, a business plan is relatively short, and your readers can find their way around fairly easily.

Date

Because securing financing can take a long while, be careful about distributing a plan that appears outdated. A reader who in November receives a plan dated March can easily assume that you have met with nothing but rejections for many months. Thus, it may be advisable to use only the year on the cover sheet: "Business Plan, 1992." If, on the other hand, you can easily generate new cover sheets on your computer or are using the plan internally, then include the month and year: "Business Plan, July 1992." You needn't cite anything more specific than the month.

Copy Number

Number each copy of your business plan before distribution, and keep a list of which individual has received which copy. This way you can keep track of how many copies are in circulation, and, if necessary, can ask to have a copy returned. Most important, if a copy is circulated without your permission, it's easier to trace the responsible party.

Further, since you may revise your business plan as your business develops, you may produce different versions of your plan. To keep track of which version a recipient has, use a code number or letter along with the copy number. Refrain from writing "Version 16" on your plan; it makes a poor impression. A code could look like "Copy C.4," which might indicate to you that it's the third version, fourth copy. "Copy 3.4" could indicate it's the third version, copy four, or it could be "Copy 7.4" to mean the version you completed in July, fourth copy.

Confidentiality

Once you begin to circulate your business plan, you inevitably begin to worry about the confidentiality of your information. Obviously, you don't want your competitors, or potential competitors, to know your strategy or technology.

Most new entrepreneurs are probably overly concerned about issues of confidentiality. Very few business ideas, after all, are truly new — it's the execution rather than the concept that makes a business a success. Generally, bankers and sophisticated investors respect the confidentiality of plans they receive; they're financiers, not entrepreneurs, and aren't interested in running businesses. Nevertheless, it pays to be careful.

"If you need complete confidentiality, you should most likely not pursue venture capital as a source of funds. While venture capitalists are experienced in maintaining confidentiality, for a number of justifiable reasons, in general they will not sign confidentiality agreements. Also, if you do not need a lot of money at this stage, don't seek venture capital. You will be able to demand a better price and increase the likelihood of getting funding if the company is further developed."

Eugene Kleiner
Venture Capitalist

The best way to protect your information is to be selective about to whom you send your plan. Research your recipients, and make certain they are not already funding a competitor. Check their reputations for honesty and discretion. Deal only with reputable people. On top of that, limit the number of copies of your plan in circulation and omit from your plan highly technical, sensitive information. You can provide that information later to only the most serious sources of potential funding.

To help ensure confidentiality, you can include a "nondisclosure form" for the recipient to sign. This is a fairly typical practice, and investors are accustomed to signing such statements. The nondisclosure form is delivered with your cover letter and business plan. An attorney can help you draft a nondisclosure form, an example of which is provided on the opposite page.

Disclaimer

When circulating your business plan to outside funding sources, you want to make certain you don't find yourself in legal hot water. Difficulties can arise when you offer ownership in your company in return for an investment; in actuality, you are selling stock in your company, and federal law regulates the sale of stock.

The best way to protect yourself is to consult an attorney. You can also include a disclaimer on the front cover that indicates your plan is not an offering for sale but rather a document for information purposes only. The same disclaimer can also be used to help protect the confidentiality of your business plan, especially when you are not adding a nondisclosure statement. Your attorney can provide you with the best language, but a typical disclaimer might look like this:

> "This document is for information only and is not an offering for sale of any securities of the Company. Information disclosed herein should be considered proprietary and confidential. The document is the property of _____ Company and may not be disclosed, distributed, or reproduced without the express written permission of _____ Company."

Improving Your Chances

When using your plan for external distribution, expending a small amount of effort preparing for the distribution process can greatly increase your chances of getting funded. The upcoming section "Looking for Money" identifies the kinds of funding sources to whom you may choose to send your plan. The information that follows suggests steps you can take to enhance the likelihood that your plan will receive the best possible reception once it reaches a reader.

Nondisclosure Agreement

Nondisclosure Agreement

Re: (Company Name)

I agree that any information disclosed to me by _____ Company in connection with my review of the company will be considered proprietary and confidential, including all such information relating to the Company's past, present, or future business activities, research, product design or development, personnel, and business opportunities.

Confidential information shall not include information previously known to me, the general public, or previously recognized as standard practice in the field.

I agree that for a period of five years, I will hold all confidential and proprietary information in confidence and will not use such information except as may be authorized by the Company and will prevent its unauthorized dissemination. I acknowledge that unauthorized disclosure could cause irreparable harm and significant injury to the Company. I agree that upon request, I will return all written or descriptive matter, including the business plan and supporting documents to the Company.

Accepted and Agreed to:

_____
Signature

_____
Printed Name

_____
Company/Title

_____
Date

Researching Your Recipients

It pays to do a little homework on your potential recipients so that you understand the nature of the investments or loans they make. It's a waste of everyone's time to send a business plan for your service business to a venture capital firm that funds only manufacturing companies, or to submit a loan for your new business to a bank that only funds companies established for more than three years. You'll end up waiting weeks or months just to hear an inevitable "No."

Instead, a little research can save you a lot of time. Often, this can be accomplished with just a few phone calls, especially if your potential funding targets are established venture capital firms or banks. These institutions are used to answering questions about their funding patterns and have definite procedures and guidelines. Don't hesitate to contact them for information; they'd much rather answer your questions now than waste their time having to process a business plan in which they have no interest.

With other sources, such as private investors, it may be somewhat harder to get information; they may not receive as many inquiries as venture capital firms and banks. Nevertheless, it is quite businesslike to send a letter of inquiry to ascertain the kinds of investments they are willing to consider before submitting your plan to them.

When researching potential funding sources, these are the questions you want answered:

- Do they fund businesses in your industry?
- Do they fund businesses in your sector?
- At what stage of business development do they provide funding?
- What are the minimum and maximum amounts of funding they consider?
- What are the minimum and maximum potential sizes of the businesses they fund?
- On what basis do they generally provide funding: equity or debt?
- What other companies in your industry have they funded previously?
- What kinds of information do they require you to submit with your plan? For instance, how many years of financial projections do they want to see?

Once you have this information, you can better determine whether a funding source is appropriate for your business. Make sure your type of business and financial scope fall within the interest areas of your potential recipient. Don't send a plan requesting an investment of $50,000 to a venture capital firm that only funds companies seeking a minimum of a few hundred thousand dollars. (Many do.)

If possible, you also want to find out less tangible information about your funding sources. What is the potential funder really like? When deciding on funding, does the funder tend to place more emphasis on the experience of management, the product or service, or the market potential? Does the funder take a very long time making decisions, or does the individual respond quickly? Once he or she has financed a company, how does the funder perform as an ongoing partner? What's the funder's reputation in the industry?

Some of these questions you can ask in a phone call; better yet, you can request an informational interview with the funder (see below). Otherwise, start by asking anyone you know in the same or a related industry about the potential funding source.

If the funder is prominent, check sources in the library, such as newspaper articles. Next, see if you can talk to any others already funded by the same source, particularly those funded in the last few years. They can supply a wealth of information, and if you hit it off with them, perhaps they will even arrange an introduction to the funder for you.

Informational Interview

If you intend to send your plan to a large or well-established funder, such as a bank or major venture capital firm, consider asking for an informational interview to get a feel for the institution and to better determine exactly what it is looking for in a business.

Request this only after you have finished researching your funding source and your plan is complete. The interview need not be long; ten to fifteen minutes may be sufficient. Your meeting doesn't have to be with a partner or decision maker: An associate or administrative assistant can be a source of a great deal of information.

Treat any interview you are able to secure as an excellent opportunity, even if it's with a secretary. This is the beginning of your relationship with the funder, and you want to make a positive impression. Moreover, you then know a person inside the company, and when you send your plan, you can send it directly to that person.

Don't make your first interview with your best potential funding source; get some experience with your second or third choice. You'll be less nervous.

Finding an Intermediary

The best way to distinguish your plan from the many others received by a funding source is to find someone known to the funder to act as an intermediary. Intermediaries can either send or deliver the plan personally or can allow you to use their name when you send or deliver the plan yourself.

"If you already have one or two successful stores, you have a much better chance of receiving funding from a venture capitalist. Venture capitalists in the retail field are looking for a proven concept with experienced management. They are looking for 'cookie cutter' concepts, businesses that can be repeated almost identically from location to location."

Nancy Glaser
President, Golden
Gate Chips

"If I get a phone call from somebody I respect about a plan, then that plan gets more of my attention. Who refers a plan to me can be quite important, but in the end the plan has to stand on its own."

Eugene Kleiner
Venture Capitalist

The best intermediary is:

- Someone in the same business as the funder.
- Someone who received financing (and whose business was successful) from the funder.
- A friend or relative of the funder.
- Someone highly regarded in the industry or community, even if not known personally by the funder.

Having an intermediary does not guarantee your receiving funding, but it improves your chances of getting a fair and careful review. If you are fortunate enough to secure intermediaries, be sure to send them a copy of any cover letters you have sent using their name (and perhaps a copy of your business plan as well). Potential funding sources may very well call an intermediary about your business, and when this happens, you want the intermediary to remember who you are.

Tailoring the Plan for Your Recipients

Once you have researched your potential funders, you should organize your cover letter and Executive Summary to highlight those aspects of your business most likely to fit the needs and interests of each funder. Is the venture capital firm particularly interested in patentable new technology? Will the bank fund only those companies established for more than three years? Does the division president want to see new market opportunities? If so, discuss these areas in the first paragraph of your cover letter or place more emphasis on them in your Summary.

Be certain to target your Executive Summary to address institutional concerns rather than an individual's preferences. Remember, your plan is most likely to end up in the hands of someone other than the person to whom it was sent originally.

Cover Letter

You must include a cover letter with any plan you send or deliver to a potential funding source. The cover letter will probably be read before the plan, so make certain it entices the reader to give careful consideration to your business.

The best way to start a cover letter is with this sentence:

> "_____ (name of intermediary) suggested that I contact you regarding my business, _____ (name of business), a _____ (type of business)."

For example, the first sentence might read:

> "Aaron Schneider suggested that I contact you regarding my business, AAA, Inc., a food products and service company."

This immediately draws attention to the person connecting you to the funding source and gives you a measure of credibility (assuming, of course, that your intermediary is credible.)

Next, indicate why you (or the intermediary) feel that the recipient is an appropriate funding source. Continuing with the above example, the next sentence might read:

> "He knows of your experience in funding food product companies and believes you might find AAA, Inc. of interest."

If you don't have an intermediary, your first sentence should state the name and nature of your company and why you have chosen to send your plan to the recipient. It should read something like:

> "Knowing of your interest in funding food product companies, I am enclosing a copy of the business plan for AAA, Inc, an established food products and service company now seeking financing to enable us to expand operations."

Generally, your cover letter should state:

- Why you've chosen the particular funder to receive your plan.
- The nature of your business.
- The developmental stage of your business.
- The amount of funds sought.
- Whether you are looking for an investment or a loan.
- The terms of the deal, if appropriate.

Keep your cover letter brief. It should motivate the recipient to read your plan, not replace the plan itself. A sample cover letter is provided for your review at the end of this chapter.

Following Up

Your job is not done once you have sent out your business plan; you must follow up on its progress to ensure receiving an answer from your funding source. Some investors or banks tell you exactly when you can expect to hear from them. Others are far less diligent in their communication with fund seekers. You must take the initiative.

Don't become a pest, however. Keep your inquiries brief and professional, and don't call or write too frequently. You might call for the first time approximately 10 days after sending your plan, just to inquire whether the plan has been received by the funder. During this first phone call it is appropriate to ask when you can expect to hear from the funding source or when you may call back. It's perfectly acceptable to request an appropriate time to follow up again: "May I call back in two weeks to check on my plan's progress?"

Generally, refrain from calling any funding source more frequently than every two weeks. And if they ask you not to call, DON'T.

"In a cover letter, I want to know how you knew who I was. How did you get to me? Who are the other people pulling for you? The first plans I read are those that come to me from a credible source."

Ann Winblad
Venture Capitalist

"For a bank, it's more important to have our fallback positions covered than our upside measured. A bank is different than a venture capitalist; we don't get larger profits if the company is very successful. So we spend most of our time assessing the fallbacks in a plan in case of error. The fallbacks we look to are receivables, guarantees (collateral), inventory, and fixed assets."

Robert Mahoney
Executive Director
New England Corporate
Banking, Bank of Boston

Updating Your Plan

Your quest for financing may take many months, and your plans for your company may change during that time, especially if yours is a new enterprise. You want to make certain that your written plan is always reasonably current with your actual business strategy and position.

So, before sending out a plan to a new financing source, review its contents and update it. Bring your financial information up to the close of the last month or quarter, revise your financial projections to reflect recent developments, and add descriptions of any new members of management.

It's best not to print too many copies of your plan at one time — you'll be more tempted to send out an old version if a stack of them are already printed and ready to go. If you're preparing your plan on a computer and printing it yourself, updating it should be no problem.

Looking for Money

Not all money is equal. When you first start to look for financing, you imagine that you'll take any money you can find, but you should exercise care. The various sources of money require different types of return on their investments, have varying levels of sophistication and comfort, and provide you with significantly different auxiliary benefits and disadvantages.

Whose money do you want? As you begin your search for financing, first stop and ask yourself these questions:

- Are you willing to give up some amount of ownership of your company?
- Are you willing to have debt that you have to repay?
- Are you willing to risk property or other assets?
- How much control of the direction and operation of your company are you willing to relinquish?
- What other help do you want from a funder besides money?
- How fast do you want to grow?
- How big do you want your company to be?
- What do you see as the long-term relationship between you and your funding source?

Keep in mind that you are going to have an ongoing relationship with your money source; make sure it is someone you can live with.

Debt Versus Equity

Everybody who gives you money for your business wants something in return. Funders either want their money paid back with interest or they want to participate in the profits your company eventually makes. There are two basic formulations for financing your business: taking on debt or giving up equity (ownership interest) in return for investment income.

Debt Financing

Debt financing gives you the advantage of keeping complete ownership of your business. You keep control, and you keep all the eventual profits. You borrow a specific amount, and you have to repay only that amount plus interest, regardless of how profitable your company becomes. The lender does not share in the profits.

Because lenders do not reap the benefits of substantial profits, they have to reduce risk as much as possible. To do so, they may ask you to secure the loan with collateral of your assets (including your home). Using debt financing may jeopardize these assets if your business income is unable to pay back the loan, and if the business fails, you may still have the debt. This is a major risk, especially for a new entrepreneur. You should be extremely cautious before risking your home, your children's college education, or any other funds on which your lifestyle depends.

Loans from banks and other lending institutions (often referred to as conventional financing) are difficult to secure for new enterprises. Many banks will only finance businesses in operation more than three years, and very small businesses may have difficulty at any time. Credit unions may be somewhat more lenient than banks. And for very short-term financing, some small companies have even used cash advances on credit cards.

Be especially careful of shady lending companies that prey on small business startups; these companies make easy loans, requiring significant personal collateral, knowing most of the businesses they fund will fail and the assets will be seized. Or they charge hefty up-front fees to supposedly help find financing they can never truly secure.

Well-established businesses are far better candidates for conventional financing than startups. A healthy ongoing business needing funds for modest expansion activities should certainly consider bank financing. If the business is incorporated, the company itself can take on the loan debt and shield the owners from personal liability in most cases.

Equity Financing

Equity financing, on the other hand, allows you to avoid the personal risk of taking on debt. Instead of committing to repay a specific amount of money, you instead give the investor a piece of the eventual profits. This takes the form of stock in the company or a percentage ownership. If your company is very successful, an equity investor may

"We funded the initial two rounds of financing ourselves from our four partners. Later we took in limited partners, then our overseas distributor as an investor. Now we're looking for an investment partner capable of competing with the largest wineries in California so we can defend ourselves at the higher levels of sales. We know we will have to give up a significant stake in the company, but we're willing to do it on the theory that a small piece of a big pie is better than a big piece of a small pie."

Larry Leigon
President, Ariel Vineyards

"If you start from scratch and you want steep growth, you have to have the ability to finance internally due to very large margins, or you'll have to reconcile yourself to either selling out or accepting financing from outside sources and giving up equity."

Larry Leigon
President, Ariel Vineyards

end up receiving many times the amount originally invested. However, if the company fails to produce sufficient profits, these investors may never get their money back.

Thus, equity investors often want to participate in decision-making to ensure that the company operates in a manner that will produce profits. They may take seats on your board of directors or even play an active role in management.

In some cases, you may have to give up so much equity that others actually have controlling interest in your company. In this case, the investors might even be able to remove you from management altogether. Still, a capable investor can bring you sound business advice, useful business contacts, and may be able to provide you with additional future financing.

Equity financing is a usual and practical method of funding start-up companies. Many of the best-known entrepreneurial high-technology firms, such as Apple Computer, were financed through equity investors.

Because it has proved so successful, equity investing has become institutionalized through venture capital firms and small business investment companies. But equity financing need not be sought only from these professional funding sources. Your accountant or attorney may put you in touch with someone who is looking for an investment, or your brother-in-law or college roommate may be willing to underwrite your business.

Sources of Money

Where do you go to find the money you need? And what are the obligations and benefits you receive from each source? Two charts near the end of this chapter outline the various sources of debt and equity financing available for businesses.

When choosing a financing source (and you do choose them, just as they choose you), pay particular attention to the personal qualities of the individual and the reputation of the professional institution you choose. Not all banks are alike, and certainly not all investors are alike. You want to choose a financing source that:

- Stands by you during difficult times and works to overcome setbacks.
- Deals with you in a professional and businesslike manner.
- Values your contribution to the company.
- Maintains open and clear communication with you.
- Is fair, ethical, and honest.

Ideally, your financing source also brings you sound business advice, excellent business connections, and the ability to help secure future financial support. These qualities are particularly important when looking for an investor or venture capitalist. Such an investor is likely to play a very active part in your company; make certain that it is someone who offers your enterprise other benefits in addition to money.

Venture Capitalists

As you search for money, you probably will hear the term "venture capitalist" quite often, but those who use the term may be referring to very different types of entities.

Two main kinds of funding sources can appropriately be called venture capitalists. The first are professional venture capital firms, which invest large sums of money pooled from various sources such as pension funds and wealthy individuals.

These private firms are established expressly for the purpose of investing in developing companies. Their partners and associates generally are experts in business management and the industries in which they invest; they are among the most sophisticated investors available. Because they invest other people's money, these firms have become more cautious over the years, often restricting investments to companies that already have income and whose products are beyond the early development stage. If your company is just in formation, you need to look for a venture capital firm that invests in "seed" companies.

The second type of venture capital firm is one operated by a venture capital partner or partners who invest only their own money. Usually, these are entrepreneurs who were very successful in business and now want to use their money and expertise to invest in companies related to their area of knowledge. Because they are risking only their own money and time, these venture capitalists may be more willing to accept the risks associated with newer businesses in return for the excitement and financial rewards of seeing a company grow from scratch.

Private Investors

A frequent source of capital for new or smaller entrepreneurial companies is the private investor. Private investors are usually well-to-do individuals who seek investments that provide more personal satisfaction and the potential of greater financial reward than are offered by conventional investments such as stocks and bonds. These investors are usually identified through professional financial advisors, accountants, and attorneys. Private investors can be an excellent source of financing.

However, private investors often have unrealistic expectations regarding the amount and timing of profits. Frequently, they are unfamiliar and uncomfortable with risk, and they may apply pressure for producing profits far earlier than a business can reasonably manage or than is

"An entrepreneur should only go to a venture capitalist if they want the added value a venture capitalist can bring. With a venture capitalist, you're asking them not only to invest money, but to use every leverage point they have, each business and industry contact, leadership and support in subsequent funding rounds, and an honest critique of your business. And it's useful to have the venture capitalist serve as a member of your Board of Directors."

Ann Winblad
Venture Capitalist

healthy. If you do pursue private investment monies, make certain that the investor understands the nature of your business and be particularly conservative in your projections of how much profit you will produce, and when.

Small Business Investment Companies

Small Business Investment Companies (SBICs) and Specialized Small Business Investment Companies (SSBICs) are private firms which exist to provide both investment financing and long-term loans to small businesses. Some SBICs provide only equity; others rely on debt, and some provide either. Each SBIC has its own policy.

SBICs are licensed by the U.S. Small Business Administration (SBA) and may receive funds from the government for the purpose of investing in small businesses. SBICs are willing to consider any small business. SSBICs restrict their investments to companies operated by minority or economically disadvantaged entrepreneurs.

SBICs are good vehicles for financing a small business. However, most of them maintain rigorous evaluation procedures, and you will have to meet some of the same criteria required when applying for conventional financing or funding from venture capitalists. Many of the SBICs now only make loans, and they will seek the same type of collateral and evidence of credit worthiness as banks.

U.S. Small Business Administration

The SBA guarantees loans from other institutions; it does not make loans directly (except for Vietnam-era veterans and disabled persons). If you are seeking financing, the SBA can provide you with a list of lending institutions active in giving loans to small businesses. Remember, these banks and institutions must approve your application, so you must meet bank criteria to qualify; thus, new businesses generally do not qualify. The SBA guarantee, however, sets interest limits and may make a difference if the lending institution is "on the fence" about your loan.

Friends and Family Members

Be careful when financing your business through family or friends, either with loans or investments. This money may be the easiest to secure, but may cause you to risk personal relationships; by mixing your personal and business affairs, you may find you make both your business and personal life more difficult. Unsophisticated investors are nervous about money — they don't understand that it takes time before profits are realized. They view every natural delay or setback with alarm.

If you do take a loan from a personal source, later repay it with the required interest, and subsequently become very successful, the friend or relative may not understand why he or she does not participate in the profits. And, if you are unable to pay back the loan, the relative may never forget and may remind you of your failure at every family occasion for the next 20 years.

Chapter Summary

As you begin to send your business plan to funding sources, careful preparation can increase the likelihood that your plan will be reviewed fairly and thoroughly. Research your recipients, and tailor the presentation of your plan to the recipient's interests and concerns. Choose your potential funding sources wisely; remember that your funding source will become an ongoing participant in your business. And be realistic. You must always give something in return for the money you receive.

"The best and most exciting way to start a business is when you're financially strapped. Then, you have to be creative to keep things going. You have to shop carefully and creatively if you don't have much money. I managed to get a lot out of a little money. The goal was to make enough product to produce at least a small income stream, enough to keep making more. '

Deborah Mullis
Founder
D.A.M.E.'S Foods

Sources of Debt Financing

	What They Look For	Advantages	Disadvantages
Banks and Lending Institutions	Ability to repay, collateral, steady current income from business.	No profit-sharing; no obligation for ongoing relationship after repayment; definite preset amount to repay. **Best For:** Established companies needing funding for specific activities; short-term cash-flow problems.	Difficult to secure for new businesses; must often risk personal assets; same financial obligation regardless of business' income. **Worst for:** Ongoing operational expenses; new companies with relatively inexperienced management.
Loans from Family or Friends	Likelihood of repayment; your personal character; other personal considerations.	Easier to secure than institutional loans; specific amount to repay; no profit-sharing. **Best For:** Companies with no other option; companies with secure future.	Can jeopardize personal relationships; unsophisticated lender often nervous about money; probably no professional expertise; often get unsolicited advice and frequent queries. **Worst For:** Very risky enterprises; entrepreneurs with difficult family circumstances.
Cash Advance on Personal Credit Cards	Ability to repay.	Relatively easy to secure. **Best For:** Businesses requiring small amounts of money for a limited time; short-term cash-flow problems.	High interest rates; limited amount of money; ties up and risks personal credit. **Worst For:** Ongoing, long-term financing.

Sources of Equity Financing

	What They Look For	Advantages	Disadvantages
Venture Capitalists	Businesses in their area of interest; companies that can grow to significant size; experienced management; new technology.	Large sums available; sophisticated investor familiar with industry; can bring expertise, connections, and future funding; understand business setbacks and capital risk. **Best For:** Potentially large companies; sophisticated entrepreneur or industry wizard.	Difficult to secure; must have exit possibilities in seven to ten years; take substantial, perhaps controlling, equity in company. **Worst For:** Small and medium-sized businesses; inexperienced entrepreneurs.
Private Investors	Good business opportunities with better potential rewards than conventional investments such as the stock market; appealing concept.	May fund small and medium-size businesses; easier to secure than professional venture capital or bank loans. **Best For:** Smaller companies; those able to locate relatively sophisticated or capable investor; those with appealing business concept.	Often unsophisticated, nervous investor; take equity in company; may want involvement in decisions without having necessary expertise; long-term relationship; expects profits soon. **Worst For:** Companies requiring long development time before profitability; companies needing additional business expertise.
Investment from Family and Friends	Interest in you and your business concept; chance to make money.	Easier to secure than other investors; no set amount to repay. **Best For:** Companies with no other options; entrepreneurs having friends or relatives with significant business or industry expertise.	Jeopardizes personal relationships; long-term involvement; unsophisticated nervous investor; makes friend or relative a decision maker in your business; doesn't understand risk. **Worst For:** Very risky enterprises; companies requiring long development time before profitability.

SAMPLE PLAN: Cover Letter

Ms. Tamara Pinto
617 North Isenman Boulevard
Vespucci, Indiana 98999

Dear Ms. Pinto:

Opens with reference to intermediary.

My attorney, Mr. Kenneth Pollock, suggested I write to you regarding my business, ComputerEase. I am currently seeking an investor, and I believe that the company would coincide with your interest in technology-related service businesses.

ComputerEase is positioned to take advantage of the market opportunities presented in the corporate software training field. This is a new field, and no companies yet dominate the market. ComputerEase, through a professional approach to marketing, experienced management, and an emphasis on out-standing customer support and service, can become the premier provider of software training in the greater Vespucci area. From that base, the company will be able to expand to become a regional force.

Specifies amount of funds sought.

We are seeking $80,000 in return for 20% equity in the company. We antici-pate this will be the sole round of funding. The funds will be utilized to add one training center location, expand staff, and increase marketing activities.

I appreciate your consideration of the business plan for ComputerEase. I will telephone in approximately 10 days to see if you have any questions or how we may proceed.

Thank you.

Sincerely,

Scott E. Connors
President

Chapter 20

Time Saving Tips

When you have time, you don't have money.
When you have money, you don't have time.

Speeding the Process

Developing a business plan takes time. It's not unusual for the entire process, from business concept to finished plan, to consume many months, especially for a new business. A plan for a new business will take considerably longer than a plan for expansion or growth of an existing company.

Nevertheless, there are a number of short cuts that can save you time and get your plan finished faster. Remember, you don't want to rush the process, but you don't want to spend so much time preparing a plan that you never get your business going.

Time Saving Tips for All Businesses

Here are ways to make your business planning process quicker and easier:

- **Develop a research plan.** During the course of your plan preparation, you will need to gather a lot of information. This often means many excursions away from your office or home, such as trips to the library and meetings with potential suppliers. You can avoid having to repeat these tasks over and over again if you outline all the information you're likely to need at the beginning of your business planning process. For instance, a vendor may be able to tell you not only about costs of goods, but may know a lot about your potential competition and also about customer preferences. You'll want to ask about all of those in one meeting, rather than going back.

So start your research plan by making a list of all the information you need and potential sources of that information. Then put them in a logical order. As you go along, you'll find you need additional information, of course, but a research plan will reduce the amount of times you'll have to go back to the same source and will keep you moving forward.

- **Prioritize the most important areas.** Not all sections of your plan are equally important. You want to make certain you have enough time to spend on those concerns that most effect your business success, so don't squander time on areas you already understand well or are relatively less crucial to your long-term goals. During the early stages of your plan preparation, identify which areas are the most important and address those first.

- **Organize all that paper!** You will amass an amazing amount of paper during the process of developing a business plan, and searching for information through stacks of reports, notes, and brochures will consume a great amount of time. So right from the start, set aside a separate file drawer or file box for your planning materials. Create individual files that correspond to the sections of your business plan, such as target market, competition, and operations and sections for miscellaneous material and possible appendices. Keep all your material together in one place, and start filing papers in their appropriate sections right away.

- **Keep track of the most important information as you go along.** Avoid having to handle each piece of paper any more than is necessary by setting up a note-tracking system to keep on top of important items of information as you come across them. The best way is to put this on a computer. Create a separate computer file for each section of your business plan (plus miscellaneous information) and enter important data into the applicable file as you come across it. These can just be notes; they don't have to be whole sentences or blocks of information. Be certain to indicate where the information came from. This method will really save you time. When you start to write your plan, you'll have almost all the information you need at your fingertips, in exactly the right place. And you'll be able to see which sections are missing sufficient detail.

  If you're not using a computer, use a colored highlighter to indicate the important information in each document and then file the material in the related file of your file drawer. You may have to photocopy some items because many documents will relate to more than one section of your plan.

- **Use a computerized spreadsheet.** If you don't have a computer and have never even used one, this doesn't mean you should go out and buy one and learn to use it and the accompanying software. That won't save either time or money. But if you have a computer and even basic computer skills, a computerized spreadsheet will make it easier and quicker to make the constant, necessary changes in your financials.

- **Get help.** It's not necessary to do every part of your business plan yourself. You can save a lot of time by spending a little money on hiring a consultant to help. Many professional services can move your business planning process forward faster and improve the quality of the finished product.

  To help with research, consider using a paid research service such as Nexus or Research on Demand — see Chapter 2. They can get a lot of the information you may need in a very short time.

  Although it may be somewhat costly, use an accounting firm to prepare your financials. Not only can this save time, it may increase investor confidence in your numbers. Use a desktop publishing service to lay out and print your plan; in many cases, they can make changes faster than you can.

  You can use a management consultant to help you prepare and write your plan. Companies like Abrams Business Strategies regularly review and prepare plans, and the expertise they have in preparing plans can help you understand exactly what the process entails. Plans prepared with the help of a professional management consultant are often more thorough and effective, yet take less time to complete.

Time Saving Tips for Existing Businesses

Sometimes, you need to prepare a business plan in a hurry, and the thoroughness of the plan isn't as important as the speed with which it is prepared. This book can be used as a short cut.

If yours is an existing business and you need to prepare a plan in a hurry, follow these steps:

1. Go straight to the plan preparation forms at the end of each chapter. These forms act as an outline for the text of your plan.

2. Go to each of the Flow-Through Financial forms. A list of these is in Chapter 13. These forms will give you the financial information you need to complete all your financial forms. The three essential financial forms are the income statement, cash flow, and balance sheet. Concentrate on those.

3. Go back to Chapter 3 to find tips on how to lay out the plan for the best presentation.

4. Follow the directions in Chapter 19 to learn how to prepare your plan for distribution.

These steps will enable you to prepare a plan quickly — possibly even in a weekend!

What to Avoid

One of the worst ways to save time on a business plan is by purchasing a computer program with *standardized* text or boilerplates, where you just add your company's name, industry, and financials. This can be tempting, because it seems as if most of the work has been done for you; but for your plan to be successful, examine your business and ask yourself the questions you need answered. Moreover, if you're using you plan to secure financing, funding sources such as banks are likely to recognize standardized text and treat your plan less seriously.

Chapter Summary

It's natural to be intimidated by the prospect of preparing a business plan if you've never done one before. But that intimidation can easily lead to procrastination, which wastes a lot of time. Try to let go of your fear and take the process one step at at time.

Remember: A business plan doesn't have to be perfect; no plan is. You just have to make an honest, best effort. You don't have to anticipate every possible situation, and it's not necessary to make revision after revision until you get it absolutely right. No plan written has ever been truly finished. Every plan could be improved, and every plan continues to change even after it's supposedly completed. So don't let the process overwhelm you. As the ad says, "Just do it!"

Reference

Section IV

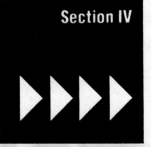

Outline of a Business Plan

I. Executive Summary

II. Company Description
   A. Legal Name and Form of Business
   B. Company's Mission or Objectives
   C. Names of Top Management
   D. Location and Geographical Information
   E. Company's Development Stage
   F. Company Products or Services
   G. Specialty Business Information

III. The Industry Analysis
   A. Size and Growth Trends
   B. Maturity of Industry
   C. Vulnerability to Economic Factors
   D. Seasonal Factors
   E. Technological Factors
   F. Regulatory Issues
   G. Supply and Distribution
   H. Financial Considerations

IV. The Target Market
A. Demographics/Geographics
B. Lifestyle and Psychographics
C. Purchasing Patterns
D. Buying Sensitivities
E. Size and Trends of Market

V. The Competition
A. Competitive Position
B. Market Share Distribution
C. Barriers to Entry
D. Future Competition

VI. Marketing and Sales Strategy
A. Company's Message
B. Marketing Vehicles
C. Strategic Partnerships
D. Other Marketing Tactics
E. Sales Force and Structure
F. Sales Assumptions

VII. Operations
A. Plant and Facilities
B. Manufacturing/Production Plan
C. Equipment and Technology
D. Variable Labor Requirements
E. Inventory Management
F. Supply and Distribution
G. Order Fulfillment and Customer Service
H. Research and Development
I. Capacity Utilization
J. Quality Control
K. Safety, Health, and Environmental Concerns
L. Shrinkage
M. Management Information Systems
N. Other Operational Concerns

VIII. Management and Organization
A. Principals/Key Employees
B. Board of Directors
C. Consultants/Specialists
D. Management to Be Added

E. Organizational Chart

F. Management Style/Corporate Culture

IX. Development and Exit Plans

A. Long-Term Company Goals

B. Growth Strategy

C. Milestones

D. Risk Evaluation

E. Exit Plan

X. The Financials

A. Income Statement

B. Cash Flow

C. Balance Sheet

D. Break-Even Analysis (if desired)

E. Plan Assumptions

F. Uses of Funds

XI. Appendix

Business Terms Glossary

See also Chapter 13, Financials, for definitions of financial terms.

Accrual Based Accounting. An accounting method whereby income and expenses are entered on the books at the time of contract or agreement rather than at the time of payment or receipt of funds.

Barriers to Entry. Those conditions that make it difficult or impossible for new competitors to enter the market: two barriers to entry are patents and high start-up costs.

Board of Directors. The members of the governing body of an incorporated company.

Capacity. The amount of goods or work that can be produced by a company given its level of equipment, labor, and facilities.

Capital. The funds necessary to establish or operate a business.

Cash Based Accounting. An accounting method whereby income and expenses are entered on the books at the time of actual payment or receipt of funds.

Cash Flow. The movement of money into and out of a company; actual income received and actual payments made out.

Collateral. Assets pledged in return for loans.

Conventional Financing: Financing from established lenders, such as banks, rather than from investors; debt financing.

Convertible Debt. Loans made to a company that can be repaid with stock ownership (or a combination of stock and cash), usually at the lender's option.

DBA: "Doing Business As . . ." A company's trade name rather than the name by which it is legally incorporated; a company may be incorporated under the name XYZ Corporation but do business as "The Dew Drop Inn."

Debt Financing. Raising funds for a business by borrowing, often in the form of bank loans.

Debt Service. Money being paid on a loan; the amount necessary to keep a loan from going into default.

Deferred Compensation. Salary delayed until a future date; often taken by principal employees as a method of reducing expenditures in early years of operation.

Disbursements. Money paid out.

Distributor. Company or individual that arranges for the sale of products from manufacturer to retail outlets; the proverbial "middle man."

Downside Risk. The maximum amount that can be lost in an investment.

Due Diligence. The process undertaken by venture capitalists, investment bankers or others to thoroughly investigate a company before financing; required by law before offering securities for sale.

Equity. Shares of stock in company; ownership interest in a company.

Exit Plan. The strategy for leaving an investment and realizing the profits of such investment.

Funding Rounds. The number of times a company goes to the investment community to seek financing; each funding round is used to reach new stages of company development.

Initial Public Offering: IPO. The first time the company's stock is sold to the general public (other than by a limited offering) through stock market or over-the-counter sales.

Lead Investor. The individual or investment firm taking primary responsibility for the financing of a company; usually brings other investors or venture capital firms into the deal and monitors the investment for all.

Leasehold Improvements: The changes made to a rented store, office, or plant, to suit the tenant and make the location more appropriate for the conduct of the tenant's business.

Letter-of-Intent. A letter or other document by a customer indicating the customer's intention to buy from a company.

Licensing. The granting of permission by one company to another to use its products, trademark, or name in a limited, particular manner.

Limited Partnership. An investment method whereby investors have limited liability and exercise no control over a company or enterprise; the general partner(s) maintain control and liability.

Liquidity. The ability to turn assets into cash quickly and easily; widely-traded stocks are usually a liquid asset.

Manufacturing Companies. Businesses which make products from raw or unfinished materials generally to be sold to intermediaries (such as stores and dealers) rather than the end-user.

Market Share. The percentage of the total available customer base captured by a company.

Milestone. A particular business achievement by which a company can be judged.

Net Worth. The total ownership interest in a company, represented by the excess of the total amount of assets minus the total amount of liabilities.

Options. The right to buy stock in a company at a later date, usually at a pre-set price; if the stock rises higher than the original price, an option holder is likely to exercise these options.

Partnership. A legal relationship of two or more individuals to run a company.

Profit Margin. The amount of money earned after the cost of goods (gross profit margin) or all operating expenses (net profit margin) are deducted; usually expressed in percentage terms.

Proprietary Technology or Information. Technology or information belonging to a company; private information not to be disseminated to others.

Receipts. Funds coming in to the company; the actual money paid to the company for its products or services; not necessarily the same as a company's actual revenues.

Sole Proprietorship. Company owned and managed by one person.

Strategic Partnerships. An agreement with another company to undertake business endeavors together or on each other's behalf; can be for financing, sales, marketing, distribution, or other activities.

Venture Capitalist. Individual or firm who invests money in new enterprises.

Working Capital. The cash available to the company for the on-going operations of the business.

Funding Sources

To find names of individuals and firms providing funding for entrepreneurial companies, contact:

Venture Capital

National Venture Capital Association

1655 North Ft. Myer Drive, Suite 700

Arlington, Virginia 22209

(703) 351-5267

(703) 525-8841 (fax)

A list of association members is available for a minimal charge. The list includes names of venture capital firms, addresses, phones, and contact persons; however, it does not provide areas of interest or stages of companies funded.

Western Association of Venture Capitalists

3000 Sand Hill Road, Building One, Suite 190

Menlo Park, California 94025

(415) 854-1322

A directory of members is available for purchase. This association has more than 120 members, representing many of most active venture capitalists West of the Rockies. The directory includes information on areas of investment interest, stages of companies funded, amounts funded, areas avoided for investment, and contact names.

Pratt's Guide to Venture Capital Sources
Published by Venture Economics
40 West 57th Street, Suite 802
New York, NY 10019
(212) 765-5311
(212) 765-6123 (fax)

This directory lists more than 800 venture capital sources in the United States and Canada available for purchase. It is cross-referenced by geographical area, contact names, industry focus for investment; it also lists key contacts, project preferences, type and amount of financing; year funded, capital under management, and areas avoided for investment. This is updated annually and is the longest-standing guide to venture capital.

AI Research Corporation

2003 St. Julien Court
Mountain View, California 94043
(415) 852-9140

AI sells VenCap Data Quest, a data base that runs on IBM-compatible computers. The data base lists venture capital firms, contact names and addresses, funding policies, funds under management, areas of investment preferences by industry, maturity stages, and geographical areas. It also lists a portfolio of companies that have received funding from AI. The data base is updated quarterly and is available in both Eastern and Western versions.

Loans and/or Venture Capital

U.S. Small Business Administration (SBA)

U.S. Department of Commerce (Offices in cities throughout U.S.)

The SBA maintains lists of banks and other lending institutions most active in making loans to small businesses in each geographical area. It also provides a loan guarantee program (not actual loans) to existing businesses and direct loans limited to special categories such as Vietnam-era veterans and the disabled.

Other Sources

State or City Offices of Business or Economic Development

Many states and cities maintain offices to encourage business expansion and increased employment opportunities. Generally, these offices only offer advice and perhaps some lists of resources. However, in some cases, actual loans or grants may be available, particularly for job creation in economically stressed areas.

Index

Establish A Framework For Excellence With The Successful Business Library

Fastbreaking changes in technology and the global marketplace continue to create unprecedented opportunities for businesses through the '90s. With these opportunities, however, will also come many new challenges. Today, more than ever, businesses, especially small businesses, need to excel in all areas of operation to complete and succeed in an ever-changing world.

The Successful Business Library takes you through the '90s and beyond, helping you solve the day-to-day problems you face now, and prepares you for the unexpected problems you may be facing next. You receive up-to-date and practical business solutions, which are easy to use and easy to understand. No jargon or theories, just solid, nuts-and-bolts information.

Whether you are an entrepreneur going into business for the first time or an experienced consultant trying to keep up with the latest rules and regulations, the Successful Business Library provides you with the step-by-step guidance, and action-oriented plans you need to succeed in today's world.

Select The Tools Your Business Needs From The Following Resource Pages

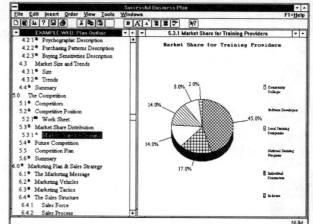

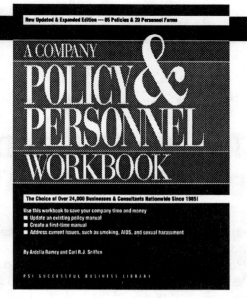

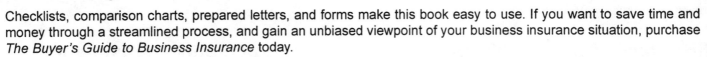

Books that save you time & money:

Learn about the hundreds of ways any business can help secure its future by starting to conserve resources now. This book reveals little-understood, but simple techniques for recycling, precycling, and conservation that can save you money, and help preserve resources. Also gives tips on 'green marketing' to your customers.

Business Environmental Handbook
Paperback $19.95	ISBN: 1-55571-163-4	Pages: 285
Binder Edition $39.95	ISBN: 1-55571-304-1	Pages: 285

This book was written in plain English specifically designed to help businesses regain control of legal costs and functions. Topics include: how to find the right attorney, when to take legal work in-house, what can be controlled in litigation, the use of mediation and other consumer rights when dealing with lawyers. Save up to 75% of your company's legal expenses and learn ways to keep problems from becoming legal disputes.

Legal Expense Defense
Paperback: $19.95	ISBN: 1-55571-348-3	Pages: 336
Binder Edition: $39.95	ISBN: 1-55571-349-1	Pages: 336

CompControl focuses on reducing the cost of your workers' compensation insurance, not on accident prevention or minimizing claims. This highly regarded book will provide valuable information on payroll audits, rating bureaus, and loss-sensitive points, illustrated with case studies drawn from real businesses of all sizes.

CompControl: Secrets of Reducing Worker's Compensation Costs
Paperback: $19.95	ISBN: 1-55571-355-6	Pages: 159
Binder Edition: $39.95	ISBN: 1-55571-356-4	Pages: 159

Written for the business owner or manager who is not a personnel specialist. Explains what you must know to make your hiring decisions pay off for everyone. Learn more about the Americans With Disabilities Act (ADA), Medical and Family Leave, and more.

People Investment
Paperback $19.95	ISBN: 1-55571-161-8	Pages: 210
Binder Edition: $39.95	ISBN: 1-55571-187-1	Pages: 210

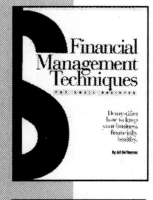

Clearly reveals the essential ingredients of sound financial management in detail. By monitoring trends in your financial activities, you will be able to uncover potential problems before they become crises. You'll understand why you can be making a profit and still not have the cash to meet expenses. You'll learn the steps to change your business' cash behavior to get more return for your effort.

Financial Management Techniques
Paperback: $19.95   **ISBN: 1-55571-124-3**   **Pages: 262**
Binder Edition: $39.95   **ISBN: 1-55571-116-2**   **Pages: 262**

Practical tips on how to turn receivables into cash. Worksheets and checklists help businesses establish credit policies, track accounts, and flag when it's necessary to bring in a collection agency, attorney, or go to court. This book advises how to deal with disputes, negotiate settlements, win in small claims court, and collect on judgments. Gives examples of telephone collection techniques and collection letters.

Collection Techniques for a Small Business
Paperback $19.95   **ISBN: 1-55571-171-5**   **Pages: 200**
Binder Edition $39.95   **ISBN: 1-55571-312-2**   **Pages: 200**

Prepares a business to enter the export market. Clearly explains the basics, then articulates specific requirements for export licensing, preparation of documents, payment methods, packaging, and shipping. Includes advice on evaluating foreign representatives, planning international marketing strategies, and discovering official U.S. policy for various countries and regional sources.

Export Now: A Guide for Small Business
Paperback $19.95   **ISBN: 1-55571-167-7**   **Pages: 316**
Binder Edition: $39.95   **ISBN: 1-55571-050-6**   **Pages: 316**

More than 200 reproducible forms for all types of business needs: personnel, employment, finance, production flow, operations, sales, marketing, order entry, and general administration. A time-saving, uniform, coordinated way to record and locate important business information.

Complete Book of Business Forms
Paperback $19.95   **ISBN: 1-55571-107-3**   **Pages: 234**
Binder Edition $39.95   **ISBN: 1-55571-103-0**   **Pages: 234**